WHITEBREAD
PROTESTANTS

Food and Religion in American Culture

Daniel Sack

palgrave

First published in hardcover in 2000 by St. Martin's Press
First PALGRAVE™ paperback edition: December 2001
175 Fifth Avenue, New York, N.Y. 10010 and
Houndmills, Basingstoke, England RG21 6XS
Companies and representatives throughout the world.

PALGRAVE is the new global publishing imprint of St. Martin's Press LLC
Scholarly and Reference Division and Palgrave Publishers Ltd (formerly Macmillan Press Ltd).

ISBN 0-321-21731-5 (cloth)
ISBN 0-312-29442-5 (paperback)

Library of Congress Cataloging-in-Publication Data
Sack, Daniel
    Whitebread Protestants: food and religion in American culture / Daniel Sack.
        p. cm.
    Included index.
    ISBN 0-312-29442-5
Food--Religious aspects--Christianity--History of doctrines--19th century. 2.
  Protestants--United States--History--19th century. 3. United States--
Church history--19th century. 4. Food--Religious aspects--Christianity--History
of doctrines--20th century. 5. Protestants--United States--History--20th century.
6. United States--Church history--20th century. I. Title.

BR115.N87 S23 2000
261--dc21   00-030899
                                                                          CIP

Design by planettheo.com

First paperback edition: December 2001
10 9 8 7 6 5 4 3 2 1

A catalogue record for this book is available from the British Library.

Transferred to digital printing 2005

For William:
brother in faith,
colleague in kitchen,
partner in life

CONTENTS

ACKNOWLEDGMENTS

WHEN PEOPLE I MEET SOCIALLY LEARN THAT I AM AN ACADEMIC, they politely ask what I'm working on and prepare themselves to be bored. When I tell them that I'm studying religion and food, however, their boredom disappears as they tell me stories—stories about the church they grew up in, or about their grandmother's potluck recipe. Everyone, it seems, enjoys talking about food.

As I've worked on this book, I have benefited from lots of interesting conversations about food—often at coffee hours or over dinners. Members of the project team of the Material History of American Religion Project—Marie Griffith, James Hudnut-Beumler, Colleen McDannell, Robert Orsi, Leigh Schmidt, David Watt, Judith Weisenfeld, and Diane Winston—have made valuable comments and asked great questions over the last four years. Marie Griffith, a fellow foodie, read almost the entire manuscript and was particularly helpful. I also appreciate the help of Courtney Bender, Carolyn Gifford, and Lynn Japinga and the rest of the Hope College religion faculty, who commented on various sections. As usual, the final responsibility for ignoring their good advice is mine.

This book has allowed me to pursue research in some interesting and varied places. Thomas Henry and the staff at St. Pauls United Church of Christ gave me unfettered access to the congregation's files. Jackie Carlson and the rest of the staff at Church World Service set me loose in their attic. William Beatty at the Frances Willard Library of the Women's Christian Temperance Union pointed me in some helpful directions. The staff members, volunteers, and clients of the feeding ministries discussed in chapter 3 answered my questions and let me lurk in their corners.

In addition to these expeditions, I also spent a good deal of time in college and seminary libraries. I appreciate the help of these libraries, some of whom didn't know I was there: Woodruff and Pitts libraries at Emory University; Van Wylen Library at Hope College; Oesterle Library at North Central College; Brimson Grow Library at Northern Baptist Theological Seminary; Beardslee Library at Western Theological Seminary; and the Buswell and Graham libraries at Wheaton College. Above all, I am grateful for the help and enthusiasm of Clay Hulet and the rest of the folks at the Campbell Library of Columbia Theological Seminary.

Along the way I've incurred other debts. I appreciate the help and support of James Hudnut-Beumler, who directed the Material History of American Religion Project; not only did he hire me and approve the topic, he also suggested the title. Jim has been a friend as well as a colleague. The Lilly Endowment, Inc., in its financial support of the project, made my research possible. Tommy Smith provided some crucial research, and Randy Tyndall helped with some of the illustrations. Stoncil Boyette pulled me out of several computer snafus—a few of my own making. Hope College—particularly Allen Verhey and the rest of the religion department—provided a good place to complete the manuscript. Michael Flamini and Amanda Johnson of St. Martin's Press have been enthusiastic and patient.

Finally, some personal thanks. I am grateful to my parents for their support over the years. I am sorry my mother—who taught me a lot about both faith and food—cannot see the final product. And I appreciate the assistance of my partner, William Tweedley. He helped develop the idea over supper one night. Since then he has listened as I talked about the book, he has read every chapter, and he has provided important distractions. Like the rest of these people, he has made the book possible.

INTRODUCTION

WHEN I WAS YOUNG, CHURCH MEANT FOOD. Decades later it's hard to point to particular events, but there are plenty of tastes, smells, and memories. There was the taste of dry cookies and punch from coffee hour—or that strange orange drink from vacation Bible school. There was the slightly sour smell of the dishcloths in the big kitchen where my mother—and all the other mothers—spent so much time. There was the weight of the big tables in the fellowship hall, as we took them down after another potluck.

Food has continued to be part of my life in the church. When I was a teenager I went from door to door at Halloween with a little orange and black box, collecting money for UNICEF. When I was in college I worked at a soup kitchen in the city—and then went out for dinner with the volunteers. When I was in graduate school I fasted for Good Friday. As a minister I celebrate Communion and drink really bad coffee at the reception afterward.

Somehow food seems to twine through my life in the church. I suspect that I am not alone.

Americans, after all, love to eat. We devote large spaces in our homes and significant parts of our incomes to preparing meals. We spend increasing amounts of money on commercially prepared food. We write and buy hundreds of new cookbooks annually. And we are more likely to be overweight than people in any other society.

Americans are also deeply religious. We have one of the highest church attendance rates in the world. We have built large institutions for religious practice and nurture. And, in a supposedly secular age, large numbers of Americans continue to identify religion as important in our lives.

This book stands at the intersection of these facets of American culture. My experience—and the experience of many others—suggests that food plays many roles in white mainline Protestant church life. It is involved in rituals and informal social life. It carries profound political and ethical meaning. Sometimes, of course, it is just food. This is a history of religion and eating, the human encounter with food. While the actual food is important, it is eating that gives food meaning. Around the Communion table, bread and wine become a connection to God. In the social hall, coffee becomes community. In the soup kitchen, rice and beans become hospitality. To understand how this meaning comes to be, this book examines how white mainline Protestants have used and understood food in their religious lives, looking at eating in the church against the backgrounds of American religious history, food studies, and theology.

I believe the way Protestants use food reveals remarkable richness and complexity in the life of the church; few scholars have studied these practices, however. Instead, theologians and clergy focus on concepts and words—creation, sin, justification, salvation, and all the rest. Historians concentrate on movements or institutions. The church these scholars describe ends up looking disembodied, with little connection to human activities and needs.

Food, however, calls attention to our senses and to our bodies, and it plays a central role in church life. Protestants eat before church, after church, and occasionally during church. They feed their infants in the nursery and their elderly at midweek luncheons. Almost every church building in the country includes a kitchen, large or small. If you ask American Protestants why they go to church, they're likely to say that they go not for the doctrine or the ethics but for the community—a community usually built and sustained around food. There is nothing more material than food, the most important substance in human life next to oxygen and water.

Other than public policy statements on hunger and food politics, the official church pays little attention to food. For theologians and church bureaucrats alike, it's off the map. Instead, food and food events are part of popular Protestantism, the unofficial part of church life. They are the concern not of the theologians or of the clergy but of the laity—most often the women in the kitchen. These dedicated Christians devote their time to preparing the gallons of coffee and hundreds of cookies in church kitchens all across the country, and see it as an important part of their lives as Christians. It is hard to imagine popular American Protestantism without food. Through this book I hope to expand our understanding of American religion, encouraging us to pay attention to popular practices that have important theological and ethical implications.

Nevertheless, this book is not an account of food in all of American religion. Instead, it explores the role that food has played in that part of American religious life known as mainline Protestantism—the cluster of denominations, many rooted in the British Reformation, that once dominated the American religious landscape and still carries influence beyond its numbers. Included in this cluster are groups such as Presbyterians, Episcopalians, Methodists, Congregationalists, Lutherans, and Baptists. More particularly, the book focuses on the white majorities within those denominations—hence, whitebread Protestants.

Why white Protestants? First, a history of religion and food in all of American religion would be next to impossible. Everyone eats, from Amerindians and African Americans to more recent Asian immigrants, and they frequently endow their eating with religious meaning. There is a rich variety of rituals, meals, dishes, and taboos in the landscape of American religious life. Focusing on just one tradition risks covering up the diversity of both American religious and American culinary life, but that very diversity overwhelms any attempt at a general treatment. Concentrating on white mainline Protestants allows for depth instead of superficiality.

Second, white mainline Protestantism needs to be studied as a particular religious tradition. Once upon a time, all histories of American religion put what we now call mainline Protestants at the center of the narrative—largely because the historians were Protestants themselves. These historians assumed that their culturally dominant tradition was the universal tradition and that all other religious communities were, at best, variations on that main theme. When discussed at all, Catholicism, Judaism, Eastern religions, and even non-British Protestant traditions appeared as exotic exceptions to the general rule.

In the last decade or two, scholars have challenged this scheme by writing narratives that focus on the experience of African Americans, Catholics, Jews, and Asian Americans. In doing so they have presented a far different account of American religious life. By focusing on the particularities of these groups, they have robbed the mainline of its pretensions to universality.

This challenge gives us the opportunity to view mainline Protestant-ism as yet another particular tradition alongside the rest. Just as whiteness studies and men's studies have put previous claimants to universality in a new light, we can look at the mainline as a specific tradition, perhaps even as an ethnic tradition. This perspective reveals the diversity within the mainline tradition as well as patterns of change and development.

Finally, most studies of food and religion in America focus on cultures that appear "exotic." Anthropologists and folklorists are fasci-nated with the foodways of Jews and ethnic Catholics, which are rich with rituals and traditions. On the other hand, scholars tend to ignore food practices among white middle-class Protestants; those practices appear either nonexistent or boring—supposedly made up of nothing but Jell-O salads and coffee. But focusing on mainline Protestants—clearly not "exotic"—forces us to turn the analytic lens on mainstream culture and to recognize the rituals and taboos that run through much of American society. Paradoxically, looking at the dominant culture might help us to see the variety in all of American culture.

Looking at mainline Protestant food events reveals the richness and creativity within this tradition itself. Some events, such as Communion, are rooted in European theology and liturgy but have been reshaped in the American environment to include new practices. Others, such as the potluck supper or the coffee hour, are part of a folk culture unique to North America. All of these eating experiences were shaped by the American context. The pressures of the free market in money, ideas, and time helped to create church-based social events. Political structures and denominational bureaucracies unique to the United States helped shape the church's role in hunger politics. From the food court at Willow Creek Community Church to the work of Bread for the World, this book places the tradition's creativity in the context of American religious life.

Because food plays so many roles in whitebread Protestant life, it is hard to fit them all into one neat narrative. Instead, the five chapters of this book are, to a certain degree, independent. Each one focuses on a different topic, a different function of food in church life. To get at these different roles, they use different disciplinary approaches and work with different time schemes. Instead of a chronological arrangement, the chapters are thematic, arranged to reflect different understandings of food. In the first three chapters, we see mainline Protestants concerned with the actual food; the last two chapters show their greater interest in its symbolic meaning. Rather than surveying the entire history of each topic, the chapters concentrate on important moments—times when whitebread Protestants used or fought over a particular function of food. While they are independent narratives, however, the chapters form a coherent whole, arguing that food plays an important symbolic role for whitebread Protestants.

The book begins with Communion—also known as the Eucharist or the Lord's Supper—a central ritual of the Christian faith. For most Christians, Communion is the paradigmatic church eating experience, setting the pattern for all the rest. Over the centuries of the church's history, Christians have squabbled over the proper celebration of the sacrament. Some of the least studied—but still important—squabbles have been over the proper menu and method for the meal. In the late nineteenth century and again in the mid-twentieth, whitebread Protestants argued over whether to serve wine or grape juice at Communion and whether to use individual or common cups. Drawing on the writings of clergymen and reformers, chapter 1, an essay in liturgical history, reveals important tensions in American Protestantism.

While Communion is a central ritual of the faith, the meals in the fellowship hall are often a more important part of church life for many whitebread Protestants. In church basements across the land, men and women, youth and children have gathered around Formica tables for potluck suppers, family nights, coffee hours, and mother-daughter banquets. But these events are more than just meals. They both reflect and reinforce members' worldviews, including assumptions about the structure of the family and the mission of the church. Chapter 2 is a piece of social history, exposing the meanings of these food-centered social events in the lives of Protestant congregations.

In many such congregations, the fellowship hall is used to feed hungry strangers as well as church members. There is a deep strain of social responsibility in whitebread Protestants; with their sense of noblesse oblige, they feel called to feed the hungry. Over the years they have developed a variety of motives and methods for this work. Using the sociological tool of ethnography, chapter 3 investigates the work of five different hunger ministries, showing how they have developed in response to social changes.

This sense of social responsibility extends beyond church basements. The abundance of the American breadbasket has made whitebread Protestants painfully aware of their wealth compared to the hunger of the rest of the world. This awareness has led them to try to feed the world. That attempt has given rise to hunger politics—an ethical focus on food-related foreign and economic policy—within American Protestantism. Those politics have changed, pushed by developments both in theology and in the international situation. Chapter 4, a history of religion and politics, reflects on how American Protestants have understood their place in the world.

For some hunger activists, feeding the hungry requires changing American eating habits as well. In the 1970s some whitebread Protestant church leaders built the "lifestyle" movement, which advocated a simpler and less environmentally destructive way of life—including a change in diet. They echoed the work of nineteenth-century diet reformers who also challenged American eating habits. Chapter 5 examines the rhetoric of these two diet reform movements, looking at food not as an object or a symbol but as a moral issue.

Put together, these chapters argue that food is a central part of Protestant church life. In their food choices, I believe, whitebread Protestants express deep faith convictions. Their eating practices reflect their understandings of ritual, community, hospitality, and justice. While food often gets taken for granted in the church, it has important and multiple meanings. Eating has an essential place in the religious lives of whitebread Protestants.

The following parable, snatched from the Internet, reflects the importance of food for Protestants. A second-grade class was doing a project in comparative religions; each child was asked to say something about his or her faith and bring in a symbol of their belief. On the day of the assignment, the first child stood up and said, "My name is Joshua. I go to Beth Shalom. I am Jewish, and this is a Star of David." The second child stood up and said, "My name is Marguerite. I go to St. Mary's. I am Catholic, and this is a crucifix." The third child stood up and said, "My name is Fred. I go to Grace Church. I am Protestant, and this is a casserole." For Fred—and for many whitebread Protestants like him—church is about food. For all the Freds and for all their casseroles, thanks be to God.

CHAPTER ONE

LITURGICAL FOOD: COMMUNION ELEMENTS AND CONFLICT

IT WAS A DARK AND HOLY NIGHT. The small group gathered in Jerusalem, prepared for the sacred Passover meal. Before this dinner, the central celebration of their faith, their charismatic young leader foretold a stunning series of events. He told them that he was about to be arrested; after they betrayed and denied him, he would die. His revelations complete, he passed them the holy meal—small cubes of white bread and little cups of grape juice.

It's an absurd—some might say sacrilegious—image, but most American mainline Protestant churches use these foods in their reenactment of that Last Supper. Most people in the pews probably have never thought about what they were eating or why—they've always done it that way and assume that's the way it's supposed to be. They probably realize that Jesus and his disciples didn't use Wonder Bread and Welch's but don't stop to ask why they do.

Communion is one of Christianity's sacraments, acts that manifest closeness to God and indicate inclusion in the faith community. Roman Catholics celebrate seven sacraments while Protestants recognize two—Baptism and Eucharist, also called Communion, the Lord's Supper, or the Last Supper. Whatever their name or number, all Christians see these rituals as instituted by Jesus Christ and as an important part of their worship life. Participation in the sacraments is a requirement for full membership, and in some traditions receiving Communion is one key to salvation.

Despite—or perhaps because of—the important role played by Communion, the Communion table has long been a place of conflict. Through the centuries churchmen and rulers have debated the meaning of the rite: Is it a sacrifice or a memorial? The Protestant Reformers argued about how often the sacrament should be celebrated: daily, weekly, monthly, quarterly? Others have debated over who is welcome at the table: only members of the local church, all adults, or everyone who is baptized? These conflicts grow out of Communion's importance to the faith; in these struggles wars have been fought and anathemas have been hurled.

Compared to these weighty theological issues, the form of the practice—the menu and the method—may appear trivial. Next to the doctrine of transubstantiation, the plastic Communion cup seems preposterous. But underlying these apparently insignificant concerns are profound theological questions. This chapter looks at conflicts concerning two parts of American mainline Communion practice—one involving a menu item and one involving its serving method—to reveal the sociological and theological issues underlying the debate.

The first half of the chapter investigates the often very public debate, beginning in the middle of the nineteenth century, over the use of wine for Communion. The argument pitted traditionalist clergy against reforming women and became an important part of the larger campaign for temperance and prohibition. Throughout, however, all the participants were concerned with authenticity—the need to do Communion "right." The section reveals the role that authentic practice played in the Communion wine debate.

The second half of the chapter turns from the menu for Communion to the method of serving. Starting in the late nineteenth century, many American Protestant churches began using small individual cups for Communion in place of a single common cup. As with the wine debate, the individual-cup question was part of a larger campaign, in this case the sanitation crusade. But here the antagonists were men of science—physicians and "sanitarians" looking to change church practice over the protests of liturgy-minded clergy. The argument also revealed deep anxieties about cleanliness and the borders of the church and of society. The Communion cup question turned on issues of authority and purity.

Few historians have studied these conflicts, perhaps due to a degree of myopia on the part of religion scholars. Like theologians they have focused on the spiritual and doctrinal aspects of Communion practice, to the neglect of the very material, embodied food substances. These questions of menu and method are not grand ideas—they are the stuff of everyday religion. Yet for millions of Christians, this is where Christ is revealed—somehow or another. Communion is Christianity's most important ritual meal, making it a good place to begin an investigation of American mainline Protestantism's food culture.

THE CONTENTS OF THE CUP: THIRSTING FOR AUTHENTICITY

Nineteenth-century Protestant evangelicals, the forefathers and foremothers of the Protestant mainline, found themselves caught in a theological bind. They wanted to celebrate Communion exactly as Jesus did. Yet they also were committed to a political and social cause—temperance. While the first commitment may have led them to use wine at the Communion table, the second explicitly forbade it. To get out of this bind, temperance-minded Protestants adopted a creative interpretation of the Bible that allowed them to have their wine and drink it too.

The difficulty—and resulting creative interpretation—was unique to evangelicals. In the Roman Catholic Church, ritual food choices—the menu for the Eucharist—are determined by tradition and written into church law. The tradition requiring wine for Communion dates to at least the thirteenth century, when theologian Thomas Aquinas stated that "only wine of the grape is the proper matter of this sacrament." He noted that Jesus compared himself to the vine, and thus grape wine— not the wine of pomegranates or mulberries—was essential. Aquinas observed that the Bible praises wine, while nonalcoholic grape juice— called must—"is at the stage of incomplete generation, and therefore it has not yet the species of wine." Correct celebration of the sacrament thus required alcoholic wine.[1] The Second Vatican Council in the 1960s significantly changed the celebration of the Mass for the Roman Catholic Church, most notably allowing laypeople to receive the wine as well as the bread, but canon law still requires the use of wine. These traditions must be followed, for incorrect practice makes the sacrament invalid if not—literally—sacrilege. Protestant communities with a strong commitment to liturgical tradition, including the Episcopalians and the Lutherans, also require the use of wine.

Generally, however, most Protestant churches have few laws or regulations around ritual behavior. They proudly proclaim their freedom from the "dead hand" of tradition. Such traditions, they believe, are human inventions. Instead, these Protestants base their practices on their interpretation of biblical precedent, trying to do everything "the way Jesus did it." This is a phenomenon called primitivism—looking to the first-century church as the model for all behavior. For instance, Presbyterians defend their polity—their system of church governance—as following the way the apostles organized the church. Some churches forbid the use of musical instruments because they are not mentioned in the New Testament. The Disciples of Christ celebrate Communion every week because they believe the first-century church did. Primitivism means that the only authentic practice is the original practice. What counts is not church law or tradition but replicating the religious experience of being with Jesus.

Early Protestants followed Rome's lead and served wine at the Communion table. Sixteenth-century reformer John Calvin specifically spoke of wine when describing the proper celebration of the sacrament.[2] Presbyterian clergy in seventeenth-century Scotland told their congregations that, as wine "warmed the cold stomach, so did Christ warm the cold heart."[3] The Protestants shared the Roman church's conviction that the sacrament was not valid without wine. One sixteenth-century Lutheran bishop told communicants who could not tolerate wine that they should refrain from receiving Communion at all.[4] In 1567 a minister of the Church of England was suspended from office when he "indede did minister the communion with beare, but it was onelie for necessitie and want of wyne."[5] A seventeenth-century Scottish Presbyterian observed that communicants "eate and drink in such measure, as they may find themselves refreshed sensibly." For some larger Communion festivals sensible refreshment required wine by the gallon or even by the barrel.[6] Thus for Protestant as well as Catholic churches, wine was the standard beverage for the Eucharist.

The use of wine at Communion meshed well with American culture in the years just before and just after the Revolution. Foreign visitors commented on the huge amount of alcohol consumed by Americans, observations borne out by statistics—in 1820 the young nation consumed over five gallons of rum per person.[7] Communion practices reflected this acceptance of alcohol. In the middle of the eighteenth century a pastor on the Pennsylvania frontier communed two hundred people with six gallons of wine, providing about four ounces of wine per person.[8] And there was other alcohol at frontier revivals; officially banned liquor found its way onto revival grounds, often upsetting the sobriety of the meeting.[9] For many American Christians, particularly on the frontier, alcohol and religion were a natural combination.

But by the early decades of the nineteenth century, this combination clashed with an opposing force: temperance. It had its roots in the intersection of evangelical morality and industrial capitalism that characterized the time; together they decisively shaped the bourgeois standards of the 1830s and 1840s. They demanded sobriety and self-control on the part of their devotees, attitudes that clashed with the alcohol-centered conviviality of the frontier. Middle-class temperance campaigners sought both to reform their own class and to gain control over the social lives of immigrants and working people. [10]

While temperance began as a health issue, through a religious movement it seized hold of the public imagination. The movement began in 1812 when a group of students and faculty at Andover Theological Seminary organized the Massachusetts Society for the Suppression of Intemperance. While health campaigners such as Benjamin Rush focused on the health dimensions of alcohol use, the religious temperance movement emphasized morality. Arguing that drinkers would be damned as well as diseased, this moral exhortation captivated the populace. [11] The crusade's morality demanded total abstinence, not just moderation.

The movement found strong support from the churches, especially among Methodists. They (falsely) claimed John Wesley, the denomination's eighteenth-century founder, as a teetotaler, and continued the tradition; in 1816 the Methodist General Conference barred clergymen from selling liquor, and in 1832 it urged total abstinence. [12] Other evangelical denominations, particularly the Presbyterians and Congregationalists, followed the Methodist lead. The nineteenth century was a heyday for church-related reform movements, including abolition, diet reform, and dress reform; temperance was one of the strongest. The strongest organization in the movement was the Women's Christian Temperance Union (WCTU), founded in 1874, made up mostly of evangelical Protestant women. Nonevangelical Protestant churches, such as the Episcopalians and the Lutherans, were less enthusiastic for the cause.

The temperance movement's mission was to convince the American people of the evils of alcohol and the necessity for abstinence. Its members sought to save Americans—particularly young men—from the captivity of the barroom. Although its mission was inherently religious, the movement was inevitably political—it was engaged in a battle for public opinion. The movement's opponents were the makers and sellers of alcohol—those the movement called the "liquor interests." It was a righteous war, requiring every resource the crusaders could muster.

In all of the reform battles of the nineteenth century, the evangelicals' prime weapon was the Bible. The scriptures were the only authority in Protestant churches; every theological and ethical argument was answered by looking to the Bible. For Primitivist Christians, the scriptures were the guide to building a church and a society faithful to Jesus; in these communities, authenticity—close adherence to the biblical model—was essential.

In the temperance crusade, unfortunately, the Bible appeared to be a chink in the evangelical churches' armor, for it appears to support the use of alcohol. In Genesis Isaac blesses Jacob, praying that God would give his son "plenty of grain and wine."[13] In Psalm 104 God is praised for bringing "forth food from the earth, and wine to gladden the human heart."[14] Through the prophet Isaiah, God calls people to "come, buy wine and milk without money and without price."[15] In his letter to his young associate, Paul advises Timothy to "no longer drink only water, but take a little wine for the sake of your stomach and your frequent ailments."[16] Thus wine appears to be an important part of the Bible's world.

In fact, the text suggests that Jesus himself drank wine. His critics called him a drunkard.[17] His first miracle was making wine—reported to be good wine—for a wedding banquet at Cana. The steward said to the host, "Everyone serves the good wine first, and then the inferior wine after the guests have become drunk. But you have kept the good wine until now."[18] And at the Last Supper, Jesus himself gave wine to his followers, blessed it, and commanded them to continue to drink the wine in his name. This supper provided the model for the Eucharist, a central ritual for the Christian community, and the use of wine appeared to play an essential role.

To be sure, the scriptures are not unanimous in praise of wine. According to the Psalms, wine can be judgment as well as blessing; God "will pour a draught from it, and all the wicked of the earth shall drain it down to the dregs."[19] Isaiah condemns those "who linger in the evening to be inflamed by wine."[20] Paul urges his followers not to "get drunk with wine, for that is debauchery; but be filled with the Spirit."[21] In the same book where he recommends wine for Timothy's stomach, he warns deacons to "be serious, not double-tongued, not indulging in much wine."[22] The Bible's attitude toward wine appears to be ambivalent, at best.

This mixed testimony on alcohol presented a challenge to temperance crusaders. They could point to the scriptural condemnations of wine to support their cause, while their opponents could use the scriptural blessings of wine—and, most important, Jesus' blessing of wine at the Last Supper—to support theirs. Temperance-minded evangelicals feared that the Bible, the basis of their morality, could be used as a weapon against them. The Lord's Supper, an essential ritual of the faith, was a potential stumbling block to moral reform.

The case for temperance, its advocates felt, rose and fell on an unambiguous biblical condemnation of wine. Starting in the early nineteenth century, they worked to solve the ambiguity through careful—and sometimes complex—interpretation of the Bible. Their starting point was their ethical objection to alcohol. They looked for a way to read scripture so that Jesus—the real, authentic Jesus—would not be understood as blessing wine. This exercise in what theologians call hermeneutics—scriptural interpretation—had a political goal in mind.

Central to this interpretation was what came to be known as the "two-wine" theory, first suggested in the 1830s by Moses Stuart, a professor at Andover Theological Seminary. Inspired by Stuart, pro-temperance Protestants—in theological journals, sermons, and a flood of pamphlets—began arguing that there were two beverages in biblical times, both translated in the English Bible as "wine." One, the wine praised by the psalmist and blessed by Christ, was nonalcoholic; the other, cursed by the psalmist and warned of by Paul, was alcoholic. Both were known as wine, but one was good and life giving, while the other was the beverage of disease and death. Such an exegesis gave temperance advocates both original, authentic practice and temperance principles. They could have their "wine" and criticize it too.

These arguments drew on a variety of sources. The most important, of course, was the Bible itself. Biblical scholars engaged in long and complex lexical investigations, identifying and distinguishing the various Hebrew and Greek words translated as "wine" in the English Bible. In 1880 two writers prepared a voluminous commentary showing the prominence of temperance sentiment in the Bible.[23] Two years later a church leader named Leon Field devoted lengthy articles over four issues of the *Methodist Quarterly Review* to the question, including a close linguistic analysis of sixteen Hebrew words and five Greek words. After exhaustive—and often exhausting—discussion, Field identified all the positive references to wine as nonalcoholic and all the negative ones as alcoholic. He concluded that "there is no term in the Old Testament or in the New which invariably indicates a fermented liquor, while there are nine which signify an unfermented article, and six others . . . which leave us free to decide, by reference to the context or circumstances of the case, whether or not a fermented wine is intended."[24] Given his devotion to both the Bible and his temperance principles, Field shaped his interpretation of these last texts to exclude any positive biblical references to alcoholic wine.

Among all the biblical references to wine, the most important were those regarding the Last Supper. Almost all of the temperance crusaders were convinced that the beverage Jesus served to his disciples was unfermented grape juice, not wine. There were two major arguments. First, they pointed out that "by a careful study of the New Testament, we find that the word 'wine' is not used in connection with the Lord's Supper. Nine times it is simply called 'the cup,' and our Saviour's own descriptive term is 'the fruit of the vine.'"[25] Second, they felt that the nature of wine was totally contradictory to the meaning of the Lord's Supper. As the newspaper of the WCTU asked in 1910, "How can a priest of the living God give to the communicant at the altar the cup containing alcohol—'the enemy of the human race' and say that it represents the blood 'shed from the foundation of the world' for us!"[26] With the temperance advocates' assumptions about the nature of alcohol and the meaning of the sacrament, using wine at Communion was unimaginable. The two-wine interpretation gave temperance-minded evangelicals biblical warrants for using non-alcoholic wine as authentic practice.

There was a great deal at stake, for Jesus' use of wine at his last meal would threaten the reputation of the Lord as well as his sacrament. Alcohol being what it is, temperance advocates could not conceive of their Savior having drunk it, let alone blessed it. Stuart was "quite certain that persons of such a character as the holy Savior and His disciples, as on an occasion of such deep distress as that when the Lord's Supper was first instituted, did not use undiluted wine."[27] "The disease, corruption, and sin associated through the coming centuries with alcohol—alcoholic wine not excepted—may have been in the mind of the prescient and divinely foreseeing Christ," Gordon argued; there is no way that Jesus could have intended to sanction its use.[28] Field points out that biblical descriptions of the Last Supper speak only of "the cup," not of wine. The cup was

> the subject of thanksgiving, the medium of blessing. Such, indeed, would be the pure and nutritious juice of the grape. Such never could be the wine upon which God has poured his maledictions, and upon which he had warned his children not to look. We cannot conceive of Christ bending over such a beverage in grateful prayer. The supposition is sacrilegious. The imputation is blasphemous. No cup that can intoxicate is a cup of blessing, but a cup of cursing. It does not belong to a eucharistic feast, but is the fit accompaniment of scenes of revelry and riot.[29]

If the beverage created in the miracle at Cana truly was wine, "that must stand as the single exception to all his other miracles. It was a malevolent and mischievous manifestation of power. There was no glory in it, but shame."[30] Since the temperance advocates assumed the evils of alcohol, a Jesus who drank alcohol could not have been a savior. They read their antialcohol agenda back onto the first century and declared that Jesus, too, must have been a teetotaler. It was the only way to keep him divine.

To support their argument that fermented wine was illicit for the Passover—and thus for the Eucharist—the temperance scholars engaged in an early kind of practical ecumenism, looking to ancient and contemporary rabbis for evidence. Field argued that since the Last Supper was a Passover meal, Jewish law allowed no leavened food to be served. Hence the beverage in the cup must have been unfermented grape juice. "The Jews have so understood the law. The Mishna expressly specifies certain fermented drinks whose use would be a violation of the feast." He cited several "leading rabbis" who claim that "fermented wine, as everything fermented is rigidly excluded from our Passover fare." Perhaps Reformed Jews use wine, he acknowledged, but the strict Orthodox bar it.[31] In 1884 the WCTU newspaper quoted a "learned Jewish Rabbi" of Albany, who said of Jesus, "To suppose that He used fermented and consequently intoxicating wine on that memorable occasion,—an occasion on which the Jews were strictly forbidden the use of any fermentation whatever, is too absurd to be entertained for a moment."[32] One of the most commonly cited authorities was Mordecai Noah, a leading New York Jewish layman, who shared with the temperance press his recipe for unfermented "raisin wine." Because it was unfermented and thus had no leaven in it, Noah told inquiring Christians, it was the traditional drink for Passover. For many evangelicals this may have been their first encounter with rabbinical authority. For these Jews, on the other hand, this may have been the first time they were respected as an authority by Christians.[33]

Having proved that alcoholic wine for Communion was not historically authentic, temperance advocates argued that unfermented grape juice—called must—was the historically correct beverage for Communion. They believed that Jesus and the disciples would have used must at the last supper. Since the Bible offered no explicit evidence for the existence of nonalcoholic wine in biblical times, they had to look beyond the scriptures. Referring to texts from classical authors, Field argued that "it is without doubt or question that both the Greeks and the Romans had a beverage which consisted of the pure, unfermented juice of the grape."[34] They knew what caused fermentation, and they knew how to stop it. Even when they did drink alcohol, he concluded, "all wines, until the last hundred years, were comparatively weak."[35] Stuart agreed, stating that all "sober men" in Greece and Rome drank only wine mixed with water; only barbarians drank pure wine.[36]

The testimony of Western missionaries in service in the Middle East, these writers argued, confirmed that nonalcoholic wines were still common in biblical lands. One man accumulated a large collection of unfermented wines from throughout the Middle East, seeing it as evidence of unfermented wines in biblical times.[37] Field concluded that "there was and is such a beverage as the unfermented juice of the grape, that it was used as freshly expressed and when carefully preserved. That it was a common drink is amply attested by the frequent references to it in the writings of almost every ancient author . . . from the earliest to the latest." And, he stated, it was often known as wine.[38] The network of Protestant missionaries in the Middle East confirmed the temperance argument.

Nonalcoholic grape juice was not only historically accurate, the reformers believed, it was also natural and pure. Unfermented grape juice, they contended, was the perfect food. "The constituent parts actually of blood and of the expressed [unfermented] wine are strikingly analogous," Field wrote.[39] A leader of the WCTU noted that physicians favor grape juice, as "there is no other fruit which contains so large a proportion of building materials for the body. . . . All of these are retained, unchanged, in pure and properly prepared grape juice."[40] While grape juice is the pure and natural creature of God, temperance advocates preached, fermentation is the mark of decay; alcohol is thus the result of decomposition and death. The WCTU minutes saw it as "obvious; leaven, ferment, is the principle of decay in the material world, hence God uses it as a fitting symbol of sin in the spiritual, and excludes it from any offering made to him, and from all his solemn feasts."[41] Field cited a scientist who stated that alcohol is "an artificial product, devised by man for his purposes."[42] One twentieth-century crusader argued that "fermentation destroys the life blood of the grape, making it a liquid corpse, unsuited to represent the uncorrupted blood of the Savior."[43] While nineteenth-century evangelical Christianity sometimes had an adversarial relationship with modern science, here it served their purpose; in the case of fermentation, two bible scholars stated, the church "has there been taught a *practical lesson* of physiology and dietetics, which it would never adopt on mere principles of self-denial."[44] This scientific material allowed the Christians to make a natural law argument for temperance and thus convince nonevangelicals. "Those who do not admit the authority of the Bible will concede that intoxication is injurious to health, usefulness, estate, morals, and reputation," Stuart concluded.[45] Science and scripture both confirmed the inappropriateness of using wine.

Drawing on this broad variety of sources—scripture, the nature of the sacrament and of the Lord, rabbinical and classical texts, the testimony of contemporary missionaries, and science—temperance advocates concluded that using alcoholic wine at the Lord's table was inauthentic. They wanted to return to the original practice, to celebrate the Last Supper *exactly* as Jesus and his disciples did. Through almost a millennium the church had used alcoholic wine for Communion, but the principles of the pro-temperance evangelicals kept them from accepting that practice as authentic.

Some evangelical Protestants, however, did want to keep alcoholic wine for Communion. They did not support the temperance movement, and they did not accept the arguments of the wine opponents. The wine advocates also based their stance on their interpretation of primitive practice. They read the same Bible as the temperance advocates, but very differently. Like the two-wine advocates, they mounted arguments from the Bible, Jewish tradition, and missionaries in supporting the one-wine theory. Presbyterian theologian Charles Hodge argued that the "fruit of the vine" cited in the institution narratives refers to alcoholic wine. "The plain meaning of the Bible on this subject has controlled the mind of the church, and it is to be hoped will continue to control it till the end of time."[46] In 1897 his son Archibald supported the pro-wine argument with references to "the unanimous testimony of all competent scholars and missionary residents in the East."[47] A Methodist clergyman conducted a long analysis of the language of the biblical texts and concluded that the wine used by Jesus was alcoholic. He also stated that the Talmud does not ban the use of wine in the Passover.[48] Another minister cited missionaries who reported that unfermented grape juice is unknown in the modern Middle East.[49] A Presbyterian stated flatly that the Bible testifies to Jesus using wine, which "is sufficient evidence that the act is right."[50] Like the two-wine crusaders, the one-wine camp looked to history but interpreted that history to suit its assumptions. Both sides were searching for the authentic supper, but that search led each side in a decisively different direction.

The debate between the one-wine and two-wine sides was not always friendly. Temperance advocates accused those in favor of using wine of selectively interpreting the Bible to serve their own ends. The editors of the *Temperance Bible Commentary* suggested that "social customs and personal habits of diet and indulgence, continued from childhood upwards, may induce a state of mind inconsistent with the unbiased interpretation of Holy Writ." If a person grows up with alcohol, they concluded, he will easily interpret the scriptures as supporting it.[51] A WCTU leader wrote in the *Union Signal,* the union's newspaper, about the publication of a pamphlet critical of the two-wine argument. She concluded, however, that "the sophistry that so palpably characterizes the whole argument of this book, the cynical tone and pettifogging style of the entire work, would render it harmless to all educated, thinking people into whose hands it may be thrust."[52] In the eyes of the temperance side, wine supporters were misled at best, corrupted at worst.

The one-wine theorists, on the other hand, accused the two-wine advocates of extremism and emotionalism in their arguments. One stated categorically that the wine at Passover was alcoholic and then observed that "neither lamentations nor maledictions can change it. Instead, then, of bewailing or misrepresenting the opinions that others have been led to form on this subject, let us accept them as what they really are." Modern interpreters should "not change the immutable past to make it harmonize with our present ideas of policy and right; but by wisdom and faith, candor and courage, patience and self-sacrifice, to bring in a better future."[53] A Presbyterian asserted that "persistency and force of assertion will never convert fiction into a fact, however they may impose on the credulous and unreflecting."[54] One of Stuart's critics stated that "the uniform practice of the church as it now exists, and as it has existed for ages, is right; if *you* say that it is *not* right, then surely it behooves you to prove that it is not,—not to call upon me to prove that it is."[55] Another accused the anti-wine faction of "perversion of scripture."[56] The one-wine supporters returned the charge of selective interpretation and extremism.

For many temperance crusaders, there was more at stake in the two-wine argument than authentic ritual practice. Many—especially the members of the WCTU—were concerned that taking alcoholic wine at the Communion table would encourage reformed alcoholics to drink themselves to destruction. Reflecting the union's commitment "to make the whole world homelike," these women focused particularly on the need to save men—husbands and sons—from the scourge of alcohol.[57] The *Union Signal* is full of stories like that of the son of an alcoholic father. After his first Communion "he immediately expressed to his horrified parent the delights of that one sip, and never stopped until he had obtained more; to-day he rests in a drunkard's grave, by the side of his dishonored father and heart-broken mother."[58] Through its work against wine at the Communion table the union sought to prevent such tragedies. In 1886 another woman meditated on "a lovely sight: a little boy, perhaps six years of age, going to the Lord's table and kneeling between father and mother to partake of the emblems of Christ's broken body and shed blood. Would a mother dare do this if thereby her boy was likely to learn to love the taste of that which might prove his eternal ruin?"[59] The men could debate the authority of the tradition and the interpretation of the Bible until they were blue in the face, but for the women of the WCTU this pastoral concern for their children demanded action. It was also a wise strategic move; even if the two-wine theory did not stand up to scrutiny, "the Bible doctrine of expediency assumes all the importance and authority of a divine command not to 'do anything whereby thy brother stumbleth, or is offended, or is made weak.'"[60] Care for the weak brother trumped all other aspects of the Communion wine question.

The wine debate was also part of a larger political battle. A member of the WCTU told her sisters that "if all the wines of the Bible are fermented wines, we may as well cease our temperance work, for we can never make the great army of loyal hearts in the church and out of it believe that God has made a mistake and that what Jesus blessed will curse mankind."[61] It was part of an intense political battle. Another WCTU leader lamented that "there are many new advocates of the one wine theory whose utterances are giving new strength to the saloon power." With his expiring breath the enemy will "hurl in the face of the temperance host, 'You are seeking to destroy a divine institution.'"[62] The entire temperance cause depended on the Communion wine question.

For the sake of their movement, temperance leaders adopted a variety of strategies to change the behavior at Protestant Communion tables. The first proposal was a simple compromise. In 1835 Moses Stuart acknowledged that "the cup which Jesus gave to His disciples, when He instituted the sacrament, contained *the fruit of the vine*, i.e. wine." But he argued that in the custom of the time, it was most likely mixed with water to reduce its alcohol content.[63] Stuart proposed that modern churches also dilute their wine. "Let your wine be *mingled*, like that which eternal Wisdom prepared for her guests. Thus may you eat and drink, discerning the Lord's body aright."[64] Stuart hoped that diluted wine on the table would preserve the church's purity on the wine question.

But as the temperance cause became more absolutist, the leaders called for total elimination of alcohol from the Lord's table. When it came to concrete action the WCTU was in the vanguard. In the 1880s and 1890s it was active and radical; under the leadership of Frances Willard, the union advocated for women's suffrage, labor rights, and other progressive causes. Members brought the same intensity to the Communion wine issue, directly challenging the authority of male pastors and lay leaders. Central to its strategy was a propaganda campaign aimed at congregations and denominations. At its second annual meeting in 1875, the National WCTU examined the question of wine at Communion and resolved "to do all in our power to induce our churches to cease from a practice so baneful."[65] In 1878 it created a standing committee on Unfermented Wines in the Sacrament, with national and state superintendents who surveyed the problem, made speeches, and distributed pamphlets.[66] In 1884 the superintendent recommended "a personal interview with every pastor in the cities, town or villages where a local union exists. I would also urge that articles on this topic be sent to all denominational papers." With the conviction of a political campaigner she concluded, "if you will conscientiously follow the directions here given, we shall find that our churches will be purified, and that no holy sanction will be given by them for the use of fermented wine."[67] As the Pennsylvania secretary for Unfermented Wine at the Sacrament reported, they were up against considerable clerical ignorance. "A minister replied to an inquiring sister, 'When I am sure that any soul has been endangered by the use of fermented wine at the sacrament, then I will adopt the other.' Several among the clergy had never heard of unfermented wine, therefore could not be expected to obtain it."[68] The department's task was to overcome that ignorance with pamphlets and newspapers. For instance, it issued a temperance catechism for Sunday school lessons "in which unfermented wine at the sacrament occupies a number of pages, [and] is being introduced into many churches."[69]

The women weren't above a little denominational politicking alongside their educating. One superintendent "earnestly recommended" that members lobby delegates to the 1890 General Conference of the Methodist Episcopal Church South, "to secure the vote of each delegate in favor of a resolution to be presented to that body at that time, recommending the use of unfermented wine at the sacrament of the Lord's Supper."[70] In 1892 the superintendent of the Department of Unfermented Wines reported to the WCTU national convention that "about two-thirds of the churches in our country are using unfermented wine at communion service." But the battle was far from won. The remaining "one-third are men of iron wills, minds set like flints, prejudices deep and firmly rooted. . . . Of the leading orthodox denominations, not one as a *whole* uses unfermented wine at Communion service." The temperance movement was strongest in the Methodist church, "and yet, there is scarcely a northern state in which there are not to be found M.E. [Methodist Episcopal] churches using alcoholic wine at sacrament, and a large majority of the M.E. churches South still use it." Presbyterians had been passing strong resolutions that ministers "have failed to put into practice." With their strong dedication to tradition the Episcopalians presented the greatest obstacle to the Department's work. In her report a superintendent suggested that "in your efforts to influence the Episcopalians, I would urge special caution against seeming in any way aggressive."[71] Although denied the right to vote in church meetings, the women of the WCTU used their moral authority to advocate for policy change.

When politics didn't work, the sisters of the WCTU turned to direct action. The union recommended refusing Communion, or at the very least refusing the cup, when there was wine in it. Avoiding the Communion wine did not start with the WCTU, however. In 1844 the session of the Presbyterian church in Seneca Falls, New York, considered the case of Rhoda Bement, charged with "disorderly and unchristian conduct." First among the charges was that she divided "the Lord's Supper, partaking the bread and refusing the cup."[72] While Bement replied that she was "not conscious of being guilty of disorderly and unchristian conduct," she did acknowledge that she had refused the cup at the Lord's Supper; "the reason given was that she acted from conscience in this case not knowing that it was the fruit of the vine."[73] After several days of hearings, the session found Bement guilty and suspended her from the Communion of the church until she showed signs of repentance. The record does not indicate that she ever did so.[74]

The WCTU took such a radical step hesitantly; the third annual convention in 1876 voted only narrowly to refuse alcoholic Communion wine.[75] Ten years later, however, the superintendent of the Department of Unfermented Wine urged members to "use your personal influence by declining to take alcoholic wine at the sacrament, for yourself and children."[76] Another stated that she did "not see how any white-ribboned woman can, with any degree of consistency, accept it. Many churches have been induced to change to unfermented wine by the persistent refusal of some of their members to accept the fermented." She recommended to members that they "get up a petition addressed to the pastor and officials of the church, signed by all the membership if possible, asking for the change, and present it to the next official meeting."[77] The strategy was effective. The New Jersey state union reported in 1879 that "devoted Christian women, after much prayerful consideration, folded their arms when the cup of fermented wine was offered at the Lord's Supper, and this silent protest has banished it from the Communion."[78] For these women, the clergy were the main opposition. Through this direct action they took advantage of polities where the congregation was more powerful than the tradition; although officially disenfranchised, they used the power of numbers to change church policy. Their moral authority overwhelmed the authority of the tradition and the clergy.

The women of the WCTU did not just advocate for grape juice; they provided it. The superintendent of the Department of Unfermented Wines regularly included in her reports a recipe for grape juice produced along the same lines as home-canned fruit. She urged that each member "suggest to the pastor of each church, the appointment of some lady in his society, who shall have special charge of the communion wine, preparing it herself if necessary."[79] If they did not want to prepare it themselves, there were a number of other sources. Perhaps a local druggist could "keep for sale the pure juice of the grape."[80] Frances Willard, longtime president of the WCTU, recommended a member in Massachusetts who prepared the juice in bulk. "As she is an earnest white-ribboner and dependent, like some of the rest of us 'Protestant nuns' on her own exertions for the support of herself and her mother, I think it 'meet, right and our bounden duty' to pass along the good news of her success in preparing just what we want."[81] The WCTU urged greater nonsacramental use of grape juice as well, arguing "that it ought to have a wider use for social and economic reasons." Technology was overcoming the problem of preserving and transporting the grape juice, but it still needed better marketing. It also required "a new style of drinking glass and decanter, or receptacle of graceful and attractive shape." The WCTU's goal was to "win by good taste and pleasure given to the eye those who would reject ugliness, and the assurance in a distinct cup that our liberty should not be misjudged."[82] By encouraging the young grape juice industry, temperance campaigners could ensure a proper drink for sacramental and nonsacramental purposes alike.

DR. WELCH'S GRAPE JUICE..

Is from Choicest Concord Grapes, pressed and sterilized by improved apparatus. Bottled and hermetically sealed within one hour after skin of grape is broken.

Contains No Alcohol—A desirable beverage for the sick or well.

Sample 4-oz bottle free to Druggists.

OVER 21,000 Gallons sold in 1894.

Capacity 10 Tons of Grapes per day.

EVERY BOTTLE GUARANTEED.

DR. WELCH'S GRAPE SODA . .

A big success. Only with Dr. Welch's Grape Juice can you get the desired color, with strong grape aroma and flavor.

Sample, formula and circular free upon application.

THE WELCH GRAPE JUICE CO.
VINELAND, N. J.

Charles Welch, a temperance advocate and Methodist communion steward, opposed using alcoholic wine for the Lord's Supper. He developed a technique to produce nonalcoholic grape juice for the sacrament; it soon developed into a substantial business. (Advertisement courtesy Welch Foods Inc.)

A confluence of temperance principles and modern business methods soon led to the production of grape juice on a mass scale, all through the work of a Methodist dentist. Thomas Welch was born in England but grew up in the "burned-over district" of upstate New York. Deeply committed to reform causes such as temperance and abolition, Welch briefly served as a preacher before pursing careers in medicine and dentistry.[83] In 1868 he became a Communion steward at the Methodist church in Vineland, New Jersey. But he was bothered by using alcohol for Communion. One Sunday a visiting preacher staying in the family home offered Communion and became drunk on the Communion wine. The experience inspired Welch to find a nonalcoholic replacement for wine. Working from Pasteur's 1850 discovery of yeast, Welch looked for ways to prevent fermentation. In 1869 he settled on a way of boiling grape juice in bottles so as to kill the yeast.[84]

The discovery did not take off at first, as church resistance was strong. In 1875 Welch's son Charles, another dentist, revived the grape juice idea and founded a company. As Welch's grandson put it some years later, "The demand had to be created. The public had to be educated. Prejudice had to be overcome." Charles started by placing ads in the Methodist *Christian Advocate* and by producing his own newspaper.[85] He advertised in handbills mailed to churches and promoted the juice at the 1893 World's Columbian Exhibition in Chicago.[86] One ad read: "Churches will find Welch's Grape Juice as economical as fermented wine, and certainly the preference should be given to the pure and the harmless, even though the price were [*sic*] a little more."[87] When Charles Welch died in 1926, his will noted that "unfermented grape juice was born in 1869 out of a passion to serve God by helping His Church to give at its communion 'the fruit of the vine,' instead of the 'cup of devils.'"[88] Along the way, the passion created a multimillion-dollar company.

Through these various strategies, the temperance leaders carried the day; while most of America's mainline Protestant churches used wine for Communion in 1850, most were using grape juice by the time Prohibition became law in 1920. Prohibition ended in 1933, and the temperance crusade has largely faded away. But the two-wine theory occasionally reappears, particularly in more conservative branches of the Protestant community. One scholar stated in 1984, "If God approves of the beverage, read 'grape juice'; if He condemns its use, read 'wine.'"[89] Others, on the other hand, question this kind of interpretation. One modern temperance supporter noted in 1957 that "the Bible offers little encouragement to those who approach it in search of proof texts as props with which to shore up the cause of abstinence." This does not mean that "temperance workers must abandon either their pleas for abstinence or else the use of the Bible in support of their cause." But it does "call for use of the Bible in some way other than the proof-text method."[90] Most of these scholars acknowledge that Jesus and his disciples used alcoholic wine but advocate the use of grape juice for pastoral reasons. An evangelical liturgical scholar acknowledged in 1980 that the earliest Christians may have used wine, but "certainly with the increasing problem of alcoholism in this country and with the numbers of converted alcoholics attending our churches, many of whom dare not even taste an alcoholic beverage, it would seem wise to make use of grape juice, which is in plentiful supply and certainly is the fruit of the vine."[91] These modern temperance-minded evangelicals have drawn back from the more categorical statements of the nineteenth century, acknowledging that the use of wine is more historical. They still choose grape juice on moral grounds, however.

The wine debate also has shifted among liberal Protestant churches. The 1960s saw the beginnings of a "wine revolution," as wine drinking became acceptable, even fashionable, among the professional classes that make up much of mainline Protestant culture.[92] Perhaps not coincidentally, the liturgical reform movement of the mid-twentieth century—discussed in more detail below—encouraged a return to traditional liturgical practice, including the use of wine at Communion. As a result of these two revolutions some churches began to use wine again.

Many in the liberal churches, however, resisted the return to wine—not on historical grounds but from pastoral sensitivity. Like most Americans, they have adopted a medical—as opposed to moral—model of alcoholism. As Methodist preacher and writer William Willimon put it, "the 'demon' in the alcohol is not in the product itself but in our abuse of it. The problem is in the abuse of one of God's gifts, not in the gift itself."[93] While the WCTU warned of alcohol's moral danger, the medical model allows wine as a viable option for those who can handle it but requires alternatives for those who cannot. A Presbyterian pastor told the *Christian Century* in 1975 that he smells the cup before taking Communion, to see if it is fermented. "No, I am not a liturgical purist. No, I am not a temperance buff. I am an alcoholic . . . in my 25th year of sobriety." He had no sympathy with the two-wine theory, which is "contrary to biblical scholarship." He carefully distinguished himself from the crusaders of the previous century and offered no condemnation of alcohol itself. Yet he thought it "liturgical arrogance to offer only fermented wine on a 'take it or leave it' basis."[94] Since alcoholic wine at the Communion table remains a problem for some, the church needs to at least offer grape juice as an alternative. A reader responded, acknowledging that "Jesus used fermented wine at the Last Supper. But being a

Christian is not a matter of imitating this or that detail of the outward actions of Jesus."[95] These clergymen requested pastoral sensitivity, not liturgical correctness.

Over more than a century American mainline Protestants have debated the proper contents of the Communion cup. They have wanted authenticity—to do Communion as Jesus did it. Their understandings of authentic practice, however, depended on their interpretation of scripture and history—interpretations shaped by their commitments to temperance. A similar debate involved the choice of Communion cup, which involved both the authority of religion in an age of science and the social purity of the church.

THE CUP: PURITY AND AUTHORITY

On the night of the Last Supper, how did Jesus and his disciples drink their wine (or grape juice)? Did they drink it from one cup, or did each man have his own? The question of first-century dining etiquette appears inconsequential at the beginning of the twenty-first century. When it comes to liturgical practices, however, a glass is more than just a glass. In the late nineteenth century and again in the late twentieth, clergy and laity engaged in another debate about the correct way to celebrate Communion. Alongside the question of menu was a question of method—whether to use the common cup or individual cups. There was a great deal at stake. First was a question of authority—the authority of the church's tradition versus the authority of modern science. It pitted clergymen and theologians against medical doctors. Second was a question of purity—many of the objections to the common cup arose from a fear of contamination by other worshippers at the Communion rail.

While at the beginning of the nineteenth century virtually every Christian community used wine for Communion, different traditions served that wine in different ways. The Roman Catholic Church used a single chalice, but since 1415 had limited it to the priests, denying it to the laity. The liturgical Protestant churches—the Anglicans, the Methodists, and the Lutherans—served the Communion at an altar, with each communicant drinking the wine out of a common cup. The Reformed Protestants—the Presbyterians and Congregationalists, among others—passed several common cups either around a table or through the pews. In the Orthodox churches, priests put a piece of bread into the chalice and then served it to the laity with a spoon. The Moravians served the wine in glasses at each place at a common meal. Compared to the unanimity regarding the use of wine, there were a wide variety of practices. With the exception of the last, however, each of these traditions agreed on using a common cup.

As the use of wine at Communion fit in with the alcoholic culture of early nineteenth-century America, the common Communion cup mirrored general practice. Most Americans were used to drinking out of a common cup, whether at a community well or in a railway waiting room. With little concern for cleanliness and little understanding of the transmission of disease, few people saw any reason not to use the same cup.

By the later decades of the nineteenth century, however, this tradition of the common cup ran up against the combined might of science and gentility. Before the middle of the century, physicians were fairly certain that most diseases were in some way communicable, but they had not identified the means of transmission. Most connected disease with "miasma" or general filth, but they could not point to a particular agent. Beginning in the 1870s, however, European and American scientists began developing the germ theory of disease transmission. With the help of newly powerful microscopes, they discovered bacteria and other microorganisms and began connecting illness to specific organisms.[96] Armed with this theory, epidemiologists and public health specialists began looking everywhere for practices that could contribute to the spread of the newly identified bacteria; by the last decade of the nineteenth century, sanitation became the order of the day. As part of its crusade to stamp out tuberculosis, for instance, the Metropolitan Life Insurance Company put 20 million disposable drinking cups in American railroad cars. Municipalities passed laws banning common drinking cups in public places.[97]

But the sanitation crusade went beyond science. The bacteriological discoveries coincided with the rise of the American middle class in the years after the Civil War. Unlike their parents, members of this new class lived in the rapidly growing cities. They were neither laborers nor owners but white-collar workers—professional, clerical, or commercial. This work made them moderately wealthy but not rich; wives did not have to work outside the home. Most families belonged to a Protestant church that fit the broad definition of evangelical and that taught lessons of personal responsibility, private morality, and social gentility.

Despite its economic success, the middle class was not able to isolate itself from the turmoil of late nineteenth-century America. The cities were booming, creating both wealth and barely controlled chaos. They were filled with growing crowds of immigrants, who had exotic beliefs and behaviors. Laborers in new industries struck for better wages, threatening both the owners and the public safety. Josiah Strong, a Congregationalist minister and leader of a transatlantic alliance of evangelical churches, described all these trends—plus the rise of "Romanism"—as perils to "Our Country." "There is no more serious menace to our civilization than our rabble-ruled cities," he warned.[98] Strong's audience, the new middle class, feared the city that made their social status possible.

To secure their social and economic position, the men and women of the middle class sought to reshape the culture to fit their expectations and norms; inspired by people like Strong, they organized reform crusades to save their country and their class. They worked to limit immigration. They waged campaigns against "impurity," including prostitution. Through the temperance campaign, they attacked the "liquor interests." As with that cause, women were in the vanguard of many of these crusades. Frances Willard, led members of the WCTU in an assault on a multitude of social ills besides alcohol, including bad diet, smoking, and impurity. "The mission of the ideal woman," Willard declared, "is to make the whole world homelike."[99] The home Willard invoked was a middle-class one—clean, safe, and orderly.

When the crusade mentality coincided with the advent of germ theory, it fueled a campaign for sanitation. By the 1890s Americans saw the danger of contagion everywhere—streetcars, paper money, and most of all in the person of the unwashed immigrant in the slums. They moved to control any possible source of disease.[100] Anthropologist Mary Douglas would suggest that there was more involved in this sanitation campaign than just germs. She argues that a culture worried about the borders of its society expresses that anxiety through a concern for the purity of the physical body.[101] Seen in this way, the sanitation obsession of the Protestant middle class reflects worries about the broad changes in American society. By controlling disease white Protestants hoped to control a society slipping out of their grasp. This does not mean that these middle-class Americans weren't concerned about actual physical disease, but it does suggest that there was more involved than just fear of contagion.

As with many of the reform crusades, the evangelical churches were at the forefront of the sanitation campaign, for in the battle against disease, morality and health were as inextricably connected as vice and disease. Cleanliness was not just next to godliness, in many cases it *was* godliness. In 1895 the newspaper of the United Brethren urged clergymen to join their local sanitary societies, because the clergy "well know that physical and moral uncleanliness are inseparable . . . that the first steps on the ladder of moral purity are clean faces, clean bodies, clean clothes, clean food, clean houses, and clean surroundings."[102] To be morally pure (and thus Christian) meant being physically pure—clean and sanitary. Physical dirt and disease, on the other hand, implied moral impurity. Just as the temperance crusaders could not think of Jesus as drinking alcohol, sanitation crusaders could not think of Jesus as being dirty.

As with the liquor question, the cleanliness issue involved the Communion table; sanitation crusaders wanted the church to practice what it preached. Beginning in the middle of the 1880s, as a result, some Protestants began criticizing the use of the common cup. Most of this agitation came not from ministers but from laypeople, most often doctors. Two issues were involved in their campaign. The first was science's attempt to be the authority for understanding the world, supplanting religion in that traditional role. The most important example of that claim came in the rise of the theory of evolution. In

Individual Communion Cups

Why permit a custom at the commun-ion table which you would not tolerate in your own home? Individual Communion Cups are sanitary. Let us send you a list of nearly **3,000** churches where they are in use. **Send for Free Book.**

We offer a Trial Outfit free to any church.

Sanitary Communion Outfit Co. 14th St. Rochester, N.Y.

In their marketing the makers of individual communion cups appealed to anxieties about sanitation and gentility.
(Advertisement from *The Christian Intelligencer,* 15 August 1906.)

the case of the Communion cup, this claim of authority was a challenge to the clergy's authority as definers of the faith and interpreters of the tradition. The second issue was an imprecise anxiety about purity. Both physicians and their lay supporters were concerned about the danger of infection by fellow communicants through sharing a common cup. As anthropologist Douglas suggests, this fear of infection reflects a more general concern about boundaries of acceptable society. Late nineteenth-century communicants objected to sharing a Communion cup with strangers—particularly the poor and other social outcasts. This squeamishness led them to change the practice—and the meaning—of Communion, making it a solitary sacrament rather than a communal one.

These two concerns—purity and authority—ran through the Communion cup debate from the beginning. In 1887 M. O. Terry, a doctor in Utica, New York, read a paper to the Oneida County Homeopathic Society spectacularly titled "The Poisoned Chalice."[103] In Terry's eyes, the advances of science, "the prestige of incontrovertible facts," gave the physician the authority of a prophet. "Whether it be necessary to criticise [*sic*] the saloon or the church he should not hesitate to do his duty, even though millions scorn and ridicule him." Terry acknowledged the weight of tradition behind the church's celebration of Communion, stating "that I am as deeply impressed with the sacredness of the solemn festival, the manner of administering of which I am about to criticise, as any one within the hearing of my voice." Despite this disclaimer, he used the authority of medical science to criticize centuries of church tradition.

The issue of purity also concerned Terry. The danger in the shared Communion cup, he argued, lay in the diverse community of the church, which provided a rich opportunity for transmitting disease, welcoming "the saint as well as the sinner (of the past)." This open invitation throws all kinds of people together. "The old lady, pure in mind and body, sips from the cup which has just left the lips of one physically impure . . . [while] the old lady's pure and healthy child takes the cup from the unfortunate child of heredity, the offspring of physical impurity." He asked his listeners, "is it just to humanity to administer a rite which is given as a symbol for purification, when by the process of giving it endangers or contaminates the innocent child as well as the aged parent?" Promiscuous sharing of a Communion cup—and therefore of germs—among such a mixed congregation alarmed Terry and evoked his concern for social borders.

The doctor reiterated that he was "not presuming to instruct the clergy," but he urged the church to offer pieces of bread that could be dipped in the common chalice. Such a change, he concluded, would "free the church from a just criticism, [and would] bestow upon her the laudation of thousands of those who are interested in the health of humanity and who are capable of judging of the truth of my statements." A medical journal, commenting on Terry's paper, suggested another solution to the problem: Follow the lead of the Roman Catholic Church and limit the cup to the clergy, with the laity receiving only the wafer. "It certainly would detract nothing from the sacrament if this practice would be followed by the whole Christian church in all its organizations."[104] Claiming an authority for science greater than that of the church's tradition, these doctors concluded that a more sanitary celebration of Communion would not change the ritual significantly.

While several doctors argued against the use of the common cup, it wasn't until the early 1890s that churches began acting on their concern. Again, the impetus came from a physician. In 1894 Dr. Charles Forbes of Rochester, New York, examined a drop of wine from a Communion chalice from the city's Central Presbyterian Church. Under his microscope he found dust and "epithelial scales which had been washed from the mouths of the communicants" in the wine.[105] Inspired (if not repulsed) by the doctor's report, the leadership of the church asked him to devise a more sanitary way to serve the Communion wine. Rather than dipping the bread in the wine, as Dr. Terry suggested, Forbes proposed individual cups. In early May the church celebrated its first sanitary Communion, drinking from individual cups arranged on a set of trays.

Over the next several years Dr. Forbes wrote and spoke widely regarding the danger of the common cup. He also turned his science into a business. Within a few months the Sanitary Communion Outfit Company of Rochester started marketing his Communion set, a three-tiered tray holding sixty small glasses, each containing a teaspoon of wine, priced from $8.50 to $25.00 per set.[106] Forbes soon had competition, as others—pastors and laity alike—went into the Communion set business. A Presbyterian pastor from a small town in Ohio beat Forbes by patenting his Communion set in March of 1894.[107] Communion set inventors and their agents were vocal participants in the ensuing debates over the proper celebration of Communion; their opponents accused them of sacrificing theological or scientific integrity in pursuit of their own profit.

During the 1890s several other physicians expanded on Terry's arguments on behalf of the individual cup. Howard Anders, a medical professor from Philadelphia, acknowledged in 1894 the danger of "an invasion of the sacredness of religion" but humbly stated that "sanitarians" were seeking to help humanity live longer and healthier lives.[108] Anders suggested that the common Communion cup was a relic of a more primitive age, when people were "innocently and religiously" subjected to the danger of disease—"in the black background of the historical panorama where stalked with prevailing tread the figures of cruel fanaticism, bigotry, ignorance and superstition." For Anders, the common cup was a relic of the impure past. "But is it religious heroism to suffer needlessly the martyrdom of bacillar [sic] attacks while we are strong in prophylactic defense as well as able in knowledge?" In the same scientific spirit as Terry, Anders saw a sanitary Communion as modern and progressive and thus greatly to be desired.

Unlike Terry or Forbes, however, Anders looked to the authority of history as well as that of science. After talking to unnamed "learned and progressive divines," Anders argued that "it is not unlikely that the use of individual Communion cups for the wine dates back to the time when Christ himself instituted the Communion." He supported this highly qualified statement by suggesting (without evidence) that "the Oriental drinking customs at that era were likewise unwittingly hygienic." He cited as documentation da Vinci's "Last Supper," which "represents each disciple with his own cup." As in the wine/grape juice debate, Anders offered the individual cup as having a historic precedent—and thus as being more authentic.

After Anders presented his paper to the Philadelphia County Medical Society, the society debated a resolution stating that the use of common Communion chalices was "a menace to the public health" and recommended "the adoption of an individual-cup method or system of administering the Communion wine in all churches, of whatever denomination or sect." There were a few dissenters—one suggested that the logistics involved with individual cups "would turn a solemn ceremony into a farce," and another argued that people likely to spread disease were not the kind of people who would come to the table—but the resolution passed. That the society would even consider such a resolution reflects a shift of authority in American religious culture at the end of the nineteenth century, away from the clergy and the church's tradition toward the laity and progressive science.

Three years later Anders analyzed the "individual cup movement" for the American Medical Association.[109] At the beginning of the movement, he sensed, many clergy viewed it "with mingled expressions of horror, surprise, resentment and animosity." In time, however, "calm, alert, frank and thoughtful ministers and church members" saw that the movement was "sanitary and not revolutionary, reverential and not sensational." Anders dealt with their objections. He acknowledged that "we know of not one *bona fide* instance of disease contracted from a Communion cup." But, according to modern science, it could not be denied "that many an innocent person may not have acquired disease from the common Communion cup." Given this possibility, Anders asked, "is it reasonable, is it right, is it safe, is it Christian" to risk exposing even one person to disease?

As before, Anders based his argument on religious as well as medical grounds; sanitation was not only good medicine but also good Christianity. Although he was a doctor, he professed to be concerned about the spiritual state of communicants; he doubted that their "spiritual devotion or meditation will be encouraged by diverting thoughts and fears of physical contamination." Reflecting a common conviction that people of the biblical era lived a clean middle-class life, Anders doubted that Jesus or Moses, "that prince of health officers," would have sanctioned the use of the common cup.

As he watched the development of the individual-cup movement, Anders noted that some clergy had resisted, but "the laity of the churches are quicker to see the need of sanitary Communion reform and the good features of the individual cups than are the pastors." He recognized that the debate was between tradition and the clergy on one side and science and physicians on the other. Gentility and progress were on the side of the individual cup, as were all right-thinking ministers. "Progressive clergymen," he concluded, "have argued against the common cup as being opposed to common courtesy, good manners, cleanliness, healthfulness, decency and convenience, as well as scriptural and early church history." This blend of science and gentility was typical of temperance and other middle-class reform movements.

As Anders suggested, resistance to the movement for individual Communion cups came from less "progressive" clergy. For over a decade James Buckley, editor of the *Christian Advocate,* the weekly newspaper of the Methodist Episcopal Church, attacked the individual Communion cup movement on a variety of fronts. His columns provoked reactions from pro-cup clergy, leading to a long series of articles and responses in the years before and after 1900.

Unlike the physicians, Buckley drew heavily on the tradition of the church, "the simple principle that all customs in the Church that are universally prevalent should be maintained, unless there are insurmountable reasons for changing them."[110] He reviewed scripture, particularly the narratives of Jesus' institution of Communion. Those narratives clearly showed, argued Buckley, "that the apostles drank the sacramental wine in the presence of their Lord from a common cup." The history of the church, he believed, showed that Christians had always used the common cup—for instance, he noted that the Council of Constantinople in 691 banned the practice of people bringing their own cups. The tradition had to be defended, Buckley believed, because conforming to modern science would give unbelievers "evidence—of which they have not been slow to take advantage—of the truth of their contention, that the Christian faith is a shallow crust over the depth of indifference of unbelief."[111] Buckley's aim in the debate was to defend the tradition against unbelievers and sanitarians alike. By basing his argument on church tradition, he refused to grant the physicians' claim of authority in this question of liturgical practice.

Even when supporters of individual cups claimed to offer evidence from the church's history, Buckley questioned their interpretations. In response to a minister who used da Vinci's "Last Supper" as proof, he retorted, "what could not be proved from paintings, especially when they were executed nearly fifteen hundred years after what they represent took place?" One correspondent, echoing temperance assumptions that the disciples must have been teetotalers, suggested that "judging from their cleanly habits, each [of the disciples] had an individual cup." But, Buckley pointed out, the proponent "produced no tradition, nor a single sentence which implied that any father of the Church taught or surmised such a thing."[112] He mocked "passages about the clean habits of the apostles," noting that "their association with Christ did not make them immune to the ordinary diseases of mortality. Forks were not known in the days of Christ and His apostles, and they ate out of a common dish." Early Christians touched the sick and kissed each other "promiscuously prior to the administration of the Holy Communion."[113] Once again a debate about Communion turned on the search for authentic practice, with each side claiming the weight of precedent. Buckley and other individual-cup opponents offered the authority of tradition against the authority of science.

Despite his focus on the tradition, Buckley was not above citing his own scientific evidence. He asked his readers who were physicians to write in with proof that disease could be transmitted via the cup. "None were forthcoming, but instead several physicians wrote declaring the whole movement a baseless scare." He also pointed out that those who were scrupulous regarding the cup continued to breathe in public, "far more dangerous than a common cup sipped occasionally."[114] Buckley analyzed reports of epidemics supposedly tied to the use of a common cup and found them overblown.[115]

In the intensity of the debate Buckley questioned the qualifications and motives of critics of the common cup. One expert told him that "many of those who have emphasized and exaggerated the danger of the Communion are without experience as sanitarians." Instead, they were in it for self-gain, "accelerated by inventors, patentees, and advertisers of cups."[116] Buckley accused some advocates of offering "bribes and commissions" to pastors and congregations to get them to use the cups.[117] From this conspiratorial view, the individual-cup crusade was not about theology or sanitation but about marketing.

The key to the issue for Buckley, however, was theology. For those who consider Communion nothing more than remembering a martyr or a departed friend, he wrote, "any change to suit convenience might be made in wine, bread, number of cups, or ritual, provided good taste were not violated nor pathos extinguished." But for Buckley, Communion was much more than that—it was a sacrament instituted by Jesus, who intentionally chose its form to reflect its purpose. For Buckley, "The Holy Communion is ordained to symbolize the union of the believer with Christ, and the union of all believers in One Body."[118] No matter the divisions within the church, he proclaimed, "one, and only one, rite has been maintained as a complete and sublime utterance of equality, namely the *common cup* at the Communion. Jew and Gentile, bond and free, male and female, black and white, parents and children, master and servant, ruler and subject, rich and poor, minister and layman, have all drunk from one cup. Those dressed in broadcloth and silks touch their lips to the same cup that has been tasted by those in homespun and cotton."[119] For Buckley, Communion is about community. He characterized his opponents, on the other hand, as "full of the vanity of introducing a new custom." From his perspective, they "have denied that the Lord's Supper in any way symbolizes the communion of believers with each other."[120]

Buckley's respondents accepted this characterization of their position, arguing that the Lord's Supper was not meant to be a communal experience but an individual one. After reading the Bible's accounts of the Last Supper, one stated that "there is not a hint of the fellowship of believers one with another, or of their union in one body. The ordinance is memorial of Christ, and exclusively of Christ." He concluded that the individual cup is "more suggestive of the real purpose of the supper, namely, the fellowship of the individual disciple with his divine Lord and Master[.] He takes that little cup in his hand, filled from the common wine, and forgetful of all but the sacrifice of the cross, he enters into undisturbed fellowship with Jesus."[121] These arguments suggest a radically individualistic understanding of Communion.

For both sides the Communion cup question had pastoral implications. Buckley acknowledged that some people might be anxious about the health or cleanliness of the person next to them, but he had little patience with their concerns. He urged going "to the altar to receive from the hand of the distributing deacon the Holy Communion, whether son or stranger, servant or employer, genial companion or repellent neighbor sits by our side." Thinking about the hygiene of a neighbor is surrendering "the soul to the body."[122] Buckley urged his readers to focus more on the presence of Christ than on the purity of the church.

The full implications of the purity crusade, the editor felt, were apparent against the background of Jim Crow-era America. He noted that in many churches it was customary for African Americans to go to the Communion table after the whites. Some clergymen, he observed, have "gravely suggested that individual cups might put an end to the necessity of separate congregations for the whites and colored throughout the South. The superficiality of this remark probably accounts for its brutality." The individual Communion cup, Buckley believed, would result in dividing the church along racial and numerous other lines. "The logical consequence of refusing to drink from a common cup, be it observed, merely upon grounds of taste, would be the formation of caste churches, the freezing out of such as were disagreeable, and the reducing of religious societies to clubs in which any member should be permitted to blackball unsatisfactory applicants."[123] Here Buckley came to the heart of the Communion cup issue—the desire to draw boundaries around and within the community of the church. The individual Communion cup, he believed, had serious—and dangerous—implications for the church.

At least one of Buckley's opponents, however, felt he was being insensitive to the legitimate concerns of church members. One Methodist clergyman used individual cups because his congregation wanted them. "There is an increasing number of persons who object to the common cup. . . . Some of them decline the cup when it is put to their lips, or they refuse to present themselves at the chancel rail. Among such have been some of the most loyal and devout of my members." While Buckley might dismiss such people as "squeamish," the clergyman concluded that "this is largely a matter of taste."[124] This pastor discarded tradition rather than alienate his members.

Another clergyman, disagreeing with Buckley's theological convictions, argued that "there is real Communion where a score or more persons, each with a clean cup in hand, all take the sacrament at the same time. We claim, however, that it is not nearly so important as to *how* the emblem of the Lord's passion is taken, as to the fact that it is taken by faith in him." For this pastor, the means of serving was a "non-essential." His congregation had been using the individual cups, and he felt "that it constitutes the most beautiful, chaste, solemn, and impressive sacramental service that it has ever been the privilege of the people here to attend."[125] Yet another questioned the need to conform to tradition at all. "But suppose they did use but one cup, must we conform to apostolic usage in everything? . . . Because times and customs have changed. The fact is, we have not been observing the original method. . . . The New Testament says but little about forms and ceremonies. The manner of doing things was left largely to our sense of propriety."[126] In this view, the pastoral needs of the people were more important than the tradition.

The debate was not limited to the Methodist Episcopal Church; other denominations struggled with the question of the Communion cup, raising many of the same issues. In Lutheran circles, as in Methodist, clergymen and theologians argued about the role of tradition, scriptural interpretation, and the meaning of the sacrament. Most agreed that the nature of the cup was *adiaphora,* a nonessential. An individual-cup advocate stated that "the cups had no essential import. . . . The validity lies in the *contents,* and in the efficiency in the spirit in which it is received."[127] One of his opponents, acknowledging that many parts of contemporary liturgy differ from the practice of the disciples, conceded that "in unessential things our celebration differs from the first. . . . Now the use of a common cup or of individual cups is an unessential thing."[128]

Nevertheless, there were disagreements, some of which centered on biblical interpretation. One suggested that, since the disciples had been celebrating the Passover meal, there must have been multiple cups on the table.[129] On the other hand, an opponent, noting that the Lutheran church was dedicated to the scriptures, not "mere reason"—a distinction "which separates her from the Reformed family of Churches"—engaged in detailed exegesis to show that Jesus used only one cup at the table.[130]

Whatever the scriptures said, the strongest opponents of individual cups based their arguments on tradition, which was more important for the Lutherans than for the Methodists. One Lutheran pastor wrote, "the weightiest argument for the use of but one cup at the institution of the Supper seems to us to be not the word of Scripture, but the custom of the church. From the beginning and for nearly two thousand years but one common cup is used."[131] The Lutheran church was inherently conservative, one stated, and added that "only an urgent necessity and the very best reasons will induce our church to break and part with that which is tried, proved, and historic."[132] This strong adherence to tradition, they contended, was what made Lutherans Lutherans. "If the Lutheran church is ever to become the leading Protestant denomination in America she must ever, even in externals, maintain a distinctive and peculiar character."[133] The tradition elevated the Lutherans above Reformed and other "non-sacramental" churches, where "the use of the Individual Communion Cup can be introduced with a lessened disturbance of conscience."[134] The individual cup was first introduced in "the very Churches which can see nothing but symbolism in the Holy Sacrament," but it would not fit the theology of the Lutheran church, centered on "the union of all communicants in one body in Christ, the living Head."[135] In general, Lutherans put theology at the center of the debate. "The individual Communion cup is a contradiction of the spirit and symbolism of the Sacrament. The one term implies separation and distinction; the other implies union and fellowship."[136] Rather than pastoral or sanitary concerns, the Lutheran debate over the individual cup focused on the authority of the tradition and the theological meaning of the sacrament.

By the early twentieth century, individual Communion cups had become common among American Protestant churches, especially the nonsacramental ones. While there is no way to determine how many churches chose the new cups and how many kept the common cup, individual-cup Communion sets were soon standard features in church supply catalogs. Some congregations even found that Communion sets could be objects of beauty as well as utility. A Presbyterian worthy advised that "the trays and cups should be of as fine a texture and workmanship as the means of the congregation will permit. Many churches have beautiful Communion services which they have received as memorial gifts."[137]

Some churches, recognizing that something was missing from their services, came up with various ways to hold on to the idea of a communal Communion while using individual cups. One ministerial advice book recommended adding "impressiveness to the service" and preserving "the ancient symbolism" by placing old Communion chalices "on the table between the trays containing the individual cups."[138] A Lutheran liturgy guide recommended placing individual cups in the pews or at the entrance to the chancel. At the time of distribution each communicant would bring a cup to the altar, where it would be filled from a chalice with a pouring lip.[139] These compromises sought to keep the sacrament both symbolic and sanitary.

Many congregations developed a new practice that sought to give individuals sitting in pews the feeling they were eating together. According to Buckley's description in the *Christian Advocate*, as the individual cups were passed, "the people take them in their hands, await a signal from [the pastor] and simultaneously lift the cups to their lips." Buckley snidely concluded that "a reporter observed that the spectacle was truly impressive. We doubt it not, but it was the impressiveness produced in the public when the children perform a calisthenic feat in good time."[140] A clergy advice book found the practice "of questionable value. It seems too reminiscent of drinking a toast." The author based his objections on different theological grounds, sensing "that there is something very personal about taking Communion which is lost by this regimented wholesale participation. Communion is an act of fellowship, but it is also an act of personal worship and dedication."[141] Like Buckley's critics, this author was working with a more individualistic understanding of the sacrament. Both he and Buckley, however, objected to the theatrical nature of simultaneous Communion.

For many the concern for a sanitary Communion included the bread as well as the cup. Presbyterians were told that "the bread should be cut into small cubes. The plan of slicing a loaf of bread with the crusts removed and permitting communicants to break the bread as it is passed is to be emphatically discouraged as both unbecoming and unsanitary."[142] One of those reforming women at the WCTU reported on the ideal Communion, as celebrated in her church in 1912. The bread was unleavened—as she put it, unfermented. The "wine" was nonalcoholic, for obvious reasons. And the "wine" was served in individual cups. "Why? Because to that table came the diseased, the sick, the afflicted, and there must be no destroying germs conveyed from one to other." Around that table, she concluded, "Christ [was] fitly represented. No sin-afflicted one could say that he was tempted or his appetite for drink aroused. No one with the glow of health could be tainted. The bread and the cup, like Christ, were pure, free and life-giving. Was not this supper a perfect symbol and what Christ intended when he invited his guests to the 'Lord's supper'?"[143] For middle-class American Protestantism, this was the perfect Communion—pure and hygienic.

By the middle years of the twentieth century, however, some of these middle-class Protestants were questioning the pure Communion of their youth. Pastors and scholars, participating in the liturgical reform movement of the 1950s and 1960s, wanted to shake up the practice of the Lord's Supper.[144] Their campaign often ran up against the convictions of the laity, especially regarding the individual Communion cup.

The liturgical reform movement arose from the confluence of academic, ecclesiastical, and cultural currents. Post-World War II scholars investigated the liturgies of the early church, trying to "recover" models for contemporary practice. Seminal works were Gregory Dix's *The Shape of the Liturgy* (1944) and Bard Thompson's *Liturgies of the Western Church* (1961). Much of this scholarship drew on anthropological investigations of ritual, including that of Victor Turner. It appeared in liturgical journals, including the Catholic *Worship* (founded as *Orate Fratres* in 1926) and the Presbyterian *Reformed Liturgy and Music* (founded in 1965), which shared the results with parish clergy.

Meanwhile, changes in the church encouraged changes in liturgical practice. The most important was the Second Vatican Council (1962-1965). Not only did it radically change the worship practices of the Catholic church; it also encouraged greater dialogue between Catholics and Protestants, leading to a liturgical convergence of the two traditions. Ecumenical discussions within American Protestantism—most notably the Consultation on Church Union, which began in 1961—required discussions regarding worship in the larger church. Inspired by this academic and ecumenical activity, individual American denominations—notably the northern Presbyterians (1961) and the Lutherans (1978)—revised their worship books, with practices reflecting the emerging consensus.[145]

But the liturgical revival wasn't the only revolution going on in these years. The decade's counterculture searched for spiritual vitality, for real experience, and for community but had little interest in the tradition of the church. In particular, it developed scorn for what it saw as the "hang-ups" of bourgeois American Protestantism. Two Presbyterian ministers, looking to offer "creative worship for the emerging church," proposed to "revitalize our stale, and sometimes perverted, worship methodologies." They looked to the Communion table for community, "the calling of the church to be and to become the incarnate word of God," as a means of overcoming the radical individualism of modern American society.[146] Seeking community at the table was a common theme. Another observer stated that "in Communion, in partaking of the same cup and the same loaf, we act out what we would like to be as a church; we practice eating as the Body of Christ so that we might become the Body of Christ."[147] The counterculture's search for community required the church to reexamine its Communion practices. Liturgical reform was a response to cultural trends as well as ecclesiastical ones.

One of the victims of the liturgical reform movement was the individual Communion cup. Most liturgical scholars heaped considerable scorn on the little cup, arguing that it was inconsistent with the practice of the early church as reflected in the Bible. One reminded "the reader that to the one loaf should correspond the one cup (cf. I Cor. 10:16ff) and that therefore the acquisition or use of individual cups is inadvisable as especially injurious to the communal character of the Communion."[148] Another argued that the common cup was not only historical, but also one of "two *unprecedented* actions of Jesus during the meal." It was radical—and importantly symbolic—for Jesus to have used a common cup, for usually "the guests had individual cups." The single cup, he concluded, must be historical, "since it can hardly have sprung from the creative imagination of the primitive community."[149] These scholars returned to the question of authentic practice.

Others raised theological objections to the individual cup. In 1965 one Lutheran pastor saw the "germ question" as "a Tower of Babel destroying over 1900 years of sacred practice." He argued that sinful humans, under "satanic manipulation," often have destroyed God's plans, and he wondered if "the seemingly innocent use of grape juice and individual glasses is not just one more extension of this satanic manipulation?" The individual cup, he concluded, was wrong theologically, "more concerned with the private, vertical relationship to God, at the expense of the suffering neighbor in the world."[150] A Congregationalist scholar saw the individual cup as an "element of individualism"; until they are removed, he worried, "the desirable unitive character of the Eucharist will be seriously weakened. If the sacredness of the meal and stress on unity are to be renewed, individual glasses, so reminiscent of cocktails, must be removed, and chalices and loaves must be substituted."[151] Like Buckley seventy years before, these theologians fought against individualistic interpretations of the Eucharist.

Others based their more visceral scorn on the aesthetics of the individual cup. In the 1970s William Willimon described "Communion as it is 'celebrated' in many churches today: self-contained, thimble-sized glasses and tasteless, infinitesimal bits of bread far removed from the original, biblical experience of eating with Jesus, now almost incomprehensible to the average person." Such "cold, rigid, robotlike, assembly-line, impersonal actions reveal exclusiveness, detachment, and insensitivity to the hungry."[152] Elsewhere Willimon mourned that "too many holy Communions are more expressions of holy hygiene (with their disposable, individual, antiseptic plastic cups) . . . than of worship of God. We invite them to the Bridegroom's feast and then treat them to a weight-watcher's fast!"[153] One Presbyterian, echoing the contemporary critique of the "suburban captivity of the churches," complained that the individual cup, like other Communion practices, separates the Lord's table "from the people so comfortable in their cushioned pews."[154] The liturgical radicals saw the "tiny individualized portions of grape juice [as] examples of commercialized substitutes for Christ's broken body and poured-out life."[155] For these writers, the individual cup represented much that was wrong with postwar middle-class Protestantism.

Some observers, however, defended the individual Communion cup from these attacks. One argued that "millions of people have known the sacramental presence of Christ as they drank together with their companions of the Way and received the fruit of the True Vine from individual cups." He concluded that "their means to Christ ought not to be scorned as they are in much current literature."[156] Another acknowledged that if you use the little cup, "some of the pictorial element disappears, but the gift is still there." He urged chalice crusaders not to "regard those who used other forms as weaker brothers and sisters."[157] While they did not offer an unqualified defense of the cup, these men sought to moderate the pro-chalice crusade with some pastoral sensitivity.

Most churches retained the individual cup, even though it had become liturgically incorrect. Among liturgical reformers, however, the individual cup had gone out of fashion, replaced by the traditional silver or the politically symbolic ceramic. In one modern worshipping community, reveling in the counterculture, "a beautiful crocheted tablecloth, which someone had brought from home, was placed over the table. The homemade bread and wine were brought forward and placed on the table. Large pottery mugs also were presented from the congregation."[158] Even in more traditional worship settings, scholars worked to make the common cup a norm. One stated that "the common cup was taken for granted in early thinking about this sacrament, as it was in the words of Jesus repeated in the Eucharistic prayer."[159] When a group of Lutheran denominations created a common worship book in 1978, they advocated strongly for the common cup. A commentary on the liturgy argued that scientific studies had shown the cup to be safe, while "the use of pre-filled individual glasses destroys the significance of the one cup, is excessively individualistic, and is totally undesirable historically and theologically." It tolerated the use of the pouring chalice "where circumstances prevent sharing the chalice directly."[160] The liturgical scholars were leading a return to fundamental church practice in using the common cup.

The people in the pews, however, would have none of it. A brief mention of the common cup in the magazine of the Lutheran Church in America provoked several letters in 1978, none of them positive. One reader found it "hard to believe that my church, guided by well-meaning but unrealistic theologians, is really going to take this giant step backward into the Dark Ages." Another, a doctor, agreed that "the practice might have seemed acceptable" before the advent of the germ theory, "but it is medieval and known to be dangerous at the present time. It is wholly unacceptable for the 'image of unity' which it is supposed to invoke."[161] For these laypeople, their health was more important than the theologians' integrity.

As in the 1890s, a physician crystallized the issue. In 1983 a retired public health specialist and American Lutheran Church layman criticized in a denominational magazine the proposed reintroduction of the common cup. We would never think of using one drinking glass when entertaining guests at home, "but somehow church leaders think this practice is entirely acceptable when serving the Lord's Supper." Obviously baffled by the thinking of clergy and theologians, he wrote that "the sole reason for encouraging the use of the common cup is to provide an image of unity. This reason is not strong enough to preserve a filthy, unhygienic practice."[162] A grateful reader replied that "it is about time we heard from someone with expertise, instead of accepting the unsupported assurances of clergy who are not competent in the field of disease." Another found that the "prospect of receiving wine via this odious practice" removed her interest in participating in the sacrament.[163] These laypeople placed greater stock in the physician's knowledge of disease than the clergy's concern for good liturgical practice.

In response to the article, the Worship Committee at Luther Northwestern Theological Seminary investigated the question of the common cup. It traced the variety of practices in the history of the church and concluded in 1984 that "neither the New Testament nor the Lutheran confessional writings specify that all who participate in the

Lord's Supper drink directly from the same vessel." Serving two to five hundred people in the course of a service also makes a single cup logistically difficult. The study group acknowledged the importance of "a visible, corporate, eucharistic expression of Christian unity in the form of a meal." Nevertheless, the public health specialist who wrote the original article convinced the group of the dangers of disease arising from the cup. In conclusion, the group recommended that the seminary "give consideration to methods other than many communicants drinking from the same vessel."[164] The seminary adopted the use of a pouring chalice and individual cups for its community worship.[165] Despite the school's theological concerns, the committee gave way to the possible presence of germs in its midst.

The release of the committee's report coincided with the rise of another, more dangerous germ—human immunodeficiency virus (HIV), the virus that causes AIDS. The AIDS epidemic began quietly in the early 1980s, but by the middle of the decade it was perceived as the country's leading public health threat. Numerous factors—its first appearance among socially marginal groups, its incurability, and the horrible ways it killed its victims—made the AIDS virus the most feared microbe in decades. Inevitably, AIDS became an issue in the common/individual-cup debate in almost every denomination; since the Lutherans, however, had recently made a very public endorsement of the common cup, it hit them particularly hard.

Frank Senn, a Lutheran pastor, criticized Luther Northwestern for releasing its report as the fear of AIDS was increasing.[166] The school denied any connection, Senn said, "but if the seminary wanted to make some kind of witness in the face of the irrational panic caused by the spread of this disease, its decision was badly timed." He proclaimed that liturgy "should not be conformed to the culture of this world; it should be in a position to transform it." The point in the Communion cup debate "is whether the body of this crucified Lord are ready to abandon themselves in radical obedience and in love of one another." For this pastor, retaining the common cup had significant theological and ethical importance, involving the heart of Christian identity.

As in the 1890s, the argument was as much about pastoral sensitivity as it was about theology. Some pastors felt that the liturgical reformers were out of touch with the concerns of the people in the pews. A member of the faculty at Luther Northwestern, while disappointed with its decision, stated his willingness to hear the concerns of the laity. "Can we expect the same from the liturgical gurus?" he wondered.[167] Another pastor argued that "in our discussions the pastoral needs of our parishioners, not the 'right' liturgical form, however legitimate, needs to be the prime concern."[168] For these Lutherans, the needs of their people were more important than liturgical correctness.

Like Buckley decades before, Senn dismissed these pastoral concerns and focused on the ethical and theological implications of the individual cup. He believed there was too much at stake, arguing "that sound pastoral care does not lie in giving in to people's fears or phobias." He acknowledged the problem in his own parish, where "one family left because we would not abandon the common cup, citing concern about AIDS as the reason. Another person stopped communing altogether for a while because one homosexual male, not even known to be at risk for AIDS, communed regularly."[169] But he worried that certain people, including gay men and those with AIDS, "will become as lepers—a new class of untouchables feared by society and cast out of the eucharistic fellowship."[170] In Senn's eyes, the individual Communion cup endangered the integrity of the church by drawing lines in the name of purity. Supporting Senn, another pastor concluded that concerns about AIDS made the common cup even more essential, for "in this time of exclusion and fear the gospel clearly points to . . . the Blood of the One-who-was-with sinners made to be common to us all."[171] The concern over AIDS and the common cup again confirms Douglas's insight regarding physical and social boundaries. This concern for sanitation and purity, her theory suggests, was also a concern about the boundaries of the church. The laity and many clergy, anxious about the presence of those at high risk for HIV—mainly drug users and gay men—resisted the reintroduction of the common cup with its potential for transmitting disease.

Although their debate was particularly public, the Lutherans were not the only church group struggling with the question of a common cup in the age of AIDS. The Episcopal Bishop of California pledged to continue drinking from the cup himself but encouraged those anxious about disease—and those persons with AIDS concerned about opportunistic infections—to take only the bread at Communion.[172] The National Council of Catholic Bishops consulted with the Centers for Disease Control, which believed that while the HIV virus could not be transmitted by a common cup, it "could not provide an absolute endorsement that the practice is safe." The council urged parishes to continue using the common cup but allowed pastors to inform "those who are fearful that they have the option of receiving Christ under bread alone."[173]

Meanwhile, another medical scientist proposed changing practice on the basis of the potential for disease. A microbiologist writing in a Canadian evangelical journal acknowledged that the risk of transmission is low. Further, he stated, "spiritual factors eliminate the high-risk group of persons from participation in Communion services"—implying that real sinners, the only ones likely to be infected, wouldn't come for Communion anyway. Nevertheless, he believed, the potential for infection still existed. "Good sanitation practices," he concluded, "would strongly suggest that the common chalice be superseded by individual cups at Communion services, retaining the chalice as a visual cue for personal use by the minister alone."[174] This perspective suggests the scientist was as concerned about purity as he was about his scientific research. Other medical studies presented a mixed report. Most agreed that the Communion cup *could* transmit disease, but some argued that there had never been solid proof of such transmission taking place.[175]

The last half of the twentieth century saw the introduction of two other means of distributing Communion. One was the restoration of an ancient practice, while the other was a radically new—and in many ways typically American—idea. The ancient practice was intinction, the dipping of the Communion bread into the wine and eating both together. The Western church practiced intinction intermittently in special situations—most often in the case of the dying—until it was banned by the Council of London in 1375, possibly because such dipping echoed the morsel of sopped bread Jesus offered Judas. It remains, however, the standard way of receiving Communion in the Eastern church, where the celebrating priest puts pieces of bread into the wine and then offers the mixture to communicants on a spoon.[176]

Intinction returned to the Western church through Anglicanism. In the nineteenth century some Anglo-Catholics recovered the practice as they looked to restore the worship of the Middle Ages.[177] Partly in response to sanitary concerns, the 1948 Lambeth conference of Anglican bishops passed resolutions permitting the use of intinction. The General Convention of the Episcopal Church of America in 1949 allowed churches to use intinction, subject to the approval of the bishop.[178] A British medical journal praised the move.[179] An American Episcopal priest, while uncomfortable with innovation, acknowledged "how sensitive Americans are" on the subject of hygiene and concluded, "probably something has to be done to relieve them."[180] Since the second Vatican Council, the Roman Catholic Church has permitted intinction.[181]

Thanks to the reform movement, intinction has become a more common option in mainline Protestantism, as nonliturgical churches—especially Reformed churches—became more interested in older liturgical traditions. The 1986 *Book of Worship* of the United Church of Christ acknowledges intinction as one of many options for receiving Communion.[182] Congregations of all the mainline denominations adopted intinction; they could do so because few churches had liturgical regulations that would bar the practice. In most cases advocates present it as a compromise between the restoration of single cup, so desired by liturgical reformers, and hygienic scruples. "An agreement to practice intinction can be a way of caring for one another, while preserving the important symbolism of one chalice," a Presbyterian pastor concluded.[183] The Episcopal bishop of Newark, long involved in AIDS concerns, preferred the common cup but accepted intinction in a virus-wary culture, "for it keeps the eucharistic symbols intact."[184] Some liturgical purists, however, still complained that it "undermines the symbolism of drinking from a common cup."[185] Obviously intinction was a compromise that did not satisfy everyone.

Remembrance, marketed by a Southern Baptist publishing house, combines
grape juice and a morsel of bread in one easy and sanitary package.
(Photograph courtesy LifeWay Christian Resources
and Broadman & Holman Publishers)

The 1990s saw the appearance of a fascinating variant on the
individual Communion cup—prepackaged Communion. An Oregon
pastor designed and manufactured a small plastic cup that contained
juice and a wafer of unleavened bread in separate sections. His church
of 2,800, he bragged, reduced Communion preparation time from ten
hours to forty minutes. Marketed by a Southern Baptist publishing
house under the name Remembrance, the product was sold through
Christian bookstores and used by thousands of mainly evangelical
congregations as well as by thousands of men at a Promise Keepers
rally. While some were critical, the pastor replied, "it's more important
that you do it than how you do it."[186] The prepackaged Communion
sets were a creative adaptation of an ancient rite to contemporary
American culture, with its obsessions with hygiene, bigness, efficiency,
and packaging. Methodist writer William Willimon, however, wanted
nothing to do with it. "Just when you thought that modern life had
depersonalized the gospel to the utmost, we have another break-
through—Communion without communion!"[187]

Worshippers at University Church in Chicago receive communion any way they want it—either wine or grape juice, individual cup or common cup—from stations around the table. (Author's photograph)

From antique engraved silver chalices to prepackaged grape juice, Communion practice among whitebread Protestants has covered the map. This variety of practices has grown out of a strenuous debate among clergy and laypeople about practical and theological concerns. Two issues, above all else, have shaped the debate. The first is a question of authority. Physicians, claiming the authority of science, challenged the authority of the church and its traditions to shape practice. Laypeople, afraid of infection, have listened to the physicians rather than to the clergy, opting to protect their health rather than the authenticity of the sacrament. Second, this obsession with health and purity has changed the practice—and thus the theology—of the sacrament. The individual cup, intended to prevent the spread of disease, has fostered an individualistic understanding of Communion. Afraid of contamination by others in church, whitebread Protestants have shifted their theology of the sacrament, focusing on the Communion of the individual and God rather than the Communion of the entire church. Squeamishness about disease and a concern for social boundaries within the church has changed the meaning of a fundamental practice of the church.

A Communion table stands at the center of University Church, an English Gothic building across the street from the University of Chicago. Affiliated with the Christian Church (Disciples of Christ) and the United Church of Christ, the congregation is a stronghold of liberal Protestantism. When dedicated in 1923, the church had straight rows of pews facing a raised chancel, which was occupied by the pulpit and the Communion table. At the height of the 1960s liturgical reform movement, the congregation reoriented the sanctuary, bringing the table out of the chancel and into the center of the room, with the pews facing it in the round. On the first Sunday of every month, the congregation celebrates Communion. There are six stations around the central table, each with a different way of distributing the elements—wine or grape juice, single chalice or individual cups, drinking or intinction. Catering to those concerned about sanitation or alcohol, the church allows its members to receive Communion in any way they choose.

This diversity of practice is emblematic of mainline American Protestantism. No other worship tradition would give members this variety of choices at the Communion table. Southern Baptists wouldn't allow wine. Roman Catholics wouldn't allow the individual cups. Those churches have their rules—written or unwritten. Mainline Protestant churches like University Church, however, put more importance on meeting the needs of their members than on following a particular set of liturgical rules. Depending on a person's theological commitments, this openness to a diversity of practice looks like either Christian liberty or mushy relativism.

The diversity of liturgical food practices among whitebread Protestants goes beyond the two debates considered here. Different churches use different kinds of bread, for instance. The more liturgical churches use the traditional thin breadlike wafer. Others—particularly Methodists—use a Chiclet-like pellet. Most of the churches I grew up in used cubes of Wonder Bread—perhaps the ultimate white bread. In one church I visited, the presiding minister broke a hot dog roll as part of the celebration. The wine and the cup discussed in detail here do not exhaust the varieties of Communion practice.

This diversity of practices is not accidental but reflects important tensions within American Protestantism. The individual Communion cup and grape juice both owe their introduction to nineteenth-century reform movements, rooted in the church but seeking to change all of society. In both cases the crusade for change was led by laypeople—temperance-minded women in the case of grape juice and physicians in the case of the Communion cup—and resisted by clergy, who were trying to defend traditional practice. The debates over these liturgical changes are part of ongoing conversations in American Protestantism over authority and tradition.

These debates over the cup and its contents also reflect the diversity of meanings Communion holds for mainline Protestants. Some of those concerned for authentic practice wanted their Communion to be a reenactment of the Passover Seder with Jesus, while others saw it as a traditional rite, reflecting continuity with the church of all generations. Advocates of the individual cup spoke of Communion as a mystical experience for each worshipper, while common-cup users stressed the communal experience of all participants. While some critics see this diversity as proof that Communion is meaningless for whitebread Protestants, it might also suggest that Communion has many meanings, often reflected in one event.

Eucharist, the Lord's Supper, Communion—whatever it is called, the sacrament stands at the heart of Christian worship and is paradigmatic of all Christian meals. But there is far more to eating in church than this one meal. Next we turn to fellowship food—meals that may carry more meaning for their participants than Communion itself.

CHAPTER TWO

SOCIAL FOOD: POTLUCKS AND COFFEE HOURS

IN FEBRUARY 1952, St. Pauls Evangelical and Reformed Church of Chicago dedicated its new parish house. The congregation, one of the oldest in the city, had been planning and raising funds for the building for years. It included offices, classrooms, a full gymnasium, and even a set of locker rooms. The heart of the Parish House, however, was the kitchen. The envy of some restaurants, the kitchen could serve a sit-down dinner on china plates for over four hundred people. It was the ultimate in church kitchens.

But the kitchen at St. Pauls was not unique; American churches large and small include kitchens and fellowship halls, many built in the same postwar years. Some of these kitchens are more complex than others, but out of all of them has come an endless stream of coffee, spaghetti, cookies, and salads. Church members have devoted facilities, money, and labor to make these meals possible.

Why have American Protestant churches devoted so much of their resources to feeding their members, most of whom were perfectly capable of feeding themselves? It's because Americans go to church for more than teaching and prayer. They go looking for community. We live in a society that discourages connections between people. On the frontier Americans lived miles away from their nearest neighbors. As cities grew, everyone was a stranger. Our market economy encourages competition rather than community. In the middle of this life of isolation, Americans hunger for community, for connections with other people. They find that community in church—specifically, in the church's social events.

This chapter is a history of the church social as a response to this search for community. It traces the development of the social congregation, which arose in response to the need for community on the frontier and in the growing city. It identifies the instructions for community in church-produced "fun books." It shows how church socials changed as a congregation's community changed. Finally, it looks at the theological implications of the ultimate in church socials—the church food court.

Please note that this chapter is about food-centered social events rather than the food itself; there are no recipes and only a few menus. The food is essential, however, because it provides a center for community; it meets a common need and nourishes a life together.

These food-centered social events are not religious in themselves. Jell-O salad is not sacramental, and potlucks are rarely salvific. Church dinners and coffee hours do, however, play an important role. They are crucial to the religious life of many Americans. For these people participating in a community is often the most important motivation for attending church, and shared meals are often more important to creating community than are shared worship experiences. The meals are a place where religious identity is shaped, community is built, and memories are created. They may not be religious, but they're not just another meal.

THE RISE OF THE SOCIAL CONGREGATION

Christians have been eating in church at least since the Last Supper; these meals have served a variety of purposes. Some have been ceremonial, such as communion or love feasts. Others, in contrast, have been simply practical. Still others have been instrumental, planned with the goal of creating community within a scattered congregation. This goal gave birth to the social congregation in the second half of the nineteenth century. It was a uniquely American invention, shaped by the particular circumstances of American church life.

The first church meals in America, however, were practical affairs, at camp meetings at the dawn of the nineteenth century. In these temporary communities on the American frontier, people gathered to worship, pray, and eat together. The first revival meetings were informal affairs, and visitors relied on local hospitality. But the August 1801 revival at Cane Ridge, Kentucky, tested the limits of such hospitality, with over eight hundred people in attendance. This was a lot of people in a fairly small space, with no church kitchen or fast food restaurant nearby. Barton Stone, pastor of the host church, remembered that his members shared their food with visitors, but soon the crowd grew so big that even those supplies gave out. While many worshippers may have stayed with more affluent hosts, historian Paul Conkin estimates that there may have been as many as 140 wagons surrounding the church, with people sleeping in their wagons or on the ground. They cooked for themselves and tethered their horses in nearby pastures to graze. Camp meetings were not vacations, especially for women. Even though the revival services were almost continuous, somebody had leave worship to mind the cook fires.[1]

Although meals at camp meetings were necessary because of the crowds, they were as much about socializing as they were about food; "roughing it" helped to bond the community. One account notes that "there was something cheery about clustering around an open fire to roast ears of corn or meat on forked sticks." Some camps featured boarding tents, where worshippers could buy meals at moderate prices, while campers known as "spongers" lived off the hospitality of their neighbors.[2] Church leaders, dismayed at the festivity of these communal meals, urged restraint. In 1839 the editor of the *Western Christian Herald* suggested the "plainest fare," so that cooks could spend more time before the throne of grace and less over the cook fire.[3] Despite the best efforts of revival leaders, the camps sometimes also attracted merchants peddling vegetables, desserts, and liquor—the last officially forbidden but often available. These camp meeting meals continued in the tradition, most common in the rural South, of meals "on the grounds" of the church.[4]

Other than the camp meetings, however, there is little record of antebellum churches planning meals simply for the sake of fellowship; such social events awaited what church historian Brooks Holifield calls the "social congregation." Colonial-era churches were "comprehensive congregations," he argues; each settlement had one church, which included all the residents and which served all their needs—spiritual, political, and social. The church's main function was worship, but it was also a community center. Social and political changes at the end of the eighteenth century challenged this monolithic comprehensive congregation. States disestablished churches, forcing them to be financially and politically independent. This increase in denominational competition created more religious options while the rise of benevolent organizations—including reform and fraternal societies—provided alternate social and political opportunities. Meanwhile, industrial capitalism fostered class divisions. In response to all these changes, congregations were forced to focus their energy on specifically religious functions for individuals within a neighborhood, making them "devotional congregations."

The pattern changed yet again in the decades after the Civil War, giving rise to the "social congregation." In these years, Holifield writes, congregations became centers for more than just worship. While New York pulpit prince Henry Ward Beecher encouraged seminarians to "multiply picnics," many congregations took his suggestion one step further and built gymnasiums, parish houses, camps, baseball teams, and military drill teams. These new measures were important in a rapidly growing country, Holifield concludes, as the churches hoped "that the new congregational activities could overcome the impersonality of large churches and synagogues, eliminate class distinctions, attract children and their parents, provide wholesome amusement for young people, and draw men more actively into congregational work."[5]

In an urbanizing and industrializing society, social congregations also sought to provide alternatives to the city's tempting entertainment. In rural America, churches were the only social center available and thus could exercise some moral control over their members. The growing cities, however, provided many temptations, particularly for young men and women away from the influence of home and family. In place of Sunday school and prayer meeting, the city offered saloons, amusement parks, and pool halls, places designed to attract and corrupt young minds with fun. In the urban environment, churches were just one competitor in the free market of entertainment; they knew that city dwellers had an almost infinite number of ways to spend their time and money.[6] In this competition, the church had to use every tool at hand, including food.

To retain members and attract young people, Protestant churches organized alternatives, including picnics in parks and games in the church gymnasium. In 1924 one advocate of such programs called on churches to accept and redeem play and physical training. He acknowledged that "there are forms of idling time away which are called amusements that are evil indulgences in themselves and there are others that come perilously close to falling under this classification." But he pointed to the example of the Young Men's Christian Association (YMCA), which "redeemed gymnastics, athletics, bowling, and pool."[7] In such a scheme recreation became not ancillary but vital to the church's mission.

For immigrant congregations—like St. Pauls Church in Chicago— these social events were even more important. The church, founded by German immigrants in 1843, served as their community center, where people could both feel at home and experiment with assimilation. It preserved ethnic solidarity and tradition against the homogenizing forces of the larger culture. And it provided opportunities for young people to meet and court, encouraging marriage within the community.

To meet these various social needs, congregations and denominations created a rich variety of social organizations in the late nineteenth century. Women's societies, founded to support missionary work, often became social groups as well. Men's groups, perhaps inspired by the rise of the YMCA, also served a mixture of missionary and social purposes. Perhaps most important were groups for young people, such as the interdenominational Christian Endeavor Society, founded in 1881, and the Methodist Epworth League, founded in 1889. Along with Bible study, social service, and evangelism, these organizations sponsored coed social events for members of high school age. With the aim of building community, they were the heart of the social congregation.

GAY PARTIES FOR ALL OCCASIONS: THE BIRTH OF THE FUN BOOK

The organizations within the social congregation served a variety of purposes: supporting mission work, educating members, and helping the poor. But alongside these official functions, the groups also built community, as an important part of their mission.

To serve the need for community, church groups developed a well-organized system of fun in the late nineteenth and early twentieth centuries. They planned parties, excursions, plays, banquets, and socials of various sorts, many of which were centered on food. Social events were built into the structure of many of these church organizations. The headquarters of the Epworth League, for instance, recommended that each local chapter have a social committee to plan wholesome parties and meals for its members.[8] Like other parts of American life at the end of the nineteenth century, socializing became bureaucratized.

But evidently building community wasn't easy. Whitebread Protestants, it appears, needed instruction in how to be social. According to a group expert writing in 1940, "capacity for the full enjoyment of life has to be developed. It involves attitudes, appreciations, interests, and skills. These do not come by happenstance or wishful thinking. They require time, patience, planning, and effort." In this man's eyes, fun was serious business. "Informality, spontaneity, surprise, variety, verve, fun, and good fellowship are basic necessities for the highest success," he concluded.[9] Americans needed to plan their fun.

National officials and the denominational publishing houses came to the rescue. Beginning in the 1890s they started issuing "fun books," references full of ideas and suggestions for church social events. Cokesbury Press, the Methodist publishing house, printed many of them, but they were aimed at an ecumenical audience. The authors were clergymen, successful leaders of Epworth and Christian Endeavor groups or popular in their Kiwanis chapters, or women with a gift for entertaining. With titles like *Gay Parties for All Occasions* and the *Abingdon Stunt Book,* the fun books suggested everything necessary for a good party—from theme and decorating ideas to games and menus. Even if short on time or creativity, a group leader could organize a successful social event with the help of a fun book. The author of one of the earliest such books hoped that "the volume will have a wide circulation and help to solve the problem of social evenings in our Church life."[10] Another imagined that "the plans in this book will make those eating meetings more inviting and entertaining."[11] The books gave church leaders a model for the social congregation—a community full of good wholesome fun. In the process of solving "the problem of social evenings," they also modeled what it meant to be Christian.

The fun books were an endless source of creativity. One of the first books, written for the Epworth League in 1894, suggests fifty different themes for league events, ranging from a "Literary Salad," to "Illustrated Nursery Rhymes," to a "Penny Social."[12] A "Party Book" from 1932 offers fifty-two complete parties, one for each week of the year, complete with text for an invitation, games and "stunts," and decoration and refreshment ideas. Party themes include a Valentine Party, College Field Day Party, Celebrities Party, and a Water Carnival.[13] *Gay Parties for All Occasions* was written for "a single family or . . . groups of families working together in the church, club, or community in big family night programs." Among the ideas for family parties were Let's Have a Circus, a Commencement Party, Family Jamboree, and a Hobby Party.[14] The *Abingdon Party and Banquet Book* of 1950, on the other hand, focused on banquets for adults, each with a theme; keyed to each theme was a humorous menu. Among the suggestions: the Classroom Capers

Banquet, an Irish Luncheon, and the "Kampus Kut-Up" Banquet, "planned for a group that includes both married and single young people." The menu for that banquet included Dressed Campus Fowl, Cranberryisms, Peasology, Tumbled Saladometry, Chilled Teography, Rollsalgebra, and Pastry a la Modernisms.[15] The *Cokesbury Dinner and Banquet Book,* by the same author, contained similar ideas, but added opportunities in the program for prayers and inspirational address.[16]

The parties outlined in these books have common elements. They all center around a theme; as one author notes, "a good theme helps. 'A Mother Goose Banquet,' 'A Rainbow Banquet,' 'A Circus Banquet'— the very mention of these themes sets the mind to working with the idea."[17] They all include games of some sort—a mixture of "active" and "quiet" games. One book's Valentine Party featured a mixer, a "Heart Puzzle," a "Valentine Relay Race," and "Heart Archery."[18] Alongside the games were "stunts," goofy skits strictly done for fun—often at the expense of one or more of the party guests. One collector of stunts traced the idea back to church young people's conferences in the early twentieth century, where it was the custom "to put on a stunt night during the week of Conference or Assembly, at which time the group from each city in the state is requested to produce a stunt." Stunts were often a feature of Rotary and other service club meetings. Through the stunts the author hoped "that the burdens of life will be lightened and our courage to meet the more serious problems of life will thereby be renewed."[19] Finally, all of the suggested programs allowed time for refreshments; most recommended a menu, whether it be a heart-shape cake and heart-shape sandwiches for a Valentine's party, or "Stewed Rabbit" and "Seance Vegetable" for a "Mystery Banquet."[20]

With all of these elements, the fun books provided more than ideas for a successful program—they provided a middle-class Christian worldview. The parties the books suggest are proper entertainments for Christians, although the program ideas have few explicit Christian or ecclesiastical elements. Some allow time for prayers or an address, but mainly they are just parties. Nevertheless, these books present a world that is supposed to be fun, creative, wholesome, and well ordered.

Coffee is essential for any church committee meeting, including this sophisticated
gathering in the parlor of St. Pauls Church, from sometime in the late 1950s.
(Photograph courtesy St. Pauls Church)

Designed specifically for whitebread Protestant churches, the books
reflected the congregation's class, religious, and social norms.

The focus on middle-class churches is never explicit, but it is
inescapable. To throw most of these parties, for instance, a church would
need a fellowship hall, complete with a reception room, a full kitchen,
and a contingent of volunteer, if not paid, staff. The books also encourage
a strong sense of etiquette and middle-class propriety. A 1953 book
entitled *Christian Etiquette* argued that Jesus "performed his first miracle
to save an embarrassing situation for a bridegroom at his wedding
reception" and offers "some suggestions for good manners at a church
social." It encourages party organizers to

> plan the entire social. It is rude to invite people to a social and then
> not plan for their entertainment. Plan every detail in advance. Plan for
> an icebreaker to start the evening. Have plenty of good games. Check
> to be sure that everyone on the program is prepared. Be sure of your
> menu. Plan the music. Decide how the new people will be introduced.

Plan what you will say in introducing your honored guests. Arrange transportation if any is needed. Decide what time refreshments will be served. In essence, plan your church social until the evening is worthwhile for every one.

A good social committee chair was, in effect, a good hostess. The etiquette book further recommended that a church dinner should be sophisticated, noting that "it is the finishing touches which make or fail to make a church dinner whether it be a pot luck or banquet. Provide center-pieces for tables. Use candles. Pick pretty teen-age girls for waitresses and have them wear identical aprons. Provide dinner music on records if musicians are not available."[21] Just because the dinners are for the church, these books seem to argue, doesn't mean they shouldn't be elegant.

And yet, while sophisticated, these events are to be *church* socials—they aim to be Christian, or at the very least not worldly. Religious elements occasionally sneak into the programs. One book suggests a "Bible Party" for a youth group meeting, planned "not for study, but for an evening of fun. At the same time no one can play the games given here without getting a lot of Bible knowledge that will be helpful." (Preceding this suggestion is the outline for "An Evening With the Gods," based on Greek mythology, so there is a certain ecumenism afoot.)[22] An etiquette book suggests closing the Sunday school picnic with "a campfire devotional period."[23] Another party suggestion concludes with the admonition that Saturday night is not a time for dating but for studying the Sunday school lesson and an early bedtime.[24]

While few of the parties feature prayer or sermons, they are Christian in their wholesomeness. None of the menus, of course, includes alcohol. The books shun rough language, and occasional sexual double entendres are lodged safely in the context of courtship or marriage. Church social events were meant to provide an alternative to the morally dangerous parties of the "world." Nevertheless, they made the excitement and etiquette of the "worldly" available to Christians.

All of the parties suggested in the fun books were for subgroups within the church, divided along age, social, and gender lines, with few for the entire church. For each group there was appropriate entertainment and a menu. Parties for the youth group tended to focus more on games, while events for older groups included stunts or speeches—funny or serious. Adult parties also were segregated along social lines, generally for either couples or singles, with little mingling between them. Some, finally, were only for men's or women's groups. This segregation reflects the organized nature of the social congregation and of American life. As society became more institutional and bureaucratic in the late nineteenth and early twentieth centuries, middle-class Americans spent more time in specialized settings. Men (and a few women) spent a majority of their waking hours in the workplace, a generally homosocial setting. The schools divided children into classes along age (and sometimes gender) boundaries. Even outside work, men and women tended to socialize in gender-segregated settings. This increasingly balkanized social system shaped the church's social life as well.

Perhaps because the parties often were planned for adolescents and young adults, many focused on love, romance, and dating—all in a wholesome context, of course. The party suggestions make powerful assumptions about gender and relationships. In particular, they depict women as out to catch and control innocent young men. The *Cokesbury Party Book* suggests a party to honor a new bride and groom, beginning with the verse "Needles, needles, and rolling pins, / When a man marries his trouble begins." Throughout the plans for this party, wives are seen as bullies, interested only in making their husbands behave and earn more money. In the script for a mock wedding service, the "father of the bride" says, "I gladly give her into the board and keep of this unfortunate man. My gain is his loss."[25] A 1951 collection offers an "Opportunity Party" for Leap Day, when young ladies are allowed to be the aggressor and invite the men. "The reception room may be filled with all kinds of mechanical traps, such as mousetraps, bear traps. . . ." When a man arrives, he is captured by two or three women, blindfolded, and sent through "Old Maid's Row," where he is molested by women acting as man-hungry spinsters.[26] While recommended for a church, these parties had little to do with Christian understandings of marriage. Rather, they reflect cultural images of marriage as a trap for men and of women as desperate for a husband.

The books also advocated games as a social control mechanism. The author of the *Fun Encyclopedia* noted the problems of planning events for certain kinds of people, including the Dignified, the Timid, the Blasé, the Know-It-All, the Subnormal, and others. For those who set themselves apart from the group or try to take it over, he recommends making them the "victims of 'goat stunts,'" games that intentionally embarrass the victim and bring him or her to the level of the group. Others, he writes, are "Religious Dyspeptics," who object to fun and games on moral grounds, looking "with disfavor on harmless fun, and sometimes are very critical," having "a depressing effect on the rest of the group." The author suggests educating them "in the values of wholesome play."[27] In the world of the fun book, there was little room for those who don't want to have fun.

The fun books played an important role in the development of the social congregation. They provided guidelines for the building of Christian community, telling whitebread Protestants how to plan their meals, find their fun, and meet potential spouses—all in a properly Christian way. The books seem to have reached their peak around the 1950s, cresting with the postwar church growth boom. Offering exemplars to pastors and group leaders around the country, they helped to develop congregations' social life just as church supply catalogs helped to foster the decoration of the sanctuary. To get a sense how this social life developed, we turn to the experience of one congregation and its social life through the twentieth century.

BUILDING COMMUNITY IN CHICAGO

Over its more than 150 years, the members of St. Pauls Church in Chicago have consumed tons of spaghetti, numerous salads, and countless cups of coffee. All of these food-centered social events were designed to create community in a complex city. The history of these food events reveals how the congregation's expectations of community have changed.

By the end of the nineteenth century, St. Pauls was a typical "social congregation." In 1869 a group of young men and women founded the Jugendverein, or Young People's Union, which held social events and pushed the congregation toward greater integration in American society. Men in the church formed the Men's Club, the Ushers Association, the Edgewood Bowling Club, and the Athletic Association. In 1892 the congregation's women, under the leadership of the pastor's wife, formed the Frauenverein, or Women's Union. In addition to their own social events, these "Mothers of the Church" took responsibility for taking care of the church building and cooking its meals. While these organizations had a variety of purposes—study, service, or education—many of their meetings centered on food. Many of the church's meals, particularly before the middle of the twentieth century, were not only strictly for adults but were also gender-segregated. In their program and their menu, these separate men's and women's meals reflected gender roles prevalent in the larger society.[28]

Starting in the early years of the twentieth century, the Men's Club held annual dinners at the church. To a more casual age these dinners appear quite formal, mirroring the huge secular feasts of businessmen and fraternal organizations of their day. The menus were large, involving multiple courses (often with French names) and always featuring at least one kind of meat, usually beef. The club's annual dinner in 1913 was a four-course banquet, featuring trout and beef tenderloin and concluding with cigars.[29] This menu was a common one for men's dinners in the early twentieth century; food historian Laura Shapiro writes that "the dinners planned for men were mighty, sometimes blatant, symbols of maleness. Commonly recommended for a bachelor supper or a men's club dinner were saddle of mutton, woodcock, strong cheese, brown bread, and hard-crackers."[30] In this gendered understanding of food, a meal for men must be substantial—and include meat.[31]

Like the menu, programs for the Men's Club dinners were weighty. The 1913 dinner, presided over by a toastmaster, featured a song from the men's quartet and the church's orchestra, a poem from the assistant pastor, and a special address by social gospel leader Graham Taylor, "A

Church for the City and a City for the Church."[32] The 1918 dinner attracted more than three hundred men to a room decorated with "many American flags . . . in harmony with the spirit of the evening." "Forty gracious young ladies waited on the tables, while twenty more women, some young and others not so young, worked like Trojans in the kitchen." According to the church newsletter, the meal, featuring beef again, was "one of the finest meals ever served at a Men's Club dinner."[33]

The club's meals changed as circumstances changed. The meals went into some decline during the 1930s, reflecting the pressures of the depression and perhaps a decline in the availability of willing "ladies."[34] After World War II, however, Men's Club dinners returned with enthusiasm. In 1948 the club's leadership announced that all future meetings would be preceded by a meal: "We anticipate that the dinners will encourage more of our members to attend regularly, and will also spare the wives the trouble of preparing dinner on at least one night each month. We believe that most of you will agree that there is nothing quite like a good dinner to get any meeting on its way." These meals were prepared by the women of church and served by girls—suggesting that not all the wives were "spared" the trouble of preparing dinner.[35] By the late 1950s, however, men from the church's Catering Committee were sharing in the food preparation. In the church newsletter the group crowed about these men-cooked meals: "Do you know, that we have the best cooks in Chicago to prepare the delicious food served at our meetings?"[36] A 1958 "Ladies Night" dinner featured a male member's famous fried chicken as well as "fellowship, entertainment, and 'Gemut-lichkeit'" in the form of games and group singing.[37] When the men did the cooking at St. Pauls in the 1950s, it was a major item in the newsletter.

Women's organizations also revolved around food, with meals that were as feminine as the Men's Clubs dinners were masculine. One such group was the Dorcas Society, made up of younger women interested in studying the social issues of the day. The newsletter reported in 1930 that members of the society felt that "joining in at coffee parties or being studiously present at all society functions, bringing good friends together from time to time for a pleasant pastime is well and good enough in its place, but the Dorcas society is organized for greater purposes."[38] Nevertheless, the society did indeed eat at its meetings. A luncheon in 1938, the society reported, was quite enjoyable; "the hour that is spent around the festal board surely creates a friendly feeling and closer fellowship between one another."[39] On the menu for these luncheons may have been the "dainty, delicious sandwiches" recommended by a fun book, *How to Plan Church Meals*. The author argues that "sandwiches for the tea table are quite a different thing from the 'he-man' sandwiches you want for a picnic, or the meal-in-one you serve to teen-agers. They are delicate, made for nibbling—and looking pretty is far more important than providing nourishment."[40] Or lunch may have been a salad, as recommended for women by a generation of domestic scientists. As Shapiro notes in her *Perfection Salad*, "as a kind of non-food, the salad course had a non-nutritive function: it enhanced the femininity of the whole meal and made the scientific cook herself more socially palatable. Decorative, seemingly ephemeral, salads were perceived as ladies' food, reflecting the image of frailty attached to the women who made them."[41] Whether fragile salads or dainty sandwiches, the menus for the women's luncheons were appropriately feminine.

Like the men, the women of the church also held more formal social events. A good example is the tea held to celebrate the dedication of the church's new parish house in 1952. The menu included "a plentiful supply of dainty tea sandwiches and cookies [which] added to the completeness of the occasion." The entertainment featured a "delightful and well-known reader" performing her writings, including "humorous verses, stories about gardening, household experiences, and family living which everyone recognized as true to life. All were told in such a happy manner that everybody's spirits were refreshed."[42] An annual event for the church's women, perhaps parallel to the Men's Club annual banquet, was the annual Easter Monday luncheon, the cooperative effort of the various women's organizations. In 1961 the menu included "potato salad, jello molds, pickles, olives, meat balls, ham, fried chicken, and all the rest of the goodies." Over 180 women attended, "replete with all their Easter finery." A woman comedian doing Swedish ethnic humor provided the entertainment.[43] Like the luncheons of the Dorcas Society, these formal meals modeled the femininity expected of the church's women.

Not all of the church's meals were exclusively for adults. The men's and women's organizations each invited their children to join them for the annual Father-Son and Mother-Daughter banquets, meals that reinforced these food-structured gender roles in the younger generation. The Mother-Daughter Banquet in 1934 featured a play called "Ruth, the Loyal," produced by the women and extolling devotion to mother.[44] In later years the mothers and daughters welcomed visiting entertainers, such as "the Gypsy Troubadours," a balloon artist, or a fashion show provided by the Cotton Council of America.[45] Each of the banquets included singing (with songs such as "What a Faithful Friend Is Mother," sung to "What a Friend We Have in Jesus") and concluded with a candlelighting ceremony, marking the passing of wisdom and tradition from mother to daughter. The Father-Son banquets were more obviously masculine, both in program and menu; in the place of poetry and songs of devotion, the 1966 banquet began with a Boy Scout-led pledge of allegiance, with a dinner of roast beef followed by a tumbling act and Disney cartoons.[46]

As the adult meals at St. Pauls presented a model of society's gender roles, food-centered social events for the congregation's young people presented a wholesome model of youth, an alternative to dangerous adolescent activities. Wholesome church-sponsored programs for youth have a long tradition in American religious life. Colonial Massachusetts pastor Jonathan Edwards gathered his Northampton youngsters into neighborhood groups for lectures and "social religion."[47] One fun book author, an Epworth League leader and self-proclaimed expert in "Phunology," argued in 1923 that "young people will seek to satisfy the social instinct. It is God-implanted." But he warned that "if the church and the community do not provide their social life in other wholesome modes of expression, for this God-implanted instinct, young people will seek outside the church for places, many of them undesirable, or positively dangerous."[48] The church had the duty to model a wholesome adolescence; it conveyed these models partially through food events. These activities were even more important to an immigrant church like St. Pauls, as it sought to assimilate its children into the mainstream while providing them a place to meet and court young people from the same ethnic group.

To serve these purposes, St. Pauls put great emphasis on wholesome entertainment for its children and teenagers. Soon after the turn of the twentieth century the Young People's Union hosted a "necktie party" to encourage young men and women to socialize. "Each girl brought a necktie and an apron made of the same cloth. She would put on the apron and leave the tie at the door. As they arrived, each of the boys would choose a necktie, then enter the social hall to discover who was to be his partner for the evening."[49] At a 1924 supper for the confirmation class, "the girls of the class furnished the entertainment while the boys furnished the best appetites and the noise, ably assisted, of course, by the girls. So it proved to be a real homelike party."[50] In 1939 the congregation's youth welcomed the Young Peoples Federation of the Chicago area to the church; the main course was an increasingly common treat, chop suey, which fortunately could be extended to satisfy the larger than expected crowd.[51] Since that dinner had depleted their budget, the Young People's League had a simple potluck Thanksgiving dinner. The church newsletter detailed the "simple" menu of "casserole dinners of noodles, vegetables and bean varieties, meat loaves, three kinds of potato salads, three varieties of cole slaw, salmon mold, five fruit and vegetable jello molds, potato chips, pickles, olives, bread and butter sandwiches, cakes, cookies, candy and coffee!" A member made the buffet table "look even more enticing, by directing two blue floodlights upon it."[52] The "Chuck Wagon" at the Junior Congregation's 1941 Western night featured a menu that "was true Western style (at least the Council members who planned the meal seemed to think so)—beans, beans, and more beans, then dry bread, coffee, and doughnuts."[53] Kids, after all, will eat anything—no matter what color light is on it.

If the congregation worried about the temptations awaiting their young people after World War I, the anxiety reached a fever pitch in the

1950s and early 1960s. This was the era of *West Side Story* and *Rebel Without a Cause.* Anxious parents, worried that their children growing up in the city might join a gang or drive a Mercury over a cliff, turned to the church for help. In these years the congregation organized a variety of activities to keep the youth coming to church; the planners knew that if you fed young people, they would come. Confirmation class "graduates" were invited to join the junior high fellowship at a party; the youth pastor wrote breathlessly, "if you don't come, there is something wrong with you because they always have a very good time and I sincerely hope that you will become a very active member of that group for they do a great deal of good and have lots of fun as well."[54] In the late 1950s the church turned the basement of the new sanctuary into a "Youth Center and Lounge" where the young adults "had a Smorgasbord supper followed by entertainment."[55] In March 1961 the senior highs went swimming and then went back to the church for pizza, which soon became a youth group standby.[56] At the peak of the national folk music craze in 1964, the youth group hosted a "Hootenanny" that attracted over one hundred teens from neighboring churches. "Pizza and coke were served by hard working mothers. When the evening was over, $33 was collected for the Mental Health Drive."[57] The young people also presented three short plays as a "cafe-style theatre-in-the-round," modeled after Chicago's increasingly famous Second City company. "Food? Of course," the newsletter promised. "Pizza, beverages, and other refreshments (all soft!) will be sold at intermissions."[58] Members of the congregation were urged to turn out and show their support for the young people's programs, events that kept the church's youth out of real nightclubs and in the church.

These programs for church youth were part of a larger concern about families; to serve them congregations like St. Pauls organized "family nights." In 1962 the church sponsored "a Night of Knights" which "found our gym transformed into a kingly banquet hall as well over 200 'knights, ladies, and little jesters' enjoyed a scrumptious pot luck 'feast' and a delightful movie: 'The Mouse That Roared.'"[59] A Mardi Gras in 1963 featured games, cartoons, and dancing for everyone (including "twisting for the teens"). In place of gumbo and jambalaya, the menu

A family night supper at St. Pauls featured a Polynesian theme, including
appropriate decorations, plus two impressive buffet lines.
(Photograph courtesy St. Pauls Church)

was most un-Cajun: hot dogs and taffy apples.[60] The "Family Roundup"
in 1966 featured the same menu at the "chuck wagon," plus square
dancing with the "Hi-Kickin' Chickens."[61] An international night in
1967 brought out three hundred people for lasagne, Swedish meat balls,
chicken teriyaki, and sauerkraut and bratwurst prepared by families in
the congregation. "The menu made all dieters wish they had stayed at
home." Guest performers from local Filipino, German, and Spanish
American communities provided the entertainment.[62] As the young
adult group said about their own meetings, the family nights "brought
all of us closer together, sort of like a big happy family."[63] None of these
social events was explicitly religious, but all were aimed at strengthening
the nuclear family and giving it the church's blessing.

Throughout much of the twentieth century the church's food events
built community and presented its members with models for society.
Adult dinners reflected gender roles, youth events encouraged wholesome and churchly behavior, and family events built togetherness.

Changes in urban America after World War II, however, challenged these traditional models. Economic growth and the rise of the automobile culture allowed Americans to move to the suburbs. This exodus destabilized city neighborhoods and their churches, while causing a building boom of suburban churches. The church's once-stable neighborhood, Lincoln Park, changed as longtime German residents moved farther away from the center city. Landlords divided large row houses, built for families, into small apartments to house an influx of single young people. The construction of the now infamous Cabrini-Green public housing complex just south of Lincoln Park brought African Americans into the community. St. Pauls, no longer a neighborhood church, needed to change its identity and its program to survive.

In 1947 the church council contracted with Booz Allen, a nationally known consulting firm, to evaluate the church, its neighborhood, and its prospects and to propose solutions. The consultants argued that St. Pauls had gone from being a neighborhood church to being a "First Church"—a prominent congregation serving a city-wide constituency. No longer serving an ethnic enclave, its future lay in being the leading church of its denomination (Evangelical and Reformed) in Chicago. To attract members from a larger area, however, the church would need to provide more services. The consultants recommended that the congregation build a new parish house, including up-to-date facilities for children's and family programs. With expanded facilities and programs, the church would need an assistant pastor for pastoral care, a director of Christian education, a program director, and a full-time dietician/cook. With a food service staff, the church could offer regular Sunday dinners, which "help to build fellowship in a large church as well as to meet a growing interest of people in going out for Sunday dinner. Committees take advantage of them to meet afterward." They also encouraged the formation of small groups, called colonies. To keep people coming into the building during the week, the church also could offer "mid-week dinners around which a variety of activities are built such as choir rehearsals, young peoples groups, various group meetings of the church school, church officers meetings, a joint meeting of the colonies with

The dedication festivities for the St. Pauls Parish House, in the spring of 1952,
featured a formal banquet for over four hundred people.
(Photograph courtesy St. Pauls Church)

outstanding speaker or special music and other groups." In addition, the
kitchen could cater special dinners for outside organizations, to provide
a service for local nonprofit organizations and to help raise some money
for the congregation. "Most dining rooms operated on the above basis
are not only self supporting but often are able to make a contribution to
the total budget of the church. It eliminates putting the burden of church
dinners on women's organizations except to help with table waiting
which may also be shared by young people."[64] Thus the consultants
pinned the congregation's future on food.

Following these recommendations, the church built a parish house
in the early 1950s. The building's architect understood the new challenges that the city presented to the church and its mission. In his note
in the dedication program, he wrote of "the great need for off-the-street
recreational, spiritual and cultural opportunities for youth." Outreach
to youth lay at the center of the church's plans for the new building, and
the design addressed these plans. The architect noted that St. Pauls was

"a large, cordial family, and one of the blessings of family life is the privilege of gathering in Christian fellowship. This is well provided for in your new Parish House for its dining and kitchen facilities make the preparation of large-scale dinners comparatively easy. The scientifically-ventilated and attractive dining hall-auditorium-gymnasium, with its spacious stage, makes possible a festive setting unsurpassed in church units."[65] The architect saw the church's facilities, including its kitchen, as vital in its outreach to family and youth. A sampling of congregational histories suggests that the decade after World War II was a boom time for the construction of church kitchens.

The kitchen and dining room provided ample facilities for the congregation's traditional family- and youth-centered social events. But as the neighborhood changed, with increasing numbers of elderly residents and a growing community of single young people, the family night suppers and youth activities did not appeal to these new constituencies. One pastor observed after a 1975 picnic that many families and new members attended, but "missing in our family gathering . . . were older adults and single persons."[66]

In response, the congregation created food-centered social events to welcome these missing groups. In 1977 the church planned a "Family of Faith Thanksgiving" dinner on the Sunday before Thanksgiving. "Invitations have been sent to our shut-ins and it is hoped that other members of St. Pauls who may have no family nearby will join us."[67] The congregation's strategic plan of 1984 called for specific fellowship programs to reach the elderly, including "at least one new, annual program that improves the sense of fellowship, appreciation and understanding of St. Pauls' German heritage."[68] Food-centered socializing changed to include the elderly.

Given the need to revitalize the church, the outreach to young singles was even more important. In 1960 St. Pauls began to sponsor a series of "after church 'coffee clatsches' for the young 'career' men and women who so often join us for morning worship but who yet remain strangers to St. Pauls and to each other."[69] As the neighborhood rebounded in the 1970s, Lincoln Park became the haunt of Chicago's yuppies, and the church looked for ways to attract them. It opened the gym for a monthly volleyball game, mainly for the young adults. "We then retreat to a home where repasts of various sorts are offered on a Bring Your Own basis (usually wine and cheese)." The church also started a monthly series of restaurant visits and hosted progressive dinners to attract more singles.[70] Previous food events at St. Pauls modeled traditional gender roles and nuclear family structures. In response to a changing urban environment, the congregation adopted a more inclusive model, accommodating single adults.

This shift also affected traditional family nights, which were broadened to include the whole congregation. The Family Life Committee wanted its meals to "be a time when groups of people having diversified interests (such as the volleyball group and the Frauenverein) could enjoy together some of the life at St. Pauls."[71] In 1980 the Board of Elders organized a "Prom Night" but felt that it was "very important, given the theme, that this be 'billed' as an intergenerational event and that single people feel comfortable in attending."[72] The newsletter promised that "there will be dancing, music, and just the kind of refreshment you would expect at a high school dance (with the little-something-extra to be found in the locker room)."[73] A Mardi Gras party several years later moved further from the "family night" model; the newsletter warned parents that there would be no activities for children and so encouraged them to leave the kids at home.[74] These food events reflected a change in the congregation and a shift away from traditional family models.

In general, however, St. Pauls shifted away from large social events in the 1960s and 1970s, for a variety of reasons. Most practically, there were fewer volunteers available to make the food. In 1967 the pastor asked the Mothers Club "to cook and serve dinners for some of the church functions." While happy to help, they replied, "we could not give him a definite answer at this time because most of our members are working mothers, and this leaves it up to those few mothers who are at home (working) and for the help of the others in the evening only." Nevertheless, "we always enjoy working together and helping our church."[75] This decline in volunteer time reflected a larger trend in the congregation, as members had less and less time for church activities. In 1985 the Congregational Life Committee abandoned its monthly "Fun 'n' Games Nights" during daylight savings time, when people were distracted by other claims on their time.[76] A year later the committee announced that it was reducing the number of church-sponsored social events "to prevent 'burn-out.'"[77]

Less practical trends might also help to explain the decline in food events at St. Pauls. The 1960s saw a tide of theological and ethical critiques of the church, especially social events, that focused on wealthy mainline churches like St. Pauls. Around the beginning of the decade a group of social critics, the most important of whom was sociologist Gibson Winter, attacked Protestant "organization churches" for their "trivialization of the religious enterprise." In *Suburban Captivity of the Churches,* Winter wrote that churches were marked by "the bustle of activities which are only indirectly connected with the sacred aspects of religious life." Defined by their place in political and economic structures, organization churches become "a cult of consumption rather than mission and ministry."[78] Winter was not alone. Church historian Martin Marty warned readers that "laymen can become so organized and their activities so routinized that the machinery of church life, smoothly oiled, takes the place of the deity in many a hierarchy of values."[79] Critics like Winter and Marty called the churches to turn their attention away from organizations and activities—such as potlucks and family nights—and to focus on mission and ministry in the city.

In the face of this critique, liberal congregations like St. Pauls shifted their food events from feeding their own members to feeding strangers. At St. Pauls the "mothers of the church" had been doing this work for years. Often during the Christmas holidays, members of the Frauen-verein and the Dorcas Society visited the indigent, taking food along. In 1940 the Dorcas Society distributed twenty-eight baskets of food at Thanksgiving and "23 at Christmas. The Christmas visit to the County Hospital brought gifts of 150 glasses of jelly, 337 boxes of cookies and candy, 30 shoulder capes, 200 oranges and 134 gifts for the 'forgotten men.'"[80] This distribution continued into the 1970s, as the women of the Dorcas Society and the Sunshine Club took Christmas fruit baskets to "the sick and shut-ins."[81] Another group of women baked fifty dozen cookies for a Christmas party for the children of state prisoners.[82]

In the 1960s, however, church members began to turn their attention—and their food—to urban problems. In 1968 the congregation helped to sponsor a summer education and work program for city youth, mainly minorities. "As with all teenage students they get extremely hungry while studying and working. To help solve the hunger problem, women in the congregations are preparing hundreds of sandwiches for daily lunches."[83] As the neighborhood changed, more poor people appeared on the streets and in the houses of Lincoln Park. In response, a group of churches organized an open pantry to "provide food and other necessities for families which have been unable to make ends meet."[84] Within nine years it had served over a half-million meals to needy families.[85] The first Sunday of the month was "Pantry Sunday," when members brought contributions of canned goods to worship.[86] Responding to a different needy group, the church also cosponsored a weekly lunch for neighborhood seniors in need of a good meal.[87] Another agency supported by the church hosted a Christmas dinner for street people. "Donations are needed: turkeys cooked without stuffing, stuffing, salads, cranberry sauce, desserts. Volunteers are needed for kitchen duty and to visit with the guests."[88] Food was a tool in addressing urban problems.

But while members of the church took food out to poor neighbors, it began to invite them inside as well, after a precedent was set in 1968. During the Democratic National Convention in Chicago, protesters against the Vietnam War gathered in a park near the church. When police used horses and tear gas to clear the park, the pastors of St. Pauls opened the church as a shelter for fleeing protesters. "They were invited into the gym and social hall to sleep. They were fed by some of the women of the church, many of whom could imagine their own children or grandchildren in this situation."[89] It was a controversial decision, but it set a precedent for offering the church's hospitality to strangers.

With the gentrification of Lincoln Park and the deinstitutionalization of psychiatric patients, the neighborhood's homeless population grew in the early 1980s. Working with three neighboring congregations in the fall of 1985, St. Pauls opened its doors as a temporary overnight shelter during the winter months.[90] By the end of that winter, the shelter had served hot meals and had provided 3,594 "bed nights."[91] "The Shelter provides an opportunity to do something good 'for one of the least of these, my brothers, and sisters.' It also gives you a chance to meet and talk with our volunteers." Volunteers spent the night supervising the shelter, spent an evening preparing and serving a fresh dinner, or helped shelter guests in the laundry room constructed in one of the gym's locker rooms.[92] The shelter served meals once a week during the summer months.[93] By 1991 the shelter had two staff members, visiting healthcare providers, and a literacy project. It served thirty-two guests per night.[94] The church's kitchen, built in 1952 to serve the families of St. Pauls, by the mid-1980s was welcoming shabby strangers as well as prosperous members—to eat in the basement, if not to worship in the sanctuary.

The church's social concerns even appeared in its social events. In 1988 a committee organized a "South of the Border Night."[95] The elders, however, saw it is a "relative failure," as it "was not so well attended as similar events of recent years, except that South of the Border seemed quite popular to families with children." Looking back, several board members and the pastors "noted/surmised that people may not be regarding the church as a center of social life any more; that, in fact, they look upon the church as a center for volunteer activity in the community, and perhaps South of the Border would have drawn more people if it had been tied to fund-raising."[96] In a liberal congregation like St. Pauls, there seemed to be less time for simple socializing. People were looking for parties with a purpose. In 1985 "the Youth Group [hosted] an 'all you can eat' Pancake Breakfast on Sunday, November 24. The proceeds will be used to support . . . [a] program for homeless and runaway teenagers."[97] Another youth group pancake breakfast benefited Habitat for Humanity.[98] Participants in a combination Bible study and exercise group, called "Exercise and Exegesis," began preparing and distributing sack lunches for the homeless. To support this work they sponsored "a St. Pauls Motherhood and Apple Pie Bake Sale on Sunday, October 18, during coffee hour." Members were invited to "come and get your just desserts!" "Whether baking or buying, be sure to take part in this worthwhile event that will feed both the fortunate and the less fortunate among us!"[99] Church members also attended a shrimp boil on behalf of a denominational mission program on the Gulf coast.[100] These food events were an analogy for the shift in the congregation's self-understanding and its mission, from an inward-focused "organization church" to an outward-focused and mission-oriented congregation.

To help congregations like St. Pauls, these years saw the creation of what might be called a "serious fun book." *Simply Delicious: Quantity Cooking for Churches* provides some of the same helps found in earlier books—recipes, cooking hints—but for a very different church. The book seeks "to encourage local churches to be responsible about serving food. . . . In a world where so many are hungry and malnourished, the church dare not be complacent about how much we eat, about how much we waste, and about the relationship between our greed and our neighbor's need. Also, in a nation where so many of us have serious health problems from eating too much and from eating unwisely, the church must call us to be good stewards of our bodies."[101] In place of recipes for roasted meat and Jell-O salads, *Simply Delicious* featured meatless meals and complementary proteins. In place of ideas for the Valentine's Dance, the book had hints on feeding street people and running a fast to learn about hunger. One chapter verged on heresy, arguing that "Kool-Aid and cookies have had their day." *Simply Delicious* is a cookbook for a socially conscious congregation. St. Pauls even learned some lessons here. A 1990 newsletter urged prospective hosts and hostesses of its weekly coffee hour "to be creative with the refreshments you bring. Consider a fruit tray or vegetables and dip in place of cookies."[102] The church's theological and political concerns shaped the menu for its social hour. Chapter 5 returns to this question of socially responsible food.

The fruit tray of the 1990 coffee hour is a long way from the beef and cigars of the 1913 men's banquet. These two menus reflect the changes at St. Pauls—and in the surrounding society—over almost eight decades. The banquet was overwhelming in its elegance—and in its masculinity. This was a community of men, influential within their ethnic enclave and reveling in its abundance. The fruit tray at the coffee hour, on the other hand, reflects a community struggling to be socially conscious and nutritionally moral. The food events at St. Pauls reveal the changes within the congregation's community—and changes in its expectations for that community.

WHO'S IN THE KITCHEN?

Church leaders plan food events to create community in the congregation. They bring people into the church and keep them there. But these potlucks, teas, and coffee hours don't just happen. Somebody has to boil the spaghetti, cut the cake, and make the tea. Like the social events themselves, this labor is not just practical. Working in the kitchen also helps build community. How a congregation organizes its kitchen reflects how the church understands itself. A church that relies on volunteer labor has a very different ecclesiology—a different doctrine of the church—than does a church that uses paid workers.

In most congregations, women volunteers have done the bulk of the cooking—and usually have worked very hard. At St. Pauls it was the "Mothers of the Church" who did most of the work. A 1923 reunion dinner of the church's confirmation classes, "one of the largest banquets ever held in our Church Hall," attracted almost four hundred people and was prepared by "the willing members of the Ladies' Aid Society."[103] The Mothers' and Daughters' Banquet in 1928 became a bit chaotic when a hundred more people than expected turned out. But "Mother" Pister, wife of the pastor and head of the Frauenverein, "was not to be flustered. She did not lose her mental equilibrium for a moment. Orders flew quickly and decisively. Everybody obeyed. There were no men to interfere, no fathers and brothers to give a lot of advice, and then stand aghast and finally do nothing—nozzir—the sudden rush delayed the beginning just a little."[104] Mother Pister and her coworkers made themselves indispensable with their kitchen skills, in a way the men couldn't—or wouldn't.

These men found community doing the dishes after a church supper at St. Pauls.
(Photograph courtesy St. Pauls Church)

The women of the Frauenverein were not shy about their contributions to the church; they knew they did important work, and they
reminded the congregation of it at every opportunity. In a 1937 church
newsletter, Mrs. Pister noted that "our women worked very hard for
Easter, helped cook the Lenten Suppers, assisted at the ten day Carnival
and again at the Sunday School Picnic." She concluded, "St. Pauls
Church need never worry about its Frauen-Verein, they will always do
their full duty and hope that all other organizations will co-operate in
that fine spirit of Christian fellowship."[105] On the fiftieth anniversary of
the Frauenverein in 1940, the newsletter noted that "under the leadership of our beloved Mother Pister, many a sumptuous meal has been
served." Over the preceding twenty-five years, the author speculated, "we
served 86,950 cups of coffee, together with 29,850 pounds of meat,
5,000 pounds of turkey and chicken, 500 bushels of potatoes, and many
other foods that go to make up a luncheon, breakfast or dinner."[106] The
women of St. Pauls could quantify their contributions to the church's
life. For women, barred from the pulpit and from most leadership roles

in the congregation, the kitchen was the center of their power in many churches until the middle of the twentieth century. They had sole responsibility for the social events that became increasingly important in the church's life. As these notes from the Frauenverein make clear, the women did not hide that power. At the same time, some women saw the work as important fellowship as well. The Mother's Club, a younger counterpart to the Frauenverein, continued with the food service tradition, telling the congregation in 1964 that "being together to cook and serve meals is always an enjoyable event."[107]

In the years after World War II, however, some congregations changed the way they organized their kitchens, as they moved away from volunteer labor and hired cooks. In an era when congregations were building bigger kitchens and organizing more social events, all-volunteer kitchen workers found themselves overworked. While in many cases "a strong committee chairman" was sufficient, one fun book encouraged paying committee chairwomen "to insure their continued service." The author also recommended that committee members have experience in food service, preferably from working in Red Cross canteens.[108] With many more mouths to feed in the church dining room, experience in cooking for large groups became more valuable. Other churches moved to lift the burden on the kitchen committee. The First Presbyterian Church of Baton Rouge, Louisiana, for instance, hired a hostess to supervise the kitchen in 1945.[109]

Other cultural shifts may have spurred the move to professional cooks. Women, the usual source of volunteer labor, had more responsibilities; some worked outside the home, while child psychologists pressured those working at home to spend more time with their children. In the postwar prosperity, when more people could afford to eat out, parishioners brought expectations for restaurant-standard food to the church dining room. In this boom time for the mainline church, congregations had the resources for elegant and sophisticated meals. Whatever the cause, this move from volunteer to professional food preparation also changed the relationship between the church and its members. When members of the church provided the volunteer labor to cook a meal, the church was a community, a place to work together. But when paid cooks prepared the meals, the church was simply a place to eat together, a service provider.

In the decades since World War II, professional church cooks have become more common, especially in large southern congregations. The National Association of Church Food Services Inc. has two hundred members, most in the Southeast, reports executive director Carolyn Clayton.[110] Most members of the association work at churches with at least a thousand members, most of them Baptist. "Fifteen years ago the group would have been all 60 year old white women," but now it has almost fifty men, and is about one-quarter black. Now that men are getting into the field, Clayton notes, salaries are going up.

In addition to her work with the association, Clayton is the food service director at Peachtree Road United Methodist Church, a wealthy congregation of five thousand members in Atlanta. Church meals at Peachtree serve a practical purpose, she argues. "If the church expects its members to be there, the church has to provide the facilities they want. If you're going to have them come to an all-day conference, you can't just send them to Wendy's." The food nurtures the members and provides fellowship, "but as a practical matter, it's necessary to keep the programs of the church running." The church's programs drive the food service operation. "If they didn't plan things, they wouldn't need us."

Peachtree is located in Buckhead, Atlanta's wealthiest and most fashionable neighborhood, and the church's food service serves the needs of that community. The congregation includes sophisticated world travelers, who eat out a lot and have high standards for their food. Such people won't settle for a piece of reheated lasagna on a paper plate, Clayton believes. The church hasn't had a covered dish supper for years. "In this area people don't want to cook," she says; the women work or are volunteers in the community.

Clayton and her staff serve set-price lunch buffets to members of the congregation every Sunday and Wednesday. Once upon a time churches across the South—and across the country—held prayer meetings every Wednesday night, followed perhaps by a brief social. At Peachtree Road the midweek prayer meeting has given way to a weekly Wednesday night supper called "Prime Time"; one week the dinner had a Mardi Gras theme. In addition to these meals open to all, the staff prepares the food for regular meetings of women's and men's groups as well as special events like choir dinners. Finally, it does the catering and banquets for special events hosted by the church, such as the regional meeting of the American Guild of Organists. Food is an important part of the church's work, Clayton concludes. "I don't see how Jesus saved a soul without a cup of coffee and a stalk of broccoli."

Professionally run food services like that at Peachtree Road are the next step in the development of the church supper. Since the end of the nineteenth century, church social events have sought to bring people into the church. They have given members an alternative to bars and restaurants and have invited visitors into the church by luring them with food. In an increasingly busy and specialized society, professional church cooks have taken the place of volunteers, but however elegant the table, the goal is still fellowship.

The food court at Willow Creek Community Church, the well-known "megachurch" in suburban Chicago, has taken church social events to their logical conclusion. It is the apotheosis of the church supper. The church was founded in 1975 to reach those it called "seekers"—unchurched people with spiritual needs but alienated by traditional churches. After surveying seekers, the founders designed worship services and programs to attract them and meet their needs. Seeker-friendly services include casual worship, up-tempo music, and no offertory. The church grew quickly and by the mid-1990s was attracting five thousand people to each of four weekend services. It occupies a sprawling campus in the growing Northwest suburbs; the church resembles a corporate office park.

In the early 1990s the church looked to expand its facilities again. The congregation had grown so large that there was no place for members to meet informally outside the auditorium. As food service director Frank Scimeca puts it, the congregation needed a living room, to "give the people in the Body of Christ a place to sit together."[111] The church's leadership realized that any good living room needs a "good kitchen." They built a large atrium space, walled with glass and filled with small tables set amid plants. A large food court area occupies one side of the atrium.

To run the food service they turned to a professional. Unlike Clayton, who "fell into" her role with no previous experience in food service, Scimeca had owned several restaurants and was an executive chef when he started attending the church several years ago. After being born again, he started looking for a way to serve the church. He now runs the Willow Creek operation for Creative Dining Services, a food service company specializing in running cafeterias for Christian colleges. Scimeca is assisted by nine full-time staff and almost twenty part-timers. He notes that employees must be born-again and members of the church since they are a public part of Willow Creek.

As important as the paid staff are the volunteers. Every member of the church belongs to one or more small groups, the member's primary connection to the enormous congregation. In addition to study and prayer, each small group volunteers together in one of the church's many ministries. With 240 volunteers, the Harvest ministry (the church's name for the food court) is one of the smaller ministries in the church. (A similar-size restaurant would have 70 employees, Scimeca notes.) The Harvest ministry tends to attract a lot of new members or seekers, since it is "a safe place to get into." Scimeca speculates that "most people have an interest in running their own restaurant—they love to cook." Once they get involved, however, they see it as a ministry, not just work. All the daytime volunteers are senior citizens, while the evening crew consists of all ages, evenly divided between men and women. Scimeca admits that although kitchen labor is an unusual role for men, at Willow Creek they can work in the kitchen because they "realize that there's freedom in Christ."

Scimeca acknowledges that the food court has a practical purpose; the availability of food makes it easier to convince busy people to come to church rather than force them to choose between church and a meal. But he offers a less practical and more evangelical justification for Willow Creek's food service. The atrium was designed as a place to share a meal and share the gospel. Members are encouraged to gather in the atrium after a service to discuss the sermon with potential members. Scimeca frequently sees a lot of witnessing and conversion going on over meals. "Many times walking through these aisles we see people, over a meal, getting saved. We're in the people business, in the business of saving people through grace, and if food does it, that's great." He tells members that the food court is a good way to entice seekers, encouraging them to tell neighbors, "Come to a service, and the food's great, too!" They can even help feed the hungry by inviting needy families to attend a service and then share a meal. Scimeca's latest innovation is an espresso cart, designed to appeal to the members of Generation X. "It's working—we see them coming in, sharing a cup of coffee and sharing Christ."

The food court at Willow Creek is the church supper for a free-market society. At traditional potluck meals, each family brings what they can afford to share with the rest of the community, which eats gathered around large tables. Such meals follow the doctrine of primitive Marxism, if not primitive Christianity—from each according to their ability, to each according to their need. At the food court, on the other hand, people get what they can pay for, as families or small clusters of individuals choose their food and pay for it themselves, just like the food court at any mall in America. The variety of menu items clearly aims to please a broad market. In addition to a salad bar area, there are five serving areas, offering pasta, pizza, grill items, and other entrees. Founding pastor Bill Hybels, notes Scimeca, initially wanted the food court to serve just healthful food, but that didn't go over well. "People when they eat out tend to cheat on their diets," he concludes. Now the court offers healthful alternatives, but the best-selling item is sausage pizza, followed by desserts. With this free-market orientation, the food court serves well its constituency, drawn mainly from suburban Chicago's white-collar middle class.

In the modern church environment, is professional food service inevitable? For a variety of reasons, the answer is probably yes. In a more complex society, people (especially women) are busier and are less likely to want to spend their scarce church volunteer time in the kitchen. Megachurches, which seem to be a growing trend, are hard to feed with an all-volunteer kitchen staff. They require bigger food operations.

Complete with salad bar and multiple cash registers, the food court at Willow Creek
Community Church can serve up to three thousand people in fifteen minutes.
(Author's photograph)

Finally, churches are competing with secular entertainments for attention and with each other for market share. In such an environment, a
good food service operation helps make a church distinctive.

But what is the social and theological cost of big food operations?
As the women of St. Pauls found a half century ago, working together,
even drudgery in the kitchen, builds community in a church. The
experiences of the small groups in Willow Creek's Harvest ministry bear
this out. But there is a danger that large church food services may lose
this community-creating work in their search for more efficient and
satisfying meals. The greater danger lies in changing the relationship
between the church and its members. Operating a food service risks
making church members consumers of a service instead of fellow
participants in a community of faith.

From the camp meeting of the Tennessee frontier to the food court at
Willow Creek, food-centered socializing has played an important part in

American church life. Church meals have built community among members and brought visitors into the church. Congregational social events have provided children wholesome and safe entertainment and adolescents a good place to meet and court the opposite sex. And they have fed hungry people.

Are these meals uniquely Protestant? Catholicism has a popular piety deeply rooted in the Mass and in a variety of devotional activities. This piety has given Catholics numerous centers around which to build community. Protestantism, on the other hand, is centered on the Word. As a result, it has a well-developed intellectual tradition but lacks a focus for popular religion. To build that kind of community, Protestantism has turned to informal fellowship activities, organized by the laity around a nonliturgical but still sacral calendar—Sunday school picnics, family nights, and the like. Food provides Protestantism with a popular religion. Protestantism also needs the market appeal of food events more than Catholic churches. While the Catholic church requires people to go to Mass at the risk of their immortal souls, Protestantism needs a different motivator. Food often fills the bill. This doesn't mean that American Catholic churches do not have food-centered social events; there is a rich record of communion breakfasts and sodality dinners. Most likely, however, these Catholic meals followed the Protestant model.

Are these meals uniquely American? Without extensive comparative research, it's hard to say for sure. Anecdotally, however, food-centered social events do appear to be unique to American Protestantism. People in other societies rarely have to travel the same distance to get to church; church meals don't have the same practical function. Many other countries also have a single dominant church—there's only one game in town. In these less competitive cultures, food is not needed as a lure to get people to come in. In the free-market environment of American religion, where people are tempted to go to other churches—or to stay home—a good church meal can provide a competitive advantage. The pressures that gave rise to the social congregation—urbanization, industrialization, and suburbanization—are not unique to the United States, however, so such congregations may exist elsewhere.

Finally, what makes a church meal a *church* meal? For veteran whitebread Protestants, the question evokes a rich variety of sensory memories—fried chicken, three-bean salad, a variety of Jell-O concoctions, and the like. There is never any alcohol and rarely any spicy food, of course. Those memories also say that a church meal should be served from a Formica-topped table in a basement with light green walls.

But church food is far more than a menu and a place. It is community. Church food is prepared by and eaten with your friends and neighbors. For many Americans, it's the closest thing we get to a communal experience any more. At its best, a church meal is a mixture of cuisines and qualities, served inelegantly alongside a virtual stranger—and all for free. It is far more than a meal; it is fellowship. As novelist Frederick Buechner writes, "to eat is to acknowledge our dependence—both on food and on each other."[112]

Many people eating in church basements, however, are dependent on church food for more than fellowship; they need it to survive. Like St. Pauls, many churches have turned their social halls—places built to feed the family—into places to feed strangers as well. Across the country, churches have become a primary source of food for the hungry and the homeless. The next chapter shows how mainline Protestants have responded to hunger in their communities.

CHAPTER THREE

EMERGENCY FOOD: THE DEVELOPMENT OF SOUP KITCHENS

EVERY NOW AND THEN A GROUP OF STUDENTS from the college chapel would go downtown and help out in the soup kitchen. The kitchen was started by the local Catholic Worker community and held in the basement of a rundown church in one of the city's less savory neighborhoods. One of its directors was a friend of the chapel, and the rest of the congregation wanted to support her work.

We got there around three o'clock on a Friday afternoon, and—although we tried to dress down—we still looked like what we were: upper-middle-class white kids from a fairly elite university. When we pulled up the first "guests" were starting to line up outside on the cold gray afternoon. We spent the next two hours making dinner. Our friend joked that the menu varied between rice and beans and beans and rice; we wept over mounds of onions to try to add a little flavor to the plain fare. Just before five we put on aprons and got our assignments: Serve the soup, pour the coffee, clean the table, serve the next guest. The doors opened at five on the nose, and we ran our feet off for the next hour, serving about two hundred people: black and white, mainly men but a few women, mainly adults but a few children. By six they were back on the streets and we were mopping the floor. Another half hour later we were talking about the whole thing over burgers at our favorite campus bar. Later that night, when the guy next door complained about the food in the dorm cafeteria, I wanted to pop him one.

Providing "emergency food"—food for the temporarily hungry and permanently poor—is a fairly common experience for mainline Protestants. Feeding the hungry ranks close to feeding each other in their priorities. For instance, a 1994 study found that 97 percent of responding Presbyterian congregations operated or supported a food distribution program.[1] Congregations in cities run soup kitchens and congregations in rural areas host food pantries. Many whitebread Protestants have their first encounter with real poverty while working in a soup kitchen during their high school or college years.

To look at the development and diversity of feeding ministries, I headed to Atlanta, a city where churches—especially Protestant churches—dominate the social landscape. With its state's conservative politics, the city relies on those churches, instead of government, to supply many social services. As a result, the city has a rich variety of emergency feeding programs. A relatively young city, Atlanta still struggles with its growing pains, which means these ministries are coping with change. I talked with leaders and volunteers at five distinctly different hunger programs about their origins, missions, and futures.[2] I was interested in why the programs did what they did and what food symbolized in their work. I found that Christian faith played a very real role in their founding but often only a covert role in their day-to-day work. Throughout, food was instrumental—it symbolized larger ideas, such as charity, community, and choice. I also found that, along the way, these ministries had become big businesses.

THE AGENCIES

Atlanta Union Mission

Every American city has a skid row—a part of town where social outcasts gather. While the name and the population may vary from city to city, every such neighborhood has at its center a gospel mission. There warm-hearted evangelical Christians offer food and a bed—"three hots and a cot"—plus a saving gospel sermon. Such missions have been an inescapable part of the urban landscape at least since the arrival of the Salvation Army in the late nineteenth century.[3]

As in many cities, Atlanta's skid row grew quickly during the Great Depression of the 1930s. Countless men, riding the rails in search of work or escape, passed through the city, a vital railroad hub. In 1938 a group of ministers and laymen opened a twenty-bed shelter called the Atlanta Holding Mission to give these men in distress food, shelter, and counseling. In 1942 they changed the name to the Atlanta Union Mission. The first executive director was a Presbyterian minister, and among the charter trustees was the pastor of the prominent Central Presbyterian Church. By 1956 the mission was serving an average of three hundred meals a day. As a publicity piece noted, many of the men were "from good homes. Most of them are worthy men who are simply victims of misfortune, men who have lost everything that gives men courage and hope. Of course, others are derelicts, drunkards, thieves, drifters, but they are all human beings." The mission offered them "friendly understanding and that understanding begins with the fact you can't talk to a man about a new beginning when he is starving." Although the flyer stated that "our doors are open to Protestants, Catholics and Jews alike, without questions," it declared that "teaching the love of Jesus Christ is the heart of the Mission work. All else it does—the free meals it gives, the free beds it supplies—are but a means to bring men under the Grace of the Gospel of our Lord."[4] In tune with the tradition of the gospel mission as well as the religious atmosphere of the South, the mission was deeply rooted in the evangelical world.

A young volunteer stirs the soup at the Atlanta Union Mission.
(Author's photograph)

Time brought changes to the mission's population and to its focus.
By 1976 the mission had almost five hundred beds in three divisions
including a shelter for women and a farm for recovering alcoholics. But
now most of its clients were former psychiatric patients, on the streets
after being released from state institutions in the early 1970s.[5] The 1980s
saw an increasing number of unemployed young men, struggling
through a recession and the loss of manufacturing jobs.[6] The end of that
decade, with the arrival of the crack cocaine epidemic, brought more
drug addicts into the mission. These changes provoked a shift in the
mission's method. In 1990 it changed its focus to concentrate on drug
rehabilitation. While it still takes in street people—including psychiatric
patients—they are allowed to stay for a maximum of sixty days. The rest
of the beds are needed for the mission's "continuum of care" for

substance abusers.[7] Once approved by the mission's counselors, participants enter a six-month Christian-based recovery program. Successful graduates can then spend up to eighteen months in a transitional housing center as they reenter the world of work.

The largest facility of the mission is in a modern brick building on the edge of Atlanta's downtown. Once the heart of the city's skid row, the neighborhood has undergone enormous changes in the last decade. Before the 1996 Olympics the city bulldozed the pawnshops and flophouses. Nearby, town houses are replacing a public housing project. But the mission is still surrounded by a high iron fence, and its transient clients still seek the sparse shade available in its courtyard. The community kitchen—an updated term for "soup kitchen"—serves a thousand meals a day. Ten years ago a writer for the city's hip alternative paper went undercover at the mission, and reported that dinner that night was "an unappetizing blob of runny noodles with a smattering of peas, potatoes, and a fleck or two of ham floating around inside."[8] The day I was there, however, lunch was good—it was a soup of rice and peas and chicken, hot and tasty and rich. There were also bagels and other bread. The meal was prepared by the mission staff and residents, and served by a group of young volunteers from a local private school. The kitchen provides a full meal at breakfast and dinner. With its white walls, bright paintings, and tables for four, the dining room feels like a fast-food restaurant rather than a soup kitchen. This is still mass feeding, but on a more human scale.

Druid Hills Presbyterian Church Community Fellowship

Atlanta's first suburb was a development called Druid Hills. A few miles east of downtown and just south of the campus of Emory University, the neighborhood had large homes and winding roads among lush ravines. On the southern edge of Druid Hills, along Ponce de Leon Avenue, was the city's first strip mall, including a movie theater and a landmark art deco diner. Across from the diner stands a large brick Gothic church— Druid Hills Presbyterian Church, once one of the city's largest and most fashionable congregations. With the national headquarters of its denomination—the Presbyterian Church in the United States—just down the street, Druid Hills was also an influential congregation.

In the late 1960s, however, the neighborhood began to change. New highways allowed residents to move to newer suburbs, far from Druid Hills. At the same time, spurred by court cases and changes in policy, state officials began releasing patients from psychiatric hospitals. The goal was to move people from state warehouses to community care centers, to allow them to reintegrate into society. In reality, many of the patients found themselves isolated in boardinghouses, often in changing neighborhoods like Druid Hills. By the early 1970s the church found itself with a declining membership and surrounded by houses full of former psychiatric patients.

In 1974 the church's outreach board studied ways to connect with this changing community. A psychiatrist, the widow of a former pastor, proposed creating a program to meet the needs of the church's newest neighbors—the former patients. The board reported that the thirty residents of one neighboring house "receive one hundred and thirty-six dollars a month from the state, and pay one hundred and ten dollars for board. They are fed two meals a day for five days and breakfast on Saturday, and no more during the weekend." But their problems were deeper, the report stated. "Aside from feeling a financial pinch, they have the bigger problems of loneliness, lack of purpose, and a real desire to belong and to be with people who care and accept them. Above all, they need to be accepted as people." That September the congregation's governing board voted to hold a service every Sunday afternoon and invite the neighborhood's psychiatric patients.[9] It was called the Community Fellowship.

A year later the Community Fellowship was drawing twenty people a week, with at least twelve regulars. The outreach board noted that "these people are responding in a positive way to the program with increased participation in hymn singing, prayers, and general social activities."[10] Soon these "general social activities" included food; the psychiatrist who proposed the program noted that "bread, beans, slaw, spaghetti, casseroles, rice, anything green, a bit of cake or fruit—all of these are wonderful foods. We have experienced that he, or she, who feeds his hungering neighbor feeds three—'himself, his hungering neighbor and Me.'"[11] Other guests starting coming from the federally subsidized apartments for the elderly next to the church. In the mid-1980s the congregational yearbook reported that the meeting featured "an old-fashioned hymn sing, followed by prayers and inspirational talks. This meeting is attended by many who would not attend our formal morning worship in the sanctuary. It has been noted that some come from a distance far beyond our immediate neighborhood." The report acknowledged that "some come mainly for the good, free Sunday dinner which follows the service." Most important, however, the fellowship's regulars "think of this as their Church, their Fellowship of Believers."[12] Few, however, became involved with the congregation beyond the fellowship's activities.

By the early 1980s, the clientele changed, just as it did at the Atlanta Union Mission. Homeless, unemployed, and substance-abusing people began joining the psychiatric patients for the Community Fellowship. In 1982 the church opened a night shelter during the winter months, providing forty people with dinner, breakfast, and a bed. Both programs continue side by side. While a few of the members of the Community Fellowship are former psychiatric patients from the neighborhood, now the majority are homeless.

At four o'clock on Sunday afternoon people start gathering in a small one-story building tucked behind the main church building; it feels like the dining hall at a summer camp, with wood paneling, long tables down the middle, and a kitchen in one corner. Large piles of mattresses along one wall show that this is also the site of the night shelter. Today the fellowship is mainly African American men, although there are a few White men and women. Most are young to middle age, although there are a few seniors. At four-thirty a church volunteer gets the group's attention for the "worship" part of the evening—he reads Psalm 23 and prays to bless the food and the fellowship. There's no hymn signing and little response from the guests. Then, table by table, people stand in line for their dinner.

Volunteers—older if not elderly members of the church—and a few church staff members serve the meal. Tonight the dinner is sloppy joes, applesauce, and leftover doughnuts and bagels from Dunkin Donuts. The guests appreciate the food, and some come back for seconds. Volunteers greet the regulars by name, but there's obviously a social separation between servers and guests; volunteers do not eat with the fellowship. By five some guests have finished their dinner and are gathering their possessions; a few guests begin cleaning up, for which they get some extra food to take along. By five-thirty the floors are mopped, the trash has been taken out, and the doors are locked.

Atlanta Community Food Bank

Unlike most such ministries, the problem was too much food. In 1975 Bill Bolling was the director of street ministries at an Episcopal church in downtown Atlanta when he noticed the increasing number of hungry and homeless people on the city's streets—especially fellow Vietnam veterans. In response, he organized the city's first soup kitchen. Some time later an executive for a local food company offered him some out-of-date but still usable products. Pleased by the generosity, Bolling was amazed to learn that there could be more where that came from, that the food industry regularly threw away almost 20 percent of its products— material that was slightly damaged, recently expired, or otherwise pulled from the shelves. He began collecting this surplus in an old pickup truck, and soon there was more than he could use for his soup kitchen. Bolling began to share the surplus with other feeding programs, and in 1979 the Atlanta Community Food Bank (ACFB) was born.

The idea was simple: centralized acquisition, decentralized distribution. He began contacting food processors, manufacturers, wholesalers, and stores to glean their unsalable products. They delivered the food to the church's basement—nicknamed "the Cave"—where feeding agencies then came to get what they needed. The results were often unexpected—one of the first big deliveries was a semi-truck load of caramel apples—but the agencies were thrilled with whatever they could get. The new program took off. Although Bolling thought he had invented something new, he soon discovered that his brainchild wasn't unique. Food banks were springing up across the country; in 1979 the ACFB became a charter member of Second Harvest, a national network of food banks.

The statistics are staggering. In its first six months ACFB served 25 agencies, distributing 15,279 pounds of food. Two years later it gave 923,000 pounds to 187 member agencies. In 1983 it quadrupled its warehouse space, to 20,000 square feet. In 1998 it distributed 13 million pounds of food to over 700 agencies from 49 counties spread over the northern half of Georgia. In addition to food from corporations—much of it channeled through Second Harvest—the ACFB also collects canned goods. Churches and companies collect at Christmas, letter carriers collect in the spring, while others donate at concerts, opera, baseball games, and drag races.

Meanwhile Bolling developed other ways of getting food to the hungry. In the mid-1990s, the ACFB introduced Atlanta's Table, which collects leftovers from restaurants and caterers around the city and delivers them to shelters and soup kitchens. Through this "food rescue" effort, hungry men, women, and children dine on everything from stuffed lobster from the Ritz Carlton to pizzas that had been ordered but never picked up. The program hit the jackpot in the summer of 1996 when Atlanta hosted the Olympics; surplus food from sponsor parties and the Olympic Village went to its agencies. The ACFB also has developed community garden and neighborhood food co-op programs.

The food bank is located in two warehouses—now totaling 120,000 square feet—beside an active railroad spur; unlike most hunger agencies, the building is designed for efficiency, not the welcoming of the poor and hungry. Inside volunteers sort the canned goods, while representatives from the participating agencies "shop" for their needs. Most food goes for a minimal price, whether it is cereal or canned salmon, while much of the fresh produce goes for free. Meat and fresh produce fill room-size walk-in refrigerators. Large trucks deliver donated canned goods, while smaller refrigerated trucks pick up food rescued from the convention center. In a corner a group of chefs from a local restaurant show shoppers creative meals made with ACFB material. Upstairs the special events office tallies the income from the annual Hunger Walk, while the executive director talks with activists about the links between food and community.

Midtown Assistance Center

The skyscrapers of corporate Atlanta stretch in a row along Peachtree Street. Much of Peachtree, especially its southern end, has been transformed into a concrete canyon. Tucked into an occasional pocket, however, are reminders of what Atlanta's main street used to be—including several of the city's first churches.

In the 1980s residents and workers on Peachtree found—as the Union Mission, the Community Fellowship, and the ACFB found—that the population of the hungry and the homeless was increasing. Many of these poor people turned to the downtown churches for help. Each of them developed ministries, including soup kitchens and shelters, but they were all individual responses. In 1986 the Midtown Business Alliance brought together representatives of five of the churches—including the Catholic cathedral and the Temple, a prominent Reform Jewish congregation—to look for a coordinated way to help. They created the Midtown Assistance Center.

The center—now nestled in the basement of the First Methodist Church, on the edge of the Peachtree Center complex—serves the working poor of the neighborhood closest to downtown. The walls of its warrenlike office are covered with job postings, offers for child care, and information about government services. The office provides help with job searching and identification cards, discounted public transportation passes, and money for utility deposits.

The heart of the center's work, however, is the food pantry. A corner of the office is piled floor to ceiling with every imaginable kind of packaged food—from soup, to pasta, to cereal. If some of the items look a little, well, out of place, that's because the food comes from contribu-

The dining room at Café 458, with flowers on every table and the menu on a
chalkboard, resembles a trendy new restaurant.
(Author's photograph)

tions from the center's supporting congregations. Members bring what
they have to spare—which explains the wave of gefilte fish from the
Temple, for instance. A shelf near the door offers the weirdest stuff—
including a can of peeled tongue—to any taker. Nearby is a freezer full
of cakes donated by a local grocery store, on hand in case of a child's
birthday. Just next door is an office full of diapers and toiletries. Clients
are given a shopping list and are allowed to choose from this rich wealth
of food. There are even some candy bars to reward children who do well
in school.

Café 458

It could be a trendy new restaurant. There's an art deco sign outside. The
decor inside features natural wood and glass block, with walls painted in
bright colors. The music from the stereo is jazz or Motown. Each table
for three or four diners has wildflowers in a little blue bottle. The menu—

mainly comfort food—is written on a chalkboard. The cooks take great pride in using a lot of fresh food in their recipes. It could be a trendy new restaurant—but it's a full-service social agency.

In 1982 another group of Christians joined in the growing concern about the homeless. Centered at Oakhurst Baptist Church in the close-in Atlanta suburb of Decatur, the group formed the Community of Hospitality, a small but committed group of Christians dedicated to ministry with the homeless. They opened a shelter in the church and welcomed some of the homeless into their communal home. They pooled their incomes—largely earned from social service work—to support their ministry. But they noticed, as other programs appeared to meet the various needs of the homeless, that there was little to meet their social needs. Other agencies gave them food, clothing, or shelter and sent them back to the street with barely a word.

To meet this social need, the Community of Hospitality created Café 458 (for its address, at 458 Edgewood Avenue in Atlanta) in 1988. Members found an abandoned liquor store, on a major avenue well past its prime. Across the street is a thrift store with barred windows, while across the alley is the Martin Luther King Jr. Center for Nonviolent Social Change. They renovated this unlikely space and turned it into a restaurant. Unlike a traditional soup kitchen, where the homeless are given some generic food on a tray and told to sit at long anonymous tables, the café aims to give its guests dignity by offering them choices. Guests sit at small tables with a few friends and consider the menu, which offers several entrées, side dishes, and desserts each day. They order their choice from a waitperson, who brings them their lunch and refills their glass. It's just like a real restaurant—except there's no bill at the end of the meal.

There's a catch, of course. The café does not feed anyone who walks in off the street. Guests must be referred by another social service agency; if there's room, they're placed on the reservation list and come for lunch every day. To stay on the list, however, they need to keep working at their goals—finding a job, recovering from substance abuse, or receiving counseling for psychological problems. The café and its sister organization Samaritan House offer a variety of services to help clients work on their goals. There are daily Alcoholics Anonymous and Narcotics Anonymous groups. There's an office where guests can work on job searching and a voice mail system so potential employers can contact them. Each of the agency's full-time volunteers, most of them members of the Community of Hospitality, has a caseload of clients from the café's reservation list.

Café 458 is unlike any other agency feeding the hungry homeless. There's a minimum of bureaucracy and a maximum of choice. It serves a limited number of clients, so each one gets personal attention. And, after lunch, the executive director puts on an apron and does the dishes.

MOTIVATIONS AND MENUS

Christians believe that God calls them to feed the hungry and cite as evidence texts in the Old Testament that tell the people of Israel to set aside food for aliens, orphans, and widows.[13] Or they retell Jesus' parable of the rich man and starving Lazarus. In time both men died, Jesus said; Lazarus ended up with Abraham in heaven, while the rich man found himself in hell because of the poor way he had treated the beggar.[14] Feeding the hungry has been an important part of the church's ministry since its early days. Soon after Pentecost, the apostles appointed seven deacons to distribute food to the community's poor widows.[15] White-bread Protestants have added their own strain of noblesse oblige to this biblical mandate. Because of their place at the head of establishment America, they have felt responsible for society's "less fortunate." For these Protestants, feeding the hungry is a duty in response to concrete needs. In time, it also has become big business. They serve a variety of clients; in that service, food plays an instrumental role while religious faith is usually implicit.

The founding stories of the Atlanta hunger ministries just described usually focus on a concrete situation—the need to deal with a hungry person on their doorstep—rather than an abstract obligation. For the ministers and laymen who founded the Atlanta Union Mission, the hungry people were freight-train jumpers and refugees from the depression. For the Druid Hills Community Fellowship, it was the psychiatric patients, living in boardinghouses that didn't feed them on Sunday. For the Atlanta Community Food Bank, it was homeless Vietnam veterans. For the Midtown Assistance Center, it was the poor in their neighborhood. For each of these ministries, the work was simply the pragmatic response of a person or people who saw a need; later they developed goals and mission statements, perhaps at the urging of the foundations and corporations that support them.

In recounting its history, each ministry focuses on a hero—its founder, the main character in its story. In the case of the ACFB and the Community Fellowship, the heroes are individuals—entrepreneurs who saw a need and single-handedly brought resources to bear on that need. Volunteers at the Community Fellowship still remember with awe Dr. Lila Bonham Miller, the psychiatrist who first saw the social and spiritual hunger of the neighborhood's psychiatric patients and pushed the church's outreach board to act. Dr. Miller has been dead for several years, but her name is mentioned every time church members describe the program. At the ACFB, on the other hand, the entrepreneur is still in charge. Executive director Bill Bolling is the agency's idea man and guru, proposing new programs to meet new needs and offering wisdom to staff, donors, and other community activists. For Café 458 and the Union Mission, the heroes are not individuals but collectives—the group of people who conceived of the ministry and nurtured the idea. Yet the clergy group (who founded the mission) and the Community of Hospitality (at the café) are still heroes, spoken of fondly and pictured in fund-raising publicity pieces.

The way these organizations deal with changed circumstances reflects their entrepreneurial nature. The Union Mission, founded to welcome itinerant and unemployed men, developed a partnership with the city's public hospital when it started getting more psychiatrically ill people. It changed its strategy again to cope with a rising tide of substance abusers. The ACFB has developed new sources for food surpluses—

including restaurants and community gardens—as the food industry has changed. The staff of the Midtown Assistance Center was getting frustrated with the mismatch between its inventory—church member donations—and the needs of its clients. That frustration led them to change their approach to food gathering; they now directly ask congregations for particular kinds of food. Café 458, which started out to be simply a restaurant serving guests referred by other agencies, has added other programs to become a complete social service agency, after finding that the referring agencies did not provide sufficient follow-up. Even the Community Fellowship has changed its program, reducing its mission rather than expanding it, in response to a changing clientele. Previous clients—deinstitutionalized psychiatric patients—needed community, and so the program centered on worship and fellowship followed by a meal. Now the fellowship's clients are the hungry homeless, so the church provides a soup kitchen with a vestigial worship service. Although not always for the better, these ministries have learned to adapt to changing circumstances.

As they have changed, these ministries have become institutions. While they were founded to deal with an emergency, a pressing—and presumably short-term—situation demanding a response, they continue their work years, in some cases decades, later. They are in it for the long haul. These emergency ministries have become nonprofit corporations, often with enormous budgets. They have boards of directors, executive directors, and development officers; they support their work through donations and grants from governments, corporations, and individuals. The Atlanta Community Food Bank is the most obvious example. From its start with one man and a pickup truck, it now has a staff of forty-four and over a thousand volunteers a month, the largest volunteer program in the city; its 1999 budget was close to $5 million. As executive director Bolling says, "we [are] a ministry that had to start operating on business principles—good food handling, good accountability, and so forth." The Atlanta Union Mission now has six facilities, serving 850 men, women, and children a day on an annual budget of $8 million. Although they identify themselves as ministries, these programs are good-size corporations. With its intentionally limited size and its communal origins, Café 458 tries to avoid the corporate image. Most of its full-time volunteers still live in the Community of Hospitality, and they conduct their day-to-day business by consensus. But most of the money comes from city and county grants, solicited by the executive director. The café, too, has a professional staff and a budget of almost $700,000. Again, the Community Fellowship is the exception to this corporate model; it is the only one of these programs directly linked to a church congregation. Almost all the volunteers and almost all the money comes from Druid Hills Presbyterian Church, supported by other nearby Presbyterian congregations. As for the other programs discussed, intentionally or unintentionally they have become corporate institutions.

Some in the hunger movement want to resist this process of institutionalization, for political reasons. One group of hunger activists argues that "we cannot continue to allow the institutionalization of the emergency response to hunger for this will only reinforce the myth that the emergency system is a permanent solution."[16] They fear that charitable ministries will allow the government to ignore the needs of the hungry.[17] Thomas Reuter, director of Café 458, is sympathetic to the argument—he believes that poverty is a systemic problem requiring systemic answers. But even if hunger has become routine, it is still an emergency for the person who is hungry. Reuter feels "caught in a bind here. We have a person who is hungry and needs some assistance now. I've got a choice—I can say, I'm not going to feed you so you'll get upset so the government will respond to you. That's the dilemma I'm in—what do I do with the people who are hungry here and now?" Many in the field doubt that their business is going to go away. Dorothy Chandler, director of the Midtown Assistance Center, believes that "there'll always be hungry people, poor people, people who have times when they have a need and nobody who can help them. We'll always have homeless people." Kathy Palumbo, the ACFB's community services director, agrees, believing that "unless there are major shifts in social and economic policy, we're always going to have people who are poor." Meanwhile, she says, the "emergency" label helps psychologically and politically. "If we

Cleaning up after dinner at Druid Hills Presbyterian Church's Community
Fellowship, a more traditional soup kitchen.
(Author's photograph)

say that our service is temporary and emergency, then it's hard to believe
that poverty is a given." For better or worse, however, "emergency" food
appears to be permanent.

While hunger is hunger, not all hungry people are alike; to address
the diversity of hunger, these agencies have different missions, focused
on specific kinds of clients. They also recognize that hunger has
numerous causes. Palumbo, who coordinates the ACFB's relationship
with its member agencies, says that the average hungry person in the
United States is a child. Most of the agencies that use the food bank serve
families with children. The typical client of the Midtown Assistance
Center fits Palumbo's definition, says Chandler. She's a "single mom . . .
[with] one or two kids. She's working, but just really struggles. She
probably gets no child support." The center serves mainly the working
poor; it refers homeless people to other agencies that specialize in their
needs. The rest of the agencies studied here, on the other hand, feed the
most visible hungry—the urban homeless. The Union Mission, the

Community Fellowship, and Café 458 are all targeted at people living on the streets or close to it. Many of them are struggling with addiction or psychiatric illness or are recently out of jail. These are the people we most often think of as hungry.

The differing missions for the agencies are reflected in their different goals for their clients. The Community Fellowship and the Midtown Assistance Center focus on survival, simply making sure that their clients have enough to eat. As its name implies, the Community Fellowship was founded to create an ongoing fellowship among residents of neighboring rooming houses. It did this through worship, group singing, and a shared meal. Now the worship has shrunk to a scripture reading and prayer, and the focus is on the food. Whatever fellowship exists happens through the efforts of the guests. One staff member at the church acknowledges that "it's not intended to turn people around in any way. It's just simply hot food. We believe that's an O.K. purpose." The Midtown Assistance Center, similarly, focuses on providing food, which clients take and prepare in their own homes. The center staff discourages clients from becoming too dependent on the food. "We're not here to be a grocery store, we're here for emergencies," says Chandler. For both of these agencies, the goal is survival.

Other programs, however, have shifted their mission from survival to recovery. Frustrated with providing a "Band-Aid" for people's problems, the Union Mission and Café 458 now focus their energies on rehabilitating people, usually from some form of substance abuse. The mission allocates a majority of its beds—and meals—to people who come off the streets. But it aims to move those people into its "Personal Development Plan," a six-month program of vocational training and addiction rehabilitation. The program's graduates can spend up to an additional eighteen months in transitional housing. Robert Hunter, program director at the largest of the mission's units, says that "they're being responsible and working on issues, being productive citizens." Similarly, guests can keep coming to Café 458 as long as they continue working on their goals, whether it be addiction recovery or developing job skills. Café director Reuter believes that "it's less about offering services than it is about offering a place to get organized, to get connected with people, to find their vision for themselves." Similarly, Bolling feels that food "becomes the entry point, the way to engage, but it's not the end, it's the beginning of a relationship. It's the easiest way to begin a relationship. More successful ministries have taken it from there"—to dealing with rent, healthcare, and neighborhood development. For these ministries, food is just one part of an entire approach to helping the poor.

This shift from emergency rescue to rehabilitation seems to be a common trend in the social service world. The soup kitchen founded by Bill Bolling is now working with smaller numbers of people for longer times, with the aim of breaking the cycle of homelessness. A staff member at Druid Hills suspects that its night shelter—if not the Community Fellowship—will go the same direction. "Some of the people who become repeaters might do better if we were pushing them a little more to get back on their feet and out of here." Such a move "would gain considerable support from some parts of the congregation" and "make it stronger in the long haul." This move from survival to recovery mirrors the larger society's greater interest in addiction recovery programs.

Some of these ministries see their work as more than survival or rehabilitation; they see feeding the hungry as key to building community. For the staff at Café 458, strong relationships are a part of the rehabilitation process. Reuter believes that "the community setting is where people find the strength to make changes they need to make in their lives. We're trying to provide a hospitable place where community can happen." At the café, the community around the tables helps to support people working on their rehabilitation. To Bill Bolling at the food bank, community is not just an instrumental good but is the end goal of feeding ministries. Food, he believes, "has been one of the great organizing tools, one of the great ways to pull people together. I think the table, which we use a lot as a theme here, of bringing people to the table, is a great symbol." In 1993 the ACFB adopted a new mission statement that puts community at its center: "Our mission is to fight hunger by engaging, educating, and empowering our community."[18] Because of this mission, Bolling says, the need for food banking will never go away. "Even if there was another place for excess food to go, and if welfare programs did away with hunger, there would still be the need for community." In places like the Atlanta Community Food Bank and the café, food is more than a substance that provides nutrition; it is a metaphor for hospitality, a hospitality that builds relationships and community.

The ACFB is also working with a concept that's starting to percolate through the world of emergency food providers: food security. Food security goes beyond just having enough to eat, to having the kinds of food we want and need to make us both healthy and happy. The agency defines food security as "knowing that [people] and their loved ones will always have enough to eat, and not only enough, but plenty of healthy and delicious food. Put simply, food is a necessity for living and it is meant to bring joy to life too."[19] Food insecurity, on the other hand, is people not having "as much good nutrition as we would hope they could have," says Palumbo. Programs like the ACFB's community gardens, Bolling believes, are part of the key to food security, "because they're very food-based," they reclaim land, "it's environmental." Most important, they involve people in producing their own food, cutting out the middleman.

As these feeding ministries broaden their vision, they begin to wrestle with the causes of hunger. At the café and the Atlanta Union Mission, most of the clients are hungry and homeless because of substance abuse problems. At the mission, Hunter believes, "people have the opportunity to come out of the darkness, off the streets—not only to come to the community kitchen to eat, and to have a safe environment—but also to come into the program and possibly make a change in their lives." Café director Reuter says that the typical client "doesn't need job training to get connected, it's mainly dealing with addiction issues—that's the big issue. That's the part where a service-focused approach doesn't work— with addiction issues. What needs to happen is for someone to make a change inside." These programs that focus on the individual causes of hunger see their work as changing individuals.

The other agencies, which deal with many clients who are hungry but not homeless, see that hunger as part of the larger problem of poverty. Kathy

Palumbo says that the eventual recipients of the ACFB's food are "all poor, so food becomes another commodity of exchange. It's a supplement for the working poor." Hunger and poverty, Bolling adds, are "feminizing—a lot more women, a lot more women and children and families. It's a lot poorer, there's a lot more addiction, and it's a lot blacker." Dorothy Chandler at the Midtown Assistance Center says that clients come to her "because they don't have anywhere else to turn. If they're working and they get sick, they're not working a job where they get sick leave. They don't have any great amount of money built up. They're just getting by. They're in lower-end jobs, with low pay." For these families, hunger—food insecurity—is just one manifestation of poverty. Reuter, while focusing on the importance of addiction recovery, also sees poverty as an issue for his clients. "It's hard to pull [the issues] apart. It's kind of an artificial separation." The issue is far more complex than just drugs or poverty.

Recognizing this complexity, one of these agencies has engaged in public policy advocacy on behalf of the hungry. Café 458 helps individual clients get the benefits they need, Reuter says, by working with "other agencies, like the Georgia Law Center for Homelessness and Poverty [which] will advocate in the area of legal issues—food stamps, etc. If somebody else does that kind of stuff, we say, you're the experts, you figure it out." The café leaves public policy advocacy to the food bank's staff. "We fully support the advocacy of Bill Bolling's group and others to argue for and struggle for the government meeting its obligations." Through its history, the ACFB has paid attention to public policy issues. Recently it has lobbied the Georgia state government for greater support for food stamps and for increased commodity distributions.[20] Bolling reported on a Second Harvest meeting where national food bank leaders agreed "that we must challenge the underlying assumptions which drive new policy proposals in Congress: that food banks and volunteer organizations alone can expand services enough to feed the hungry."[21] The food bank, unlike the other agencies, pursues the policy issues that lie behind hunger and poverty.

Despite the therapeutic and political concerns, however, religion remains an influence in the lives of these institutions. Their identities as

Christian ministries express themselves in various ways—including their programs and their fund raising. The place of religion has changed in recent years, however, as these agencies have taken a more therapeutic approach and as government agencies have gotten more involved with social services. As a result, the ministries' Christian identity is sometimes more covert than overt. For the mainline-aligned ministries in particular, Christianity serves as a motive for feeding the hungry but rarely plays an important role in their program.

As the first part of the chapter showed, each of the five agencies considered here had its roots in white mainline Protestantism. The Community Fellowship and Café 458 came out of the work of individual congregations, while a cluster of congregations founded the Midtown Assistance Center. The Atlanta Community Food Bank, while the brainchild of one entrepreneurial Christian, lived under the wings of a congregation in its early years. The Atlanta Union Mission was founded by a group of Protestant clergymen and laymen, mostly from prominent downtown churches. While most of the ministries, with the exception of the Community Fellowship, have outgrown their connection to one congregation, they still include their midwifing religious communities when telling the stories of their founding. Despite changes in governance or source of funding, they have not abandoned that part of their history.

The most substantial changes have been in the oldest and most overtly Christian of the agencies, the Atlanta Union Mission. It started out with a focus on evangelism. In 1956, a fund-raising brochure declared that "only when a down and out man accepts Jesus and understands His love is he capable of regeneration. When a man repents and confesses his sins the results are often miraculous." To encourage those miracles, the mission offered "two services every day—a prayer service at 7:00 A.M. and a religious service every night of the year," led by the mission staff and pastors of local churches. The director "counsel[ed] with the men individually. He is never too busy to put a man's salvation above all other work at the mission."[22] Those who found Jesus at the mission joined the Converts Club, where they were "instructed in the growth of the Christian life, and trained to do personal work amongst the men of the Mission."[23] The evangelical focus of the mission's work continued for decades. A 1968 brochure stated that "the primary purpose of the Atlanta Union Mission . . . is to preach the unsearchable riches of God's grace as offered to lost men in Christ Jesus. This purpose is fulfilled in multiple daily worship services. . . ." The mission's ordained staff gave "Christian counsel to as many of the men as possible and without exception we point each man to seek Jesus Christ as his personal Savior."[24] Salvation was the focus, and food and shelter were only a means.

By the mid-1970s, however, the evangelical fire seems to have cooled. A 1976 brochure called the mission "a non-denominational Christian ministry" that provided "food . . . shelter . . . and clothing to homeless adults. Spiritual direction, medical attention, personal counseling, physical and vocational rehabilitation are also provided."[25] Salvation was not as prominent in the mission's identity. Newspaper accounts suggested that the guests weren't particularly interested in salvation anyway. In the late 1980s an undercover reporter spent a night in the mission's shelter; his report included "the service which [the guests] were compelled to attend each evening at that time. After they sat down, many stared straight ahead with dazed expressions on their faces, as if at any moment they were going to fall asleep." After a half hour of "bluegrass flavored spirituals and testimonials of miracles" from guest speakers, the preacher unleashed a "classic fire and brimstone barnstormer" sermon. "The preacher spoke at length about the torments of Hell, about the eternal suffering of the soul and about the need to accept the spirit of Jesus into one's life. . . . And then he stopped—and the room was silent. It was time for the audience to say 'Amen.' But nobody was speaking."[26] In another newspaper account, a few residents of the mission's women's center complained that the staff "make you hate chapel." Another woman said, "it gets to the point for some people, it can be brainwashing."[27] If we believe these reporters, the mission's evangelical work had little impact.

In the last ten years the Atlanta Union Mission has shifted its work, downplaying salvation in favor of rehabilitation. In 1990, the mission

expanded "its programs for drug treatment and rehabilitation programs—services the mission believes are more critical to the needs of the
homeless," the executive director said.[28] By 1996 the director told
supporters that the mission, "in a caring Christian context, offers
programs and services that change lives." Its message was "You have value
in the sight of God. You can be a champion. You can overcome. You can
start anew."[29] This language is still explicitly religious, but it presents the
mission's life-changing work as therapy rather than evangelism.

Nevertheless, the Atlanta Union Mission's program remains far
more explicitly Christian than that of the other ministries. Robert
Hunter, the program director of the mission's largest shelter for men,
describes it as "a faith-based ministry program that deals with
substance abuse—drugs and alcohol." For Hunter, "faith-based"
means that "this program here is a God-sent program, meaning that
God is overseeing this program." The mission's drug counseling is
based on the Rapha system, a nationwide Christian program.[30] Guests
also are told when they arrive that they are required to go to chapel.
"If a person says, 'I'm a Muslim,' we don't tell them they have to
participate, but they need to be there. We're not going to stop you
from praying the way you want, if you can do it in private." Whatever
the guest's faith, says Hunter, "that's your prerogative, but we're a
faith-based ministry, and we ask that you recognize and respect that."
The chapel plays a therapeutic rather than an evangelistic role, helping
guests "reconnect with the pain, with the guilt, with the shame, getting
your life back in order. A lot of [guests] are very Bible-based, and they
talk about the scriptures—but at the same time they've accepted this
way of life. Some feel so guilty, so convicted by it, that they can't
change." Despite this therapeutic focus, however, Hunter does see his
work as evangelism. "The purpose is allowing the gentlemen a second
chance to not only reshape their life but to give their life to Christ.
Our purpose is getting people to change their lives and develop a better
relationship with God." The Convert Club of the 1960s continues,
in the form of the program's "alumni." "When alumni come back,"
says Hunter, "that's part of the faith-based work. If these guys can do

it, I can do it too. Some of the staff members are recovering addicts. If we can do it, maybe you can do the same—or do better." Although the program is therapeutic, the mission still describes it using evangelical language.

Religious faith—rather than explicitly Christian evangelism—plays a role at the other agencies. It provides them with a motive for ministry, though they rarely discuss religion with their clients. The café's Thomas Reuter says that his program's "faith commitment is still continuing. One of the key principles is hospitality. I think that's still a driving force here." Bill Bolling of the ACFB writes that "the greatest benefit of food banking is to experience the sacred in the work of serving others."[31] In a newsletter column he remembers "early arguments with initial supporters of the Food Bank about whether we were a ministry or a business." He is quite clear that "we are an ecumenical ministry run on strong business principles."[32] This is hardly Christian language, but these agencies believe that Christianity—or religion more broadly—requires them to feed the poor. For all of them, the call to service, rather than the call to evangelism, provides the motivation for ministry.

In their day-to-day work, however, the mainline-related agencies are reluctant to talk about their religious roots. Dawn, one of the full-time volunteers at Café 458, says that discussions of religion and spirituality are common at the lunch tables, but they are initiated by the clients, not the staff. Although Christian faith played an important role in the café's founding, the café does not present itself to guests as a ministry. Similarly, Dorothy Chandler, the director of the Midtown Assistance Center, says that "the clients are the ones who see it as a ministry. That's where the spiritual part comes from. They initiate that conversation." For these programs, Christianity provides the setting and motivation for ministry, but the message is very covert. They will say that they are feeding people because that's what God wants them to do, but they are not likely to talk about God—either to each other or to their "clients"—while doing so.

Several factors explain the mainline ministries' shyness about Christianity. One is the need to reach a broad spectrum of supporters. Bill Bolling knows that the food bank's financial supporters are a diverse group, so he has to modulate his approach in the agency's newsletter. "The language we have found that seems to resonate is the language of community building, civic kind of language. You'll see some religious language, but you're talking to Christians, Jews, and Muslims, Unitarians." A program as big as the ACFB needs to reach a broad audience and cannot allow specifically Christian language to alienate possible supporters.

The second factor is mainline Protestantism's long-standing resistance to proselytizing. For a variety of reasons whitebread Protestants are reluctant to force the gospel on anyone. Jerry Coling, a staff member at the Community Fellowship, states that "other than praying before the meals there aren't strings attached. They aren't a captive audience in any way." Overt evangelization is against the rules, he says. "We have a couple of congregations this past year who have wanted to, and I've had to suggest to them that they should take people to their own churches for that purpose. If we do anything like that, we go next door to the church." The café's Reuter has ethical objections to requiring worship attendance. "We simply don't do it because we don't think it's right. The whole idea of rice Christians comes to mind." Borrowing a term from critics of foreign mission work, he doesn't want to use food to force clients into Christianity.

Coling raises a third, more practical concern. "We get government money so we can't do that." Several of these programs receive significant grants from local, state, and federal governments, which prevents them from requiring guests to attend chapel or from talking to guests about Christianity. Chandler at the Midtown Assistance Center says that "when you get government funding, that keeps you from being an open ministry." Because of these restrictions, the Atlanta Union Mission refuses any government money. Linda Howard, the mission's public relations officer, believes that faith-based nonprofit organizations like hers are more effective than government programs, and the government should change its standards and support programs like Atlanta Union Mission without requiring them to abandon their Christian principles. Thomas Reuter agrees that "the government agencies rely on non-profits to do this kind of work. We're the best at it, we're the most efficient, we're the most flexible—on and on. We get a fraction of what government agencies get, and we do so much more." Nevertheless Reuter's café takes government money; he says, however, that the program is not restricted by government regulations against proselytizing. For all of these agencies, the interaction between religion, money, and government is complex.

While all but the Atlanta Union Mission receive substantial funding from government agencies, they all raise money from Christian congregations and individuals as well. Out of a $700,000 budget, for instance, Café 458 raises $72,000 from individuals and churches—the largest category after government support.[33] The food bank raises thousands of dollars from an annual Hunger Walk. A newsletter notes that "religious groups by the hundreds have made it tradition to walk. Whether they come from churches, synagogues or temples, religious groups bring huge numbers of people who see the walk as an opportunity for fellowship as well as stewardship."[34] Not surprising given its history, the Union Mission uses explicitly religious language in its fund raising. In a fund-raising newsletter, a former executive director wrote of "the joy of changed life at the Mission—changed lives through the awesome power of the Creator."[35] Robert Hunter, the program director, feels "that God has provided [the mission's work] for us through other people." Just as these agencies see Christianity as a motivation for ministry, they raise money through faith commitment—by reaching out to congregations and by using religious language.

Religious appeals also help the agencies get volunteers. They can call upon a deep reservoir of committed labor from the religious community. Kathleen Kelly, the volunteer coordinator at the ACFB, says that "a lot of kids come with their youth groups." The youth pastor of a Presbyterian church says that his whole church rallies around the food bank's Hunger Walk "because it gives us a way to respond to Christ's call to feed the hungry. The Walk is such an important event, because it brings so many people together from all over the community to help, and the youth of our church love it because they can help too."[36] Since most of the Midtown Assistance Center's volunteers come from the supporting congregations, says Chandler, "each person who's volunteering . . . has a real sense of doing ministry." Dawn, a full-time volunteer who recruits others for the café, says that it is "still a faith-based intentional community, open to folks of different religious backgrounds, very understanding that faith has different stages, and exploring different things is all a part of that." George volunteers a few days a week at the café because of his faith—"just in terms of being able to serve your fellow man, being able to give back if one is fortunate enough to do that." Saralyn became a full-time volunteer at the café after reading theologian Henri Nouwen, "who was talking about ministries with the poor. I had no sense of what that meant. I wanted to come here to learn more about myself and to learn more about people and to learn more about my faith." Other volunteers are less theologically reflective about their involvement. Bob, who has been volunteering with the Community Fellowship for ten years, does so because "it's to help the church. It's a program that the church is interested in doing, and they need help." Although Bob's motive is not intensely theological, it does come out of a commitment to the church, which motivates important resources of time and money for these hunger agencies.

If Christianity is the motive for these ministries, food is the means. As with the church socials, food plays an instrumental role in feeding the hungry. It goes beyond simply nourishing the body, to symbolize community and independence. Through their menus and their service, these agencies are trying to help their clients return to "normal" life through what they eat and how they eat it. To change lives, the programs need more than just rice and beans or beans and rice. To improve the ministries, they have worked hard to improve their menus.

In almost all of these programs, the food is far better than the soup kitchen stereotype. Lunch at the café was chicken fingers, pizza, or hamburger pie, along with coleslaw, sweet potatoes, or green beans, and apple crisp for dessert. Dawn says, "We generally try to have two different kinds of entrées—something with beef, something with chicken, to make sure we have different kinds of meat going there." Even the oldest community kitchen has improved its food. Lunch at the Union Mission was a hearty and tasty soup of chicken and rice and vegetables. For Hunter, the improved menu is an important part of the mission's shift from survival to rehabilitation. By offering attractive food, the staff encourages clients to keep to the recovery program. Dinner at the Community Fellowship, on the other hand, was more stereotypical: a sloppy joe and leftovers from Dunkin Donuts. With this exception, these ministries have improved their menus as a means of helping their clients reach their goals.

Several reasons explain the improved food. First, these agencies are finding good cooks. Robert Hunter at the Atlanta Union Mission says that "we get a lot of people who come in who have cooked in the past— because it doesn't matter what food you have if you don't have a good cook. We don't just throw people in the kitchen to work, we look at who has had experience cooking before." The café also relies on creative cooks. According to Dawn, "We're always bringing in volunteers who always want to try new recipes." George found himself running the kitchen one week and enjoyed it, "so typically on Wednesdays I'm in charge of menu and cooking." For these cooks, feeding the hungry is more than simply producing the most food for the least money.

The meals are also better because the agencies are getting better donations. For years the food pantry at the Midtown Assistance Center accepted whatever congregations gave in their food drives—often food that didn't meet the needs of the clients. The city's largest Reform synagogue, for instance, gives them "the leftover Passover food or that sort of stuff. We got shelves and shelves of matzo one time, and we had one volunteer who was convinced that every client was going to get matzo." Despite the staff's appeals, "you'll still see people donate what they don't want, donating what they've had in their pantry for ten years." Instead of just accepting whatever churches give them, the staff has started telling the congregations what the food pantry needs, based on client requests. A direct request, says Chandler, "cuts down on people just cleaning out their pantries, and it also gives us what we need. It really helps." The café, says Thomas Reuter, has "a friend down at the Atlanta

Farmer's Market who sends us whatever produce we want, so we go down once a week and pick up fresh produce. We try to make stuff that's fresh. It's cheaper." Prepared vegetables might cost "six bucks a pop, but a free box of broccoli, it tastes better, it's better for you, and it's free. The volunteers prepare it. Since I'm in charge of fund raising, I push the healthy economical stuff." To provide good food, good raw materials are as important as the cook.

The advent of food banking has caused the greatest improvement in emergency food, simply by making these good raw materials more available. Most food from the Atlanta Community Food Bank costs agencies fourteen cents a pound. Sherrill Terry at the food bank points out that "a lot is free. Sometimes we get stuff we need to get rid of right away, and we'll distribute it to our agencies right away. A lot of bread is distributed free." Some of the canned food comes in through food drives. "This is good stuff, because people give great stuff in food drives. They give peanut butter, tuna, and soups." Other material comes from "salvage," leftovers from grocery stores or rejects from food processors. In a typical day the food bank received 850 pounds of frozen green beans, 22 cases of orange juice, 450 cases of chips, 4 cases of baby zucchini, and a truckload of canned fruit drink. The director of marketing observes that "never knowing what will be donated next makes it more interesting." Some of the donations are a little odd, the food bank newsletter reports; "there is always Christmas candy at Valentine's Day, hot cocoa in the summer, and matzos after Passover." On the other hand, there are weekly donations of bread, milk, and eggs.[37] One day's donations to Atlanta's Table, which rescues food from restaurants and caterers, included 98 pounds of fried chicken from Hardee's, 58 pizzas from Pizza Hut (ordered but never picked up), 36 pounds of hamburgers and hot dogs, and 250 pounds of food from the convention center, including lamb, mahi-mahi, beef, salad, and vegetables.[38] This kind of variety was never available to community kitchens before.

More quality and variety are important goals for the ACFB. A recent initiative to increase the donations of fresh produce, for instance, paid off, yielding "plump red strawberries; fresh bright green asparagus; crisp

Food comes in bulk lots at the Atlanta Community Food Bank—including cereal and snacks. (Author's photograph)

orange carrots, and tangy grapefruits, oranges, lemons and limes." The director of the Salvation Army soup kitchen told the food bank that "the men at the shelter thought they had died and gone to heaven when they saw fresh strawberry shortcake served up one night!"[39] Bill Bolling says that "a lot of the food that we get here would not be available if 700 programs have to go out there and ask for it. The national manufacturers just aren't going to deal with these small programs." As a distributor, "we access much more food and much more variety. We make it easy for the donor." By serving as intermediary, the food bank helps both community kitchens and the food industry.

Since its main supplier is the processed food industry, however, the food bank is captive to trends in the market. "We have in the warehouses what people eat," says Bolling. "On the whole it's not very good. In the last twenty years we have a lot more prepared food. A lot more frozen, less fresh, less nutritious, more prepared—we're a reflection of that." It's a problem for many emergency food providers, he believes. "One of the great weaknesses in this volunteer system . . . [is that] volunteers want to handle prepared food. They want it out of a can, they don't want to cook, they don't want to chop vegetables, they don't want a long preparation time." Trends in the food industry and the needs of the community kitchen work against inexpensive quality food.

To address these problems, the ACFB is working to teach community kitchens and pantries how to improve their food. It works with the Atlanta Culinary Institute, Bolling says. "We have chefs come in here, take food off our shelves, create menus, write up recipes, cook the food, and serve it to the shoppers. They may see an item on the floor that they may never see in a grocery . . . and they'll put it out in a recipe and say, you can make something good out of it." As part of this effort, the food bank sponsored a "Soup Sampling" contest. Participating agencies prepared food "from three categories: casseroles, soups, and dishes made from 100 percent Food Bank ingredients." A panel of celebrity judges selected the winners.[40] Through such programs, the ACFB tries to encourage better cooking in community kitchens.

But the effort to improve the quality of emergency food runs into conflicts, often because volunteers and guests come from different food cultures. Most of the staff, volunteers, and donors come from middle- or upper-class white communities; their food preferences are very different from those of their clients, often lower-class blacks. As Chandler at the food pantry says, "we think pasta's so cool, everyone eats pasta. But almost none of our clients choose pasta. We have shelves and shelves of pasta, and nobody chooses that." Part of the problem comes from volunteers who "have the attitude that you're needy, you should be grateful for what you get. And that was really causing some problems. If somebody looked in their bag and took it out and asked to trade it for something else, some people didn't take that very nicely." Dawn says that many of the staff at the café "are vegetarian, but we're not imposing that on our guests because by far the majority of our guests want meat-based dishes." Differences in regional cuisine have been a problem as well. "A lot of us not coming from the South, we didn't have the first idea how to cook collard greens. But the guy at Georgia Tomato was happy to give them to us, so we asked the guests how they like them prepared and we learned to do that." The needs of the guests have challenged the preconceived notions of the volunteers.

These conflicts about food have taught lessons about cultural differences. Kathy Palumbo, who works with the ACFB's member agencies, tells about a food pantry in an Atlanta suburb, run by volunteers who grew up during the Depression. "They could remember that when they were growing up, having pork and beans was a big deal. There was a little bit of meat. So they had always, always, always stocked pork and beans." But in recent years the area around the church has been attracting Muslim immigrants "who didn't want the pork and beans. It really challenged these older people. Here was something that was prized, that they kept stocked out of a personal commitment to give people something special." After wrestling with the issue, "they decided they'd only stock half the pork and beans, and that they would get some dried beans and rice." Similarly, the food bank staff debated "when M&M wanted to give us lots of candy bars. It's just junk." But Palumbo remembered talking with pantry clients, mothers who said, "I don't have any money to buy my kids a special treat. I don't have the money when my child comes home with all A's, to buy something special." This caused Palumbo to change her mind, reflecting "how wonderful to be able to reward the child for something that they've done well. Bring on the cookies. . . . We have to quit viewing the world through our own lives only." Emergency food providers have often thought, says Chandler, "we've got to give them nutritious food." "But what they need right then might not be nutritious," she responds, "it might be junk food." In the end, "we're not trying to make a statement with what we give. We're not trying to change anybody's way of eating." This has been a hard lesson for some agencies to learn.

Several of the food providers have tried to deal with the issue of cultural differences over eating by offering their guests choice of food. Unlike some food pantries that give every client a standard box of groceries, the Midtown Assistance Center gives its clients a shopping list. "We let them select the items they need," says Chandler. "And mainly, it's as much food as they can carry." The choices include simple things like toiletries, toilet paper, and diapers as well as "goodies—cakes, birthday cakes and that kind of stuff." A lead volunteer at the Community Fellowship engages in an informal market survey before planning the menu. "I just ask people what they want," he says. Dawn says that the Café 458 volunteers "chat with [guests] about what things they might like to see that aren't coming up on the menu." A guest had suggested bread pudding. "I've never made that in my life, but I'm happy to try. If it's in a cookbook, I can make it." Reuter says that the café has "always seen it as kind of the beginning of choices. We realize that each person is different; not everybody likes chicken, potatoes, and green beans. And so we recognize that—we don't all like the same thing, and so we recognize the individuality of people." When I left the café Dawn was working at the bread pudding.

Giving clients a choice is about more than a varied menu—it offers them a sense of independence. The Midtown Assistance Center allows its clients to have some food that's "bad" for them. The Union Mission has discarded the long tables, meant to seat twenty or thirty men, and replaced them with more intimate tables for four or six. The service at Café 458 rivals any of the city's bistros. For Reuter the meal is very much a part of the program's rehabilitation efforts. By giving the clients menu choices, "hopefully they'll respect their own special needs. . . . As you make choices about what you're going to eat today, you're going to make choices about work, about who you're going to call today about getting your ID together." Providing restaurant-style service stresses "each person's dignity. You're a human being, and we're not going to treat you any differently than we'd like to be treated." With conversations around the tables, "it starts to feel really normal here. That's probably pretty healthy for folks who are trying to recapture what it means to be normal." With the exception of the Community Fellowship, where people seated at long tables are called up to stand in line for their dinner, the eating experience is part of helping guests return to society.

The stereotype of the hunger ministry is a soup kitchen in a church basement, feeding homeless men simple, cheap, and often bad food. Modern hunger ministries don't fit the stereotype, however, because hunger in America is far more complex. It is caused by poverty, drug abuse, and disaster. Many kinds of people are hungry, not just homeless men. To deal with this hunger complexity many hunger ministries have expanded their missions beyond emergency food. For them, food symbolizes community and choice, not just charity.

At the end of time, Jesus told his disciples, the Son of Man will separate all people into two groups. Those on his right hand he will bless, saying "Come, inherit the kingdom prepared for you from the foundation of the world; for I was hungry and you gave me food." They will ask, "Lord, when was it that we saw you hungry and gave you food?" "Just as you did it to one of the least of these who are members of my family," he will say, "you did it to me."

This gospel text—and others like it—motivates the hunger ministries of whitebread Protestants. For many liberal American Protestants, feeding the stranger remains a central commandment of the faith, reflecting the church's commitment to inclusion and justice. In a religious tradition that resists forcing its faith on others, emergency food ministries have taken the place of evangelism. In a society that resists categorical imperatives, feeding the hungry is one of the important remaining commandments. In this community, food is a form of salvation.

Whitebread Protestantism's motives for feeding the hungry, I suspect, go beyond the scriptures and vary from individual to individual. For most of American history, white Protestants have been the establishment—the social class that has set the standards for society. At least in their own mind, Protestants have run the country. This belief has instilled in Protestants a sense of noblesse oblige—a sense that they are responsible to make sure that the poorer sort are taken care of. Some might suggest that Protestants—generally wealthier than much of society—have fed people out of guilt. To that, Bill Bolling says, "it doesn't matter how people come. Jesus doesn't tell us how we ought to go—he just says 'Come!'" He adds, "a little guilt's not a bad thing." Some activists, like Bolling, work to feed the hungry because they're concerned

The food pantry at the Midtown Assistance Center is a cave full of plenty,
gathered through donations from five city congregations.
(Author's photograph)

about building community. Others have a more explicitly political
agenda; for them, feeding the hungry is a step toward changing the system
that keeps them impoverished. Other motivations are deeply personal.
Saralyn, a full-time volunteer, says that "it is through the relationships
at a place like the café that there is a dialogue there that changes you as
a person." Thus the motivations for feeding the hungry go beyond guilt
or obligation.

The imperative to feed the hungry is not unique to white mainline
Protestantism or even to Christianity. Such ministries of mercy are an
essential part of many faiths. Whitebread Protestants are special, however, in the way they go about it. Early Christians took the hungry into
their homes, but modern American Protestants have turned ministries
into institutions. Like the colleges founded in the eighteenth century and
the hospitals of the nineteenth, these hunger ministries have become

permanent nonprofit corporations, with boards of directors, professional staffs, and dedicated contributors.

And as with those colleges and hospitals, the Christian identity of these hunger agencies has changed. Charitable institutions often began as evangelical efforts, aiming to spread the faith while doing good works. Over time, however, their missions changed. They continued doing their good works because the Christian faith requires it. But they downplay their explicitly Christian message. These hunger agencies—like the colleges and hospitals—are Christian in motive if not in content. Whitebread Protestants feed the hungry because their faith tells them to. They don't do it to spread the faith.

I'll close with another parable. It's not biblical, but it has an important place in the life of many mainline Protestant churches. Once upon a time there was a little town beside a great river. One day a villager saw a baby floating down the river. She jumped into the swift stream and rescued the infant. The next day, when she saw two babies in the river, she called to her neighbors, and together they retrieved the children. Every day there were more babies in the stream, and the town posted residents to watch for and rescue the children. Soon the villagers had created a network of baby-watchers and baby-rescuers, with committees that raised money to pay for the rescuers and food for the rescued. The town had gotten very used to this arrangement. One day, however, one villager decided that the situation had gone on long enough and set off on an excursion upriver, to find out who was throwing the babies into the water.

This parable is common in hunger relief circles.[41] In a variety of forms, it's been told in numerous sermons, hunger agency staff meetings, and fund-raising letters. I heard it often during my time in seminary. The point, of course, is that communities are very good at organizing themselves to respond to human need, but eventually someone must ask what is causing the need. As this chapter has shown, mainline churches have been effective at founding large institutions to feed the hungry. They have been less likely to look at the causes of the hunger.

This parable's tellers want to find a way to turn church people from simple acts of charity to questions of justice. It is meant to lead listeners from serving soup to questioning the economic structure of society. The next chapter discusses how American mainline Protestants made that move—from providing food to hunger politics—on a global scale.

CHAPTER FOUR

GLOBAL FOOD: HUNGER POLITICS

ONE WEEKEND IN 1975, fifty young people gathered in their church basement in Long Beach, California. Unlike most church youth groups, however, they weren't there to eat; they spent the weekend learning about world hunger. They watched films and learned about the politics, economics, and ethics of the world food system. But they did more than just learn about hunger—they experienced it. The young people—typical American adolescents—fasted for thirty hours. Family and friends pledged them money for each hour they went without food. By the end of the weekend they had raised more than $1,500 for Church World Service, an ecumenical hunger relief agency. They broke their fast with a "Third World Banquet." The food was served according to the division of food resources among the world's people, with the majority of the food going to a small group of kids.[1]

While not every church feeds the hungry directly, almost all mainline Protestant churches have raised money to feed a hungry person somewhere. The money comes through traditional channels, such as offerings and bake sales, as well as more innovative approaches, such as fasts, walkathons, and danceathons. The churches send the money on their own, through their denominational offices, or through ecumenical organizations, including Church World Service or the Heifer Project. Some mainline Protestant churches have even moved from hunger relief to hunger advocacy, challenging the systemic causes of hunger. Collectively, we can call these activities hunger politics.

The last half century has seen the development of hunger politics—an ethical focus on food-related foreign and economic policy—within mainline Protestantism. The work had its beginnings in the chaos at the end of World War II, as churches united to feed both victim and former enemy. Through Church World Service the mainline churches became involved in worldwide relief efforts, sharing the abundance of American agriculture. In the 1970s Protestant hunger politics changed, as Americans discovered both the limits of abundance and their own responsibility for world hunger. While chapter 3 looked at how whitebread Protestants have given actual food to hungry people they can see, this chapter deals with the politics of food on a global scale. It investigates the history of hunger politics among white mainline American Protestants, looking at how their churches raised both money and consciousness around the issue of world hunger. This chapter traces the changing theological, social, and political contexts of hunger politics and reflects on the history of Christian social ethics—an ethics lived out by the young people in the California church basement.

THE AMERICAN BREADBASKET

Chaos reigned in Europe in the fall of 1945. Six years of war had destroyed the fields and killed the livestock. Hundreds of thousands of refugees searched for homes. Governmental authority and institutions were in shambles. Churches found both their buildings and reputations destroyed.

Protected by its oceans, the United States escaped the turmoil of World War II. Its factories and farms continued to be the most productive in the world. During the war America served as the arsenal of democracy; after the war it became the breadbasket of the world. Responding to the crises in Europe and in Asia, American Christians took the lead in creating denominational and ecumenical agencies to feed the hungry, clothe the naked, resettle the refugees, and rebuild the churches. These agencies—most prominently Church World Service (CWS)—gave American Protestants a personal way to help the victims of war, including former enemies.

After the crises passed, CWS remained the emergency response agency for American mainline churches. Through innovative outreach strategies it raised millions of dollars and shipped tons of food and clothing around the world. In the early 1950s the American government asked it to distribute surplus U.S. agricultural products, a program that presented the churches with important opportunities and challenging questions. This global work enmeshed the church in complex geopolitical situations. In all this work, whitebread Protestants responded to hunger by cheerfully sharing the bounties of the American breadbasket— the key to Protestant hunger politics.

American mainline Protestants had been concerned about world humanitarian disasters before, but their responses had been ad hoc or through secular agencies. In the late nineteenth century, for instance, American missionaries organized their churches to help with flood relief in China. At the outbreak of World War I, on the other hand, most of the aid went through secular organizations; the Federal Council of Churches, for instance, encouraged congregations to give money to the Red Cross. After the war American Christians sent most of their relief through Herbert Hoover's American Relief Administration. A new Christian organization, the Central Bureau for Interchurch Aid, founded by American and Swiss church leaders in 1922, focused on reconstructing churches. While all of these agencies did works of mercy, none of them was a specifically church-related ministry doing relief work. In 1924 the Federal Council's Committee on Mercy and Relief proposed creating a permanent interdenominational relief agency, but it remained just a proposal.[2] Christians were left to respond to crises on an individual basis.

Two trends—ecumenism and bureaucratization—changed the pattern for relief during and after World War II. In the years after the Great War, American and European Christians worked to create the foundation for what was to become the World Council of Churches. Although the council did not meet until 1948, its organizers created a Department of Reconstruction and Relief before the end of the war. The Commission for World Council Service, closely aligned with the Federal Council of Churches, was its American connection. Meanwhile, the U.S. government and church organizations tried to give war relief efforts some kind of order. In 1942 President Roosevelt created the Board for War Relief Control; churches bristled at the idea of control but did agree to register their work with the government. In 1943 the Federal Council and the Foreign Missions Conference created the Church Committee on Overseas Relief and Reconstruction, meant to be the fund-raising umbrella for groups such as the YMCA, the YWCA, and other church-related relief agencies—sort of like a Christian United Way. In 1944 the committee raised almost $1.9 million—nearly $18 million in 2000 money.[3] The experience of these groups pointed church leaders toward ecumenical and bureaucratic responses to issues of world relief.

Individual denominations did their own relief work as the war ended—the Northern Baptists looked to raise $4 million for war relief through their annual "Sunday of Sacrifice," for example[4]—but they increasingly looked to ecumenical agencies for efficient and effective relief. In May 1946, three groups—the Church Committee on Overseas Relief and Reconstruction, the Church Committee on Asia, and the Commission for World Council Service—combined to form Church World Service, "with the intention of rendering [their services] more rapid and effective."[5] Unlike previous agencies, which were independent and founded by groups of concerned Christians, CWS was directly related to its seventeen denominations; as one of its historians notes, it was "the first inclusive and continuing, unifying and coordinating instrument for overseas relief and reconstruction."[6]

The new agency had several missions. The first was raising funds for relief in Europe and Asia through denominational budgets and appeals;

the money was channeled largely through American missionaries and the World Council's Department of Reconstruction and Relief. It helped to resettle displaced persons, rebuild churches, support ministers, and train seminary students.[7] CWS also collected material aid from American Christians—particularly used clothing, tools, and medical supplies. Women collected clothing and made baby blankets; youth groups were encouraged to "start an overseas workshop" where they could make goods—including toys and school kits—to send to young people overseas.[8] To help manage this material, the agency opened seven warehouses around the country.[9] In its first year CWS raised $10 million (almost $87 million in 2000 money) and shipped $4.5 million worth of contributed materials to thirty-four countries, far exceeding its goal.[10]

Alongside this financial and material aid, Church World Service addressed hunger directly with the Christian Rural Overseas Program, or CROP, which was a systematic way to share American agricultural abundance with starving Europe. In the winter of 1947 CWS suggested to representatives from wheat-producing states that they create a Wheat Relief Project as part of the 1947 harvest. They set up committees in Oklahoma, Kansas, Colorado, Nebraska, and both Dakotas. Newspaper columnist Drew Pearson, hearing of the effort, proposed sending a "Friendship Train" across the United States to pick up carloads of donated foodstuffs, "inspiring housewives and farmers of the nation to spare a bag of flour or a bushel of wheat and bring it down to the Friendship Train as their contribution toward friendship with the people of Europe." As Pearson put it, the effort helped Americans "convince the people of Europe that this food comes not from the United States Government but from every dinner table in America—a sacrifice from the American people to their less-fortunate fellows."[11] Conveniently, the idea helped American farmers; shipping the food overseas gave them an outlet for growing agricultural surpluses without bringing down domestic prices. This joint mission—disposing of surpluses and directly helping the hungry—became an important part of CROP's work.

Pearson's idea quickly became institutionalized. In 1948 Lutheran World Relief and the Catholic Rural Life Conference joined with CWS

These model trains represented CROP's Friendship Train campaign of the late 1940s—symbolizing both American abundance and American generosity. (Photograph courtesy of Church World Service)

to establish an office and a national campaign for CROP. It worked through state and county offices that appealed to farmers across rural America to donate produce. As a brochure noted, "most other agencies have concentrated their efforts in cities, obtaining cash. The success of CROP from its beginning shows that the American farmer welcomes the opportunity to give gifts in kind from his fields, orchards, and livestock pens." CROP made its appeals to entire communities as well as to congregations, securing contributions from farmers who didn't belong to participating churches.[12] Some farmers set aside the produce from a part of their farms—Friendship Acres—for world relief. Montana ranchers designated several hundred calves for shipment by branding them with CROP's own brand—a cross—designating them as part of the "Lord's Herd."[13] The trains multiplied. In February 1948, farmers from Nebraska and Illinois donated over two hundred carloads of grain. By December farmers collected over two thousand freight cars of grain, beans, rice, meat, cotton, and other agricultural products; the shipments were dedicated at ten different ports in services on Christmas Day. The material was then shipped in "CROP Friendship Food Ships."[14]

Church World Service, CROP, and their supporting denominations used a variety of strategies to convince American Protestants to support their work in war relief. First, CWS and the church press drew attention to the horrible conditions confronting the survivors of the European war. *Missions,* a publication of the Northern Baptist Convention, was typical. It told its readers in November 1945 that "Europe is desperately hungry." The French were eating cats, and Germans fought in the gutter over rice thrown at an American military wedding.[15] The continent faced, it warned, "the blackest and saddest winter since the chaos of the Thirty Years' War," with more than 20 million refugees wandering the continent, many trying to survive on fewer calories than Hitler gave to prisoners in concentration camps. The magazine contrasted this hunger to the "titanic feasting" for America's Thanksgiving.[16] It constantly reminded its readers of the contrast between the Old World and the New, arguing that enough food was wasted in America to feed Europe.[17] The contrast between starvation and feeding was designed to prick American consciences.

The magazine reinforced these editorial pronouncements with news from the field. In the summer of 1946 a visitor noted that Germans were getting less than 1,500 calories a day—much less in the British zones. "The world today is witnessing a vast laboratory experiment of 70,000,000 German people slowly and relentlessly starving." Meanwhile, German churches—especially Baptist churches, the reporter noted—lay in ruins, unable to help their people.[18] Even as late as 1950, an American Baptist visited families in Hamburg still living in underground bomb shelters and eating horsemeat.[19]

While *Missions* occasionally noted similar fates befalling Japanese, Korean, and Chinese war victims, the focus of the magazine—like that of most American churches—was on Europe. The Old World was familiar territory for American Baptists and other mainline Protestants; most of their members were of European stock, and they had close

Fund-raising and educational material often focused on the needs of children—
innocent and apolitical victims of hunger. This picture of a grateful Korean boy was
included in Church World Service's "Children's Packet" for 1960.
(Photograph courtesy of Church World Service)

relationships with church leaders in Europe. Unlike the strangers in Asia, these victims of starvation were friends and family—even the Germans, the former enemy. A *Missions* editorial cited Paul's words to the Romans, "If thine enemy hunger, feed him," and reflected, "it is not pleasant to contemplate history's judgment on the American people."[20] When it came to starvation in the Old Country, blood was thicker than water.

To strengthen the emotional appeal, articles and fund-raising pieces included pictures of the elderly and of children, especially children. A CROP brochure featured on its cover an old man hungrily eating soup and a young boy in ragged clothing and asked, "Won't You Help?" It noted that "particularly pathetic are the aged whose savings have been wiped out by currency reforms. Too old to be wanted when jobs are few—too destitute to buy food—they look to you for help."[21] CWS's annual report for 1953 featured the picture of a smiling Asian boy, calling him "a dramatic symbol of the difference Christian love in action makes."[22] The concentration on children and the elderly appealed to American expectations of self-reliance. While contributors might have expected young and middle-age adults to take care of themselves, the youngest and the oldest could be thought of as innocent and thus worthy of aid. Surprisingly, however, none of the material drew a distinction between the war's innocent victims and the (former) enemy. Despite the six years of war, most of the American aid went to Germans.

To drive the point home, the agencies brought a taste of the European diet to the American heartland. In 1950 CROP invited a group of Ohio farm leaders to sample the food it was sending to Europe. The farm bureau reported that "the menu was short on food. The relief meal consisted of soup, apple butter, and milk."[23] At another luncheon a minister, looking at his bowl of barley, oats, wheat, and soybeans, observed, "I wish we could send refugees more of a variety."[24] These meals carried multiple meanings. They showed the desperation of the Europeans, who had to be satisfied with such simple fare. They proved to potential donors that the low-cost menu was efficient aid, without frills. And the meals shamed Americans with their diet that was rich in comparison.

Like the guests at these meals, CWS and CROP appeals contrasted the need of the Europeans with the great abundance of America. A CROP billboard called on farmers to "Share America's blessings" with the hungry overseas.[25] A photograph to promote the food trains featured a little girl and a grandfatherly man admiring a table covered with toy railcars, which represented all the material shipped by American farmers. A 1954 flyer stated that CROP had its beginnings "in the grateful hearts of people in a land of abundance." In contrast to American wealth, it argued, poverty "translates itself into disease,

CROP often staged a public dedication for donated food as an opportunity for
publicity. In 1962 corn donated by Indiana farmers was made into corn syrup;
the local high school band gave the syrup a send-off.
(Photograph courtesy of Church World Service)

broken families, neglected children, lessened opportunities, destruction of character." In this vision, CROP shared more than just food;
it shared the entire promise of Christian America.[26] A poster for
CROP featured an American family praying over a feast—with the
picture of a hungry little girl floating over the anxious mother's head.
"Preparing a good meal was a lot of work. Mother is glad her family
can eat so well—but she's disturbed as she remembers the many
children who never have a good meal. . . . We'll share through
CROP."[27] The American Baptist women's organization suggested a
fund-raising skit for women's fellowships in 1962; at the end a
character stated, "just because we were born in a free, rich country
doesn't mean we deserve it. I think we have a lot of things just so that
we may share with others!"[28] While postwar inflation and a rocky
transition to peacetime may have left many Americans feeling uneasy,
these programs worked to remind Americans of their prosperity—and
their duty to share that prosperity.

An essential part of the outreach campaigns, CROP in particular, was allowing Americans to see how they shared their prosperity with the poverty of Europe. Unlike the work of the United Nations or the Marshall Plan, these programs were direct aid, people to people. Press releases focused on the personal nature of the gifts, and dedication events connected American communities with the gifts. Pictures featured American farmers with the cows or bags of wheat they had given. In 1962 a high school marching band took part in the dedication of 100,000 pounds of corn syrup made from corn given by Indiana farmers.[29] The Montana office of CROP advised ranchers that branding time, marking the members of the "Lord's Herd," "can be the occasion for good publicity. Pictures and stories are the best means for more donations. Every county should have some special activity to mark the occasion."[30] Church magazines, with pictures of children eating the donated food, allowed American farmers and other donors to see the results of their generosity.[31] The CROP newsletter featured a table of donated shipments, including their size, contents, and destination.[32] Unlike much foreign aid, CROP food was visible food.

While CROP food donations were personal gifts, the campaigns also placed those donations in a larger context—they were the gifts of a Christian America. Echoing Paul's first letter to the Corinthians, a magazine of the Church of the Brethren stated that "friendship wheat" was "destined to become the bearer of goodwill to lands across the seas. . . . What an opportunity America has for demonstrating the 'more excellent way'!"[33] An Oklahoma newspaper editor, encouraging donations of money to help transport Oklahoma wheat to Korea, told his readers that "CROP is more than a program to feed hungry people; with each parcel of food goes the message of Christ. By our gifts we are proving to these people that our Christianity does work and cannot fail."[34] Such gifts were important in the geopolitical context. After the Indian ambassador spoke to the general assembly of the National Council of Churches in 1952, a Denver paper wrote that "only food, clothing, and Christianity can turn back the deadly Communist challenge."[35] The *CROP Newsletter* told its readers that "for many people in the 50 nations to which CROP supplies have been sent, the voluntary generosity of millions of American rural people to unknown neighbors across the seas has been the only contradiction of the anti-American propaganda around them."[36] In the midst of the cold war, Montana CROP concluded that "CROP means FOOD Fighting for Freedom."[37] CROP food was more than food—it symbolized both Christian care and American commitment.

Finally, CROP fund raisers appealed to the American love of efficiency and size. The CROP newsletter noted that CROP provides "relief on a person-to-person basis with an absolute minimum of waste because of the vast world-wide volunteer network of religious organizations through whose cooperation this program is carried out."[38] It was able to do this work efficiently because "CROP food is distributed by the finest people in the world—your missionaries!"[39] Church World Service, another article stated, "has the machinery ready or in operation almost everywhere where true need exists. In some countries it is the only relief agency that can operate. . . . CROP walks in where diplomats and generals fail to tread."[40] By combining their forces, denominations could increase their influence and their efficiency. Protestants knew that by supporting the work of Church World Service they were participating in a worldwide institution.

The American Protestant churches founded Church World Service and CROP in response to a specific crisis arising from the end of World War II. By the end of the 1940s the crisis had largely passed—European economies were stabilizing, diets were improving, and displaced people were finding homes. With the passing of the crisis, denominational support began to fade and financial support declined.[41] One CWS historian speculates that denominational leaders were trying to protect their own programs by decreasing support for the ecumenical agencies.[42] Under similar pressures, Lutheran World Relief and the Catholic Rural Life Conference withdrew from CROP in 1952.[43] The end of the crisis changed the circumstances of CWS and CROP's work.

Rather than fade away, however, these temporary organizations became permanent institutions. In 1950 the interdenominational organizations of the American Protestant mainline united to form the National

Council of Churches of Christ. Among the merging bodies were the Federal Council of Churches, the Home Missions Council, the International Council of Religious Education, the Foreign Missions Council, and Church World Service. CWS became the world relief agency of the new organization. After the departure of the Lutherans and the Catholics, CROP became an arm of CWS within the National Council, focused on developing relationships with supporters.[44] As part of the council, CWS and CROP were institutionalized in the heart of ecumenical Protestantism's establishment.

A new national fund-raising campaign supported the work of these relief agencies. In 1949 Henry Knox Sherrill, the presiding bishop of the Episcopal Church, called on American Protestants to participate in "One Great Hour of Sharing"; at 11 A.M. on the same spring Sunday, every mainline congregation collected money for international relief efforts. National radio networks contributed airtime the night before, and CWS distributed 75,000 posters and 3 million offering envelopes.[45] In 1953 CWS secured President Eisenhower's endorsement for the campaign.[46] The denominations promoted the offering and collected the proceeds; some of the receipts went to CWS, while some remained for denominational relief efforts. This division of labor and benefit allowed the denominations to claim the offering for their mission budgets. The Northern Baptist Convention, for instance, stated in its publicity that the offering "will be used for the total Baptist Relief Program."[47] Splitting the returns with the denominations reduced their fears of an ecumenical takeover of mission work. The *Christian Century,* the unofficial house organ of mainline Protestantism, urged Americans to send a message to the displaced persons struggling to survive in Germany. "In America more than five million Christians are uniting in 'one great hour of sharing' on March 12. On that day they will take collections in 100,000 churches. Before that the great networks will carry your pleas in radio dramas. Be of good courage. Help is coming!"[48] For mainline Protestants, the imagery of a great day of sharing suggested the importance—and the generosity—of their church.

CROP gave a face to American generosity by photographing donors with a symbol of their gift. These Missouri farmers donated grain to CROP in 1964 because "it promotes world peace and good will, spreads Christianity throughout the world, and provides a worthy means of reducing the farm crop surplus."
(Photograph courtesy of Church World Service)

All of these changes—the inclusion of Church World Service into the new national ecumenical agency, the creation of a permanent role for CROP, and the foundation of a regular funding mechanism—marked the institutionalization of CWS as the first permanent and international relief bureaucracy of the American Protestant mainline. After several years of uncertainty, CWS became the outreach arm of the Protestant establishment, with support from ecumenical bureaucrats, denominational leaders, and the national media.

All of this coincided with the heyday of mainline Protestantism. During the 1950s church membership climbed and congregations sprang up in the new American suburbs. Leading preachers and theologians became media figures. Denominations built bureaucracies to serve the needs of the flourishing church. Ecumenical agencies grew in visibility and scope.[49] Helped by all these congregations, preachers, bureaucracies, and ecumenical agencies, Church World Service's work for world hunger became an important part of church life.

The most important factor in CWS's growth, however, was the U.S. government. In 1954 Congress passed the CWS-drafted Public Law (PL) 480, known later as "Food for Peace." Under the bill's provisions the government released surplus food—including dairy products, grains, and cotton—to nonprofit agencies that shipped it overseas. This law, codifying a policy that had been in place since 1949, allowed the government to kill several birds with one stone. It could dispose of a growing agricultural surplus without endangering farm prices by removing it from the domestic food system. It could strengthen pro-American and anticommunist sentiment abroad by sharing American abundance. And it could distribute the surplus efficiently by shipping it through established church-related channels.[50] CWS director Wynn Fairfield saw the act's passage as expressing "the ever-present spirit of thanksgiving in the hearts of our people" and was grateful that "they have so pointedly chosen their religious agencies to implement so largely this sharing of their good fortune."[51]

To pay for shipping PL 480 food overseas, Church World Service initiated a campaign called "Share Our Surplus"—"S.O.S." for short. Just before Thanksgiving 1954 CWS announced a three-year campaign to raise $7.5 million, which would help deliver 500 million pounds of produce, valued at over $150 million (equivalent to $942 million in 2000 money). This allowed American Protestants to help feed the hungry at the price of five cents on the dollar.[52] Publicity for the campaign included a poster picturing a grasping crowd of hungry Africans, captioned "Meet Their Need From Our Abundance."[53] Encouraging participation, the *Christian Century* stated that "each year about this time millions of diseased, hungry, orphaned children around the world discover that the Share Our Surplus program is magic. How else can you change $5 into 37,500 cups of milk?" It concluded that "Church World Service does wonders with the little we give; it could do more if it had more. In most of us there is hidden a frustrated magician; Share Our Surplus is his chance."[54] In the decade after PL 480 was passed, CWS shipped 2.5 billion pounds of commodities valued at $250 million to some fifty countries. To do the work the agency developed an overseas shipping capability equal in skill and capacity to that of a large export firm, making arrangements for shipping, insurance, and distribution around the world. It provided these services for denominational missions as well.[55] CWS was a globe-girdling organization.

Distributing government surpluses, however, entangled CWS in domestic politics during the depths of the cold war. Agency officials suspected that "the administration in Washington would prefer that voluntary agencies help only those whose political views are similar to our own." Despite politics, CWS leaders protested their independence.[56] Nevertheless, CWS promotional material reflected a strong cold war perspective. A filmstrip showed children what it would be like in East Germany. "The enemy has come into your town and changed your government and school, and even tried to close your church. . . . There's never enough to eat or wear . . . not enough food, not enough freedom, not even enough truth. They've taken away your school books and filled them full of lies."[57] A character in a women's fellowship skit said of Chinese refugees, "maybe they are homeless and poverty-stricken, but they *are* free."[58] Government influence—and CWS's concern for its independence—became even more of an issue after the passage of PL 480. One of the law's provisions, for instance, required that the distribution overseas be done by American citizens; CWS officials feared that this made the church appear to be an arm of the government.[59] The agency responded by working whenever possible through local churches so as to not appear part of a Western imperialist campaign. It also worked to keep government commodities less than two-thirds of its total distribution, limiting its dependence on the government.[60] Government surplus food offered CWS both service opportunities and political challenges.

To preserve its independence, Church World Service raised its own money through careful public relations strategies. CROP advised local chapters that "people are more apt to take part in the CROP campaign if you can get at their heart. You can do that by using material on the need overseas provided by the National Office." A media guide gave suggestions for helping reporters get "what they came for."[61] During the

This Illinois farmer set aside a part of his farm as "Friendship Acres"—
with the produce dedicated to CROP.
(Photograph courtesy of Church World Service)

1960s folk music craze, CWS recorded a song, "When I Was Hungry,"
written by a popular musician, to be used in radio advertising and in
churches.[62] The agency worked with corporations, including such stunts
as a truck caravan, co-sponsored by GMC trucks and Carnation, that
went from Seattle to New York and back to Los Angeles, carrying 32,000
pounds of applesauce for babies in India.[63] The Sperry and Hutchinson
Company redeemed "Green Stamps"—collected by church women
across the country—for cash so CWS could send blankets overseas.[64]
Local CROP chapters also organized creative fund-raising techniques.
For instance, a Kansas bowling alley contributed "50 cents of each $1.50
paid by members of a Monday night church bowling league."[65] Through
these approaches CWS spread its message.

The agency found a good audience in the churches' young people, both as advocates and fund raisers. In 1957 it recommended that church youth groups sponsor an International Affairs CROP Party. "The purpose of the activity is to stimulate interest in international affairs, offer selves in service to others and share fun." Before the party the young people went from house to house to collect for CROP. "Students from other countries . . . are guests at the party. They often have songs or games they will share. . . . Decorations can include world globes, United Nations flags, dolls dressed in costumes. . . . The evening is completed with a dedication of the young people and the gifts they have gathered."[66] Other young people organized Halloween "trick-or-treating" for CROP.[67] A CROP newsletter praised three children who contributed pennies for each night they cleaned their plates.[68] CWS drew on the energy and idealism of youth to address the problem of hunger.

In an attempt to reach children with its message, Church World Service also produced a series of curricular materials for Sunday schools. The 1959 kit encouraged teachers to "lead the children to recognize that they, too, have a responsibility in this world task and . . . help them to find ways to carry it out and thus come to understand through practice what it means to be their 'brother's brother.'" The kit included a worship service, a singing game, stories, craft projects, and photographs of children in need. It contrasted the world's need with "our land, the United States, [which] has abundant food, more than enough for the use of those who live within her borders. . . . The treasures of food from this good land, from its orchards and vineyards, ours in stewardship from God's lending hand, become ours to use that all of his children may be fed."[69] Another kit helped children "range wide over the earth and peep into the lives of many people and discover how the church, through CWS, has touched those lives." It introduced children to the "more than 2,500 workers overseas extended into some of the more than 49 countries of the world with massive efforts to feed the hungry." The material focused on stories of "the children who have been helped to life and health, some of the mothers whose hearts beat in thanksgiving because their children are alive and well, [and] some of the fathers, who, having found new homes for their families, feel the warmth of Christian love and fellowship in their welcome to the new homeland." The goal was to encourage children to "add their money gifts to those of others, that the Church in Jesus' name, may speak and minister around the world to give the blessing of hope and life."[70] The 1961 kit focused on Korea and included Korean songs and games. It featured pictures of Korean disaster victims and asked children to "put yourself into the place of the pictured people. Suppose a flood had destroyed your home? Suppose you had been injured in a war? Suppose you had to walk three miles for a bowl of hot food?"[71] The CWS materials sought to appeal to children's feelings to get their participation.

For Sunday school consumption CWS also produced a series of filmstrips. *Wait a Minute,* from the late 1950s, "was produced to interpret to children, ages 6-12, how the overseas relief money they give in the Church School classes feeds and clothes hungry and destitute children all over the world." It featured the "Wait-A-Minute Man," who appeared whenever children were about to spend money on themselves and transported them to a place of need. One boy, about to buy a Popsicle, is transformed into a refugee child in Hong Kong, where he sees what the money given by American Christians does for his family. After the dream he "was a wiser kinder lad from the lesson he learned." He and all his friends "saved those nickels to buy milk for the hungry in place of popsicles!" The "Wait-A-Minute Man" concludes, "don't wait a single minute—send that money off today! For Palestine, for Hong Kong, for Europe's needy shore. Then don't wait a single minute to go and earn and send some more."[72] *Everyone Likes to Eat* focuses on two Korean children who "need just as much food to grow strong bodies as Betty and Tommy [in America]. But there isn't as much food in Korea as there is in America. . . . CROP sends powdered milk to Korea, and when Keeja gets a cup of milk it is a special treat."[73] *A Birthday Cake for Rima* starts out with the story of a Palestinian refugee girl. It switches to Johnny, a farm boy in America who couldn't finish his dinner. "'Gee, Ma, there's more than I can eat.' More than he could eat! How often have we heard that said in this wonderful country of ours." Johnny's father and his fellow farmers organize to send American food to Palestine and elsewhere. The story concludes with the girl getting a birthday cake baked with American surplus food.[74] These filmstrips reached children by connecting them with children in need overseas.

Several filmstrips targeted adult audiences as well. In *Our World— And Theirs* CROP appealed to viewers "to rebuild the faith of hungry people the world over by sending food from America's farms. Share the Lord's bounty and build peace and friendship through CROP, a program of your church." "It is up to us," the film told the church, "to see that these warehouses are not empty and that the hungry receive food. Through CROP, we practice the word of the Master, 'Give ye them to eat.'"[75] Another film depicted CWS as "Christian America on the move! This is Christian America closing the gap between plenty and want; maintaining a flow of material relief to the refugees and victims of war and disaster in 43 countries on earth." Like other CWS materials, it contrasted American abundance with world poverty. "In America? Better health, higher wages, prettier clothes in finer fabrics, newer houses with more appliances, and elaborate patterns of plenty. But in so many places on earth—the stark and terrifying texture of want." It urged viewers to "make a tithe of your labor and time because we owe allegiance to the Christian cross."[76] In time CWS created possibly the country's largest library of films and filmstrips on hunger and poverty, all designed to show church members the good work done by their money overseas.[77]

Through the 1950s and 1960s Church World Service thrived along with its sponsors in the Protestant mainline. Soon CWS was working around the world, far beyond its original focus on the victims of World War II in Europe. Much of this success stemmed from CWS's connection with the American government through the Food for Peace program, which multiplied Christian charity through the use of surplus food. This was the Protestant establishment at its best, yoking the food stocks of government and the moral authority of the churches. Through this entanglement with the federal government, however, international and domestic political change affected the hunger policies of the mainline churches.

Geopolitical changes led Church World Service to retarget its relief programs. As the need for aid in Europe decreased, CWS began phasing out mass feeding programs in France and Germany; in 1960 German churches, once aid recipients, began contributing to relief programs elsewhere. Japanese Christians also supported the agency's work.[78] Despite that victory, upheaval and revolution created need elsewhere. The independence of India and Pakistan in 1947 led to border wars and refugees. Israel's declaration of independence in 1948 forced thousands of Palestinians to flee to refugee camps in Lebanon and Jordan. The 1949 victory of communist forces in China closed the mainland to relief work and created a flood of refugees into Hong Kong and Taiwan. The end of colonial rule in Africa through the 1950s and 1960s created new countries that struggled with poverty and underdevelopment.

In response to these changes, Church World Service shifted its focus from Europe to new areas of need. In 1964 most of its aid went to Asia—Taiwan, Korea, India, and Indonesia. Americans saw these countries as being both needy and on the front line of the cold war. The largest African recipient was Algeria, which was dealing with civil war.[79] Unlike Germany and the Netherlands, which had strong ethnic and religious ties with the New World, many of these countries were unknown to most American Protestants. To raise money for work in this terra incognita, CWS had to invest time and money in constituency education, telling American churches about the existence of these new countries as well as their need. The children's packet for 1964 was "Come Meet Our New Neighbors in Ghana and Nigeria," featuring local recipes and instructions on how to build a hut like those of western Africa.[80] The 1966 packet introduced children to Congo, Chile, and the Philippines, and told of the visit of a man with "sky-colored eyes" who brought food and gifts to an African village.[81] These new countries required a different kind of fund raising.

But these new fields of work presented new challenges. In 1962 CWS was widely condemned when it withdrew from a mass feeding program in Taiwan. Begun in 1955 as a short-term relief measure, the program soon became a tool of American and local officials seeking to control the loyalties of the Taiwanese population; it ended up feeding almost 20 percent of the island's population. Frustrated at being used as a political tool, CWS argued that the program was rightly a governmental task and withdrew.[82] In Chile the agency became embroiled in a battle between ecumenically minded Protestants and more conservative—and anticommunist—evangelicals allied with the U.S.-based National Association of Evangelicals.[83] In 1968 the people of Biafra, a province of Nigeria, began fighting for independence from the central government; the civil war caused starvation in the province. CWS flights of food into Biafra drew Nigerian protests—and antiaircraft fire; nevertheless, the agency declared itself apolitical.[84] A CWS staffer reflected later that "many may have sincerely felt that the flights were prolonging the agony of the people of Nigeria: this is probably so, I don't have the data on that. At the end of the conflict one thing was clear: the children of Biafra were alive."[85] All of these crises taught CWS and its member churches that global relief was a political minefield.

Along with the political crises came increasing fears of environmental crisis. In the mid-1960s relief officials began warning of a looming global famine. India was hit with a two year drought.[86] Sub-Saharan Africa had no rain from 1968 to 1974. Some feared that the famine would spread around the world.[87] The National Council of Churches adopted a resolution which began, "the time of world famine has begun." It stated that "at some point in the next two decades, unless present trends are drastically altered, additional millions of human beings will find release only through death by starvation."[88] Many argued that one solution to the crisis was population control.[89] Others saw promise in the "Green Revolution," which changed agricultural technology and increased production throughout Asia in the late 1960s.[90]

In response to the challenges of international and domestic political change, Church World Service shifted its program priorities over the course of the 1960s. Although CWS continued its disaster relief work, it became increasingly concerned with issues of sustainable development. This move answered the United Nations declaration of the 1960s as the "Decade of Development." In an attempt to deal with the problem of refugees in India, for instance, CWS staffers compiled a 156-page sociological analysis of the situation, and then created a four-part plan, including vocational training, a village center, and a new agency in Calcutta.[91] In the same years the agency developed training for Tibetan refugees, food-for-work programs in Algeria, and built a desalinization plant in Greece.[92] To deal with population concerns CWS developed birth control materials for use around the world.[93]

This move toward development presented a challenge to CWS's fund raising efforts. It found that raising money for disasters was easy; photographs of starving children never failed to open a church member's checkbook.[94] Desalinization plants, however, had far less emotional appeal. To increase donations, CWS had to interpret the development emphasis to its supporters. CROP shifted its focus from food collection to fund raising; it became the "community relations" arm of Church World Service.[95] A 1974 filmstrip, *Hunger or Hope,* focused on CWS's development projects and population growth work around the world.[96] *The Road to Zapotal,* from 1981, aimed to "reveal how the churches are assisting people to change the conditions of their lives through integrated development" and show "the movement from relief in an emergency to development aid in the long-term."[97] Another film from the early 1970s put the stress on the cause of hunger—poverty—and the proper response—development. It argued that CWS's major task is to help "people fight their own root causes of hunger." Unlike earlier, more paternalistic days, the filmstrip stated that "everyone in the world doesn't need to farm as we do . . . or think as we do. But CROP believes that everyone ought to have an opportunity for a 'more abundant life.' That's what Christ wished for all of us . . . and that's how root causes of hunger will be overcome. Through people development."[98] By telling church members about the causes of hunger, CWS hoped to gain financial support for its long-term development work.

With its move toward development in the 1960s, Church World Service had come a long way from the battlefields of mid-1940s Europe. From its start as a combination of relief groups sending food to war refugees, it was now a globe-girdling agency shipping millions of tons of food, material aid, and skilled assistance to almost every continent. Originally focusing on friends, family, and former enemies, the churches were now helping strangers of many faiths. But Church World Service was still trying to connect middle-class white American Protestants with the hungry around the world in a personal way. It was still seeking to share the abundance of America—an abundance of food, money, skills, and confidence.

THE LIMITS OF THE BREADBASKET

By the 1970s, however, the American breadbasket no longer seemed quite so abundant. Geopolitical and economic challenges threatened to limit the previously boundless American economy and the previously boundless American self-confidence. These changes also led developing nations—and their supporters within the American mainline Protestant churches—to see the United States as the problem rather than the solution to world hunger. In this view, America was no longer the world's breadbasket; it was the world's oppressor. All these changes—political, economic, and ethical—led American churches to change their hunger politics. Their approach shifted from direct aid to fund raising, education, and advocacy.

The early to mid-1970s was a sour time in American political culture. A two-decade-long military involvement in Vietnam ended in retreat and apparent defeat. The war cost the United States 58,000 lives, billions of dollars, and public faith in both the strength and morality of American foreign policy. As the war wound down, the president and Congress wrestled on the home front with the Watergate crisis, a complex of corruption within the White House. The scandal distracted political leaders; worse, it deepened a widespread cynicism and distrust of government stemming from the years of war in Southeast Asia. This cynicism fed a rejection of large institutions—including the church—that began to develop in the 1960s.

The biggest blow to American confidence, however, was the energy crisis of 1973 to 1975, which demonstrated the limits to the nation's wealth and power. Post–World War II America had been built on cheap oil, which fueled the car culture and the spread of suburbia. Over those decades, however, the United States had become increasingly dependent on imported oil, especially from the Middle East.[99] Coincident with this dependence on imported oil was the growth of the Organization of Petroleum Exporting Countries (OPEC) which by the early 1970s was a well-disciplined cartel, positioned to control the supply and price of oil for much of the industrialized West.

Turmoil in the Middle East gave OPEC an opportunity to exercise this control. In October 1973 Syria and Egypt attacked Israel on Yom Kippur. Despite the surprise and the power of the Arab forces, the Israeli army soon drove back the attacks; the war was over within several weeks. American support for Israel, however, provoked Arab anger; by mid-October their representatives within OPEC embargoed shipments of oil to the United States and its allies in Western Europe and Japan.

Within weeks the country was hit by fuel shortages and price increases. Americans waited in lines to buy the small amount of gasoline available. Some areas ran short of home heating oil. States instituted rigorous conservation measures. The federal government, while resisting rationing and other regulations, urged Americans to drive more slowly and to lower their thermostats. Other countries suffered much more than did the United States; the United Kingdom, for instance, had to institute gasoline rationing. For America, however, it was a psychological blow as well as an economic one. The ultimate victor of World War II and the most prosperous country in the world, the country was suddenly subject to the whims of other nations. Through most of its history Americans believed themselves exempt from problems facing other countries, but the energy crisis—combined with increased environmental concerns—forced them to consider limits to a future they had thought was limitless.

While the industrialized world struggled with a shortage of cheap oil, nations elsewhere were trying merely to survive. In the late 1960s the "Green Revolution" offered the hope of more food for more of the world. New methods of agriculture promised to feed more people; Mexico and India, for instance, were self-sufficient in grain by 1970. But continued population growth and natural disasters endangered the progress. Sub-Saharan Africa had been gripped by drought for over five years, threatening 6 million people with starvation. This crisis came on top of famines in Bangladesh and drought in India. The international oil shortage exacerbated the problem, as the agricultural technologies of the Green Revolution made poor countries suddenly dependent on oil for modern fertilizer and irrigation.[100]

Unlike previous emergencies, however, this time the threatened nations didn't beg for aid. For the first time these less-developed nations—the "Third World"—blamed their problems on an international economy that they saw tilted in favor of the industrialized West. At a special session of the United Nations in the spring of 1974, these countries demanded the creation of a New International Economic Order. They sought adequate prices for their raw exports and an opportunity to develop their own industrial base. More important, they demanded a share of the gross national product of the wealthier nations as a support for development projects in the poorer ones.[101] Third World nations were no longer willing to receive U.S. surpluses. They wanted justice.

In response to the increasing problem of famine, and in the midst of all these other crises, the United Nations convened a World Food Conference in Rome in November 1973, attended by 1,000 governmental and private delegates from 130 countries. There were lots of speeches, although not a lot of action. U.N. Secretary General Kurt Waldheim called for increased food production in developing countries. In his opening speech U.S. Secretary of State Henry Kissinger set as a global goal that "within a decade no child will go to bed hungry, that no family will fear for its next daily bread, and that no human being's future and capacities will be stunted by malnutrition." He proposed increasing food production in both developed and developing countries, improving the means of food distribution, enhancing the quality of food, and ensuring food security against emergencies, including the creation of a food reserve system. U.S. Agriculture Secretary Earl Butz, who led the American delegation and supposedly was on the same side, called for more reliance on market mechanisms and questioned the need for a reserve system. The Third World was not impressed. India's representative called for a food security council with international authority to develop and oversee a world food policy. Argentina's representative argued that the United States had exploited developing nations and should pay food in reparation.[102]

While the United Nations discussed world hunger, the United States became increasingly concerned with hunger and poverty at home. In 1962 leftist social critic Michael Harrington wrote in *The Other America* that alongside the "Affluent Society" "there existed another America. In it dwelt somewhere between 40,000,000 and 50,000,000 citizens of this land. They were poor. They still are." They were not as impoverished as those in the Third World, but "that does not change the fact that tens of millions of Americans are, at this very moment, maimed in body and spirit, existing at levels beneath those necessary for human decency." These people were "the unskilled workers, the migrant farm workers, the aged, the minorities, and all the others who live in the economic underworld of American life."[103] In 1967 a series of studies documented hunger—indeed, starvation—across the country.[104] Activists proposed a variety of responses; a pediatrician suggested a federal program to give "every person a proper diet—and without cost to him."[105] The federal government developed a more modest collection of programs, including an expansion of food stamps, school lunches, and meals for the elderly.[106] Despite these programs, however, people were still hungry. As late as the 1980s, a Massachusetts Department of Public Health study found that 10 percent of children examined were chronically malnourished.[107] It seemed that the post-war boom had reached its limit.

This new age of limits, both foreign and domestic, provoked reflection by thinkers both scientific and religious. Garrett Hardin, a biologist and specialist in human ecology, proposed what came to be known as "lifeboat ethics." Based on the environmental concept of "carrying capacity"—the idea that a given environment can support a certain number of people and no more—Hardin argued that charity, especially food aid, was usually immoral. "To send food only to a country already populated beyond the carrying capacity of its land is to collaborate in the further destruction of the land and the further impoverishment of its people." India was starving, he believed, because its population had exceeded its carrying capacity. Sending food to India would only encourage more population growth, not to mention environmental destruction, political corruption, and possible civil conflict. China, he pointed out, had received no help from the West and thus was forced to be responsible for its own survival. "Could it be that a country that is treated as a responsible agent does better in the long run than one that is treated as an irresponsible parasite which we must 'save' repeatedly?"[108] Sending aid to the hungry, Hardin declared, was simply rewarding irresponsibility.

Arguing against more communitarian visions, Hardin and his supporters pictured the world as a collection of lifeboats adrift at sea. A given boat can support so many people; any attempt to bring more on board only sinks the boat, endangering both the saviors and the saved. Thus, they suggested, it would be suicidal for the developed nations to feed the Third World—trying to bring everyone into their lifeboat would simply sink it, dooming everyone. As situation ethicist Joseph Fletcher concluded, "indiscriminate sharing is not *always* good—indeed, it may *never* be good."[109]

Lifeboat ethics provoked a strong reaction, especially from Christian ethicists. Some questioned the principles of the theory, especially its focus on survival as the highest good. "If survival is enthroned morally," one ethicist wrote, "then human life itself is demeaned. It moves from something natural to something diabolical."[110] Others pointed out that the image of the lifeboat was faulty, ignoring the interdependence of all people on Earth, made abundantly clear by the oil crisis.[111] As one observer wryly argued, "if it's our wheat, then it's their oil."[112] Another challenged Hardin's assumption that the recipients of aid would increase their population, suggesting instead that "if the exploited are given their due—employment, health care, security, education, balanced diets—and saved from the precarious brink of near extinction, birth rates will decline."[113] Finally, most of Hardin's critics turned the blame on the

United States, arguing that "there is ample evidence that the poor nations are kept that way to a degree by activities in America and the West, especially through the operations in these countries of international corporations."[114] "In all honesty," one confessed, "we must acknowledge that ours is not a lifeboat but a luxury yacht."[115] Lifeboat ethics soon sank, but the controversy reflected the worries of the 1970s.

The most constructive theological responses to this age of anxiety came from two unexpected directions. One was liberation theology, which was rooted in Latin American Catholicism and North American minority communities. African American theologian James Cone brought the movement to the United States with his *Black Theology and Black Power* in 1969. Feminist theologians, including Mary Daly and Rosemary Ruether, followed Cone's lead. Meanwhile, Latin American Catholic bishops, meeting at Medellin, Colombia, in 1968 called for a new theological approach to the pastoral needs of their people. The theology attained its classic definition in Gustavo Gutierez's *A Theology of Liberation* (1973).

While these theologians came from a broad variety of contexts, they shared several convictions. First, they believed that the heart of biblical Christianity was a message of liberation from oppression. Second, that message spoke directly to the particular concerns and needs—both spiritual and political—of their oppressed communities. The theological response to these concerns and needs required a close social and political analysis, often from a Marxist perspective. Third and most controversially, God was on the side of the oppressed; the bishops called it a "preferential option for the poor." By placing the poor and oppressed at the heart of the gospel, liberation theology was a direct challenge to the establishment dominated by white European and North American male theologians.

On occasion mainline American Protestantism used the tools of liberation theology as it responded to hunger. In 1977 Glenn Bucher argued that "given the encroachment of theologians of liberation and the realities of starvation and scarcity, the theological renewal of North American Christianity is a prerequisite for formulating an ethical response." He asked his readers, "assuming that the gospel is at least tilted in the direction of the poor and oppressed, what kinds of public and personal ethics does communal reflection on theology and economics suggest for those in privileged positions on the human pyramid?" He encouraged his middle-class Protestant readers to reflect on their own places within the political and economic system "as a means for beginning to identify with the poor and acknowledging the need to live more simply."[116] Bucher's essay was a rich but rare application of liberation theology to hunger issues on the part of white mainline Protestants.

The other unexpected theological response to global hunger came from the evangelical community. While nineteenth-century evangelical Protestants had been deeply involved in reform movements, most twentieth-century evangelicals drew back from the world, focusing mainly on souls and salvation. The late 1960s and early 1970s, however, saw the rise of a different breed of evangelical, active in the world from a leftist perspective. In 1973 these evangelicals formed Evangelicals for Social Action; one of the group's leaders was Ronald Sider, then a professor of history and religion at Messiah College.[117]

Like the mainline activists, Sider sought to get Christians concerned about social issues, especially justice issues such as hunger. Unlike the mainliners, however, he used evangelical language, such as sin and salvation. He acknowledged that contemporary evangelicals "have been more concerned with individual sinful acts than with their participation in evil social structures."[118] But the Age of Hunger, he warned, required a faithful response. "If the Christ of Scripture is our Lord, then we will refuse to be squeezed into the mold of our affluent, sinful culture." In such a time "Christians of necessity must be radical nonconformists. . . . Only if we are thoroughly grounded in the scriptural view of possessions, wealth and poverty will we be capable of living an obedient lifestyle."[119] These were challenging words to the evangelical community—and unfamiliar words to mainline Protestants.

In his work Sider delved deeply into scripture, investigating the role of wealth and poverty in both the Old and New Testaments. He also analyzed the systemic sin that causes hunger, ranging from the structures that oppress Third World nations to the "unbiblical, heretical, demonic" advertisements that "teach the Big Lie of our secular, materialistic society."[120] At its root, oppression is not Christian. "Regardless of what we do or say at 11:00 A.M. Sunday morning, affluent people who neglect the poor are not the people of God."[121]

Sider's ultimate goal was justice for all the oppressed, but he proposed starting with justice among Christians. Church members should begin by taking care of other poor Christians. He argued that "God requires radically transformed economic relationships among his people." In response to God's reconciling work, "Christians should design and institute new structures . . . [to] reduce the scandalous extremes of wealth and poverty between rich and poor members of the one body of the risen Jesus." For instance, Sider suggested that Christians carry out the biblical concept of Jubilee in 1980, when "all Christians worldwide would pool all their stocks, bonds, and income producing property and businesses and redistribute them equally." Not only would this relieve hunger and oppression, he added, but "the evangelistic impact of such an act would be fantastic."[122] Sider's was a sectarian vision, seeing the church as a minority community with a countercultural perspective. It was a radical and evangelical response to the age of the limited breadbasket.

Neither liberation theology nor social-action evangelicalism made much impact on American mainline Protestantism in the 1970s. The mainline churches did begin to change their response to global hunger, however. Rather than rely on the abundance of the country's wealth and agriculture, as it did in the years after World War II, the churches focused on political action and education as well as direct aid.

Church World Service and its international relief efforts remained at the heart of this response. CWS continued with its annual One Great Hour of Sharing offering and continued to send agricultural products directly from American farmers overseas through CROP. Its "Friendship Acres" program sent commodities abroad well into the 1970s.[123] It also developed a new way to raise money for hunger relief: the CROP Walk.

The first walk, CWS's historian remembers, took place somewhere on the east coast in 1970, but the idea quickly spread across the country. Sponsored by local congregations or ecumenical groups, participants would walk a set route of five miles or so, having secured pledges per mile from friends and family. In 1991 over 300,000 people participated in 1,856 CROP Hunger Walks nationally, raising over $12 million. CWS adopted a policy of returning up to 25 percent of funds raised in a community to help finance local hunger-fighting efforts; in 1991 the walks sent more than $3 million to more than 3,700 local food banks.[124] The hunger walk, one activist argued, was about more than money; it "is a way to show people they don't have to just accept hunger: that we can work together on solutions."[125] Recognizing America's shift from rural to urban, CROP paid less attention to gathering produce—real food—and more to raising money—virtual food.

The agency also continued its move from direct aid to international development and justice. Its new Office on Global Education, according to its first director, aimed at "helping people discover ways in which domestic and global political and economic policies and practices were significant elements in the perpetuation of hunger and poverty in the world." It went far beyond simple fund raising to an ethical challenge, arguing "that those living in economically developed countries benefit at the expense of those living in the so-called undeveloped countries."[126] In 1973 a consultation of Church World Service and National Council of Churches (NCC) staff concluded that CWS had a responsibility to "assist people in their aspirations for self-determination" and should work to "enhance man's opportunity for self-development, liberation and justice."[127] CWS was moving to a more radical view of hunger politics.

This shift soon led to dissension within the agency. CWS director James MacCracken, concerned with feeding the world's hungry regardless of politics, resisted the justice-centered agenda of his NCC superior, Eugene Stockwell. As Stockwell saw it, "to the world view that says you have to meet needs regardless, I say that at the same time we meet needs we must also be engaged in a sophisticated political analysis of the root causes of poverty and oppression." CWS's role in distributing U.S. government-supplied food relief made the issue all the more important; Stockwell felt it was the church's task to show how American food goes to prop up global injustice.[128] In the end MacCracken resigned and CWS continued to focus on the economic and political aspects of world hunger. This politicization of hunger relief remained controversial, however; CROP officials worried that too much language about justice and social change would frighten off participants in its walks and other fund-raising efforts, donors who provided the bulk of the agency's support.[129]

This debate over the politics of aid was not limited to the staff of Church World Service, however; its work was challenged from both ends of the political spectrum. In the closing years of the Vietnam War, two Methodist relief officials drew attention to the political bias of CWS charity, noting that enormous amounts of church-delivered government food aid went to South Vietnam while little went to the desperately poor of the African Sahel—or to North Vietnam. In such a situation, "the church becomes the handmaiden of the state, carrying out the latter's military and political aims rather than serving all people impartially." These critics argued that "all charitable actions have political implications" and asked whether aid supported the long-term interests of the poor and oppressed, or simply supported the status quo of oppression and poverty. They acknowledged that "apolitical" charity is more popular with American supporters, who know that supporting social change could erode their own privileged position. The result is "superficial piety" among Church World Service staffers and a theology that "conveniently gloss[es] over the costly demands of biblical faithfulness."[130] Others criticized the government's Food for Peace program as self-serving and an engagement in power politics, not aid to the hungry.[131]

Church World Service was also critiqued from the right. In 1983 *Reader's Digest* asked its readers, "Do You Know Where Your Offerings Go?" The article, relying heavily on arguments compiled by the conservative-linked Institute on Religion and Democracy, detailed how CWS aid was going to communist Vietnam and funding political activists with a Marxist bent. The fault lay in the agency's link to the National Council of Churches, which had become politicized. "Critics charge that it supports Marxist-Leninist movements in the Third World, that it has betrayed the liberal tradition and that it has become obsessed with the alleged inherent injustices of America." The article advised church members to stay within their churches but to "withhold funds from doubtful causes."[132] CBS News repeated the *Digest* accusations; CWS, NCC, and denominational officials spent months dealing with the controversy.

Besides these criticisms, the mainline relief agency also faced competition from the evangelical community. In 1945 the National Association of Evangelicals, the evangelical equivalent to the mainline National Council of Churches, created World Relief as its global outreach arm. Its theology was different from Church World Service's; it had a strong focus on conversion as well as aid. One World Relief official noted that "a lot of people . . . have come to know the Lord through our efforts. You just won't get that with secular organizations." A CWS official, on the other hand, said that his organization makes it clear "that we are the church, and we show witness by helping, but we don't try to convert."[133] The growth of World Relief and other evangelical aid groups mirrored the increasing national visibility of evangelical Christianity; by 1985 World Relief was raising $7.5 million in the United States alone.

Direct aid, such as that provided by CWS and other relief agencies, was not the only response of churches to hunger in the 1970s. As sociologist Robert Wuthnow points out, since World War II the state— in particular the federal government—had begun to take over many social services previously provided by the church.[134] Hunger relief was no exception, as the government created such programs as food stamps, free school lunches, and Food for Peace. Given this new reality, hunger activists began to realize that they could make more of an impact on ending hunger through public policy work than through direct aid to the hungry. The best example of this work is Bread for the World.

A self-described "national Christian citizens' movement," Bread for the World grew out of the same early 1970s food crisis that gave rise to the World Food Conference and Sider's theology. In 1973 Arthur Simon, the pastor of a Lutheran church in New York, met with other concerned Christians; they concluded that "the churches have the theological basis and fine resolutions, but fail to act on the crucial matter of influencing policy decisions on hunger." They set out to "change that by organizing, in every congressional district across the land, a nucleus of Christians committed to reaching their members of Congress . . . on targeted issues that affect hungry people." They created an ecumenical and national lobbying network; within ten years it had 45,000 members and many supporting congregations. Local groups educated themselves and generated letters to political leaders, advocating policies that supported the alleviation of hunger.[135]

Bread for the World took a new approach to the hunger problem, reflecting the growing influence of government. As one Sunday school curriculum put it, "the federal government has money and resources far beyond that of local churches, or even denominations." One county in Ohio "lost $7 million in food stamp benefits in 1981-1982. In 1981 churches in the area donated $500,000 in food that went directly to the hungry. Even if church donations doubled to $1 million, there would still be $6 million less available for food assistance."[136] During its first ten years of work, Bread for the World persuaded Congress to pass "Right-to-Food" and "Preventing Hunger at Home" resolutions, create a farmer-owned grain reserve, send famine relief to Cambodia and Somalia, and reform programs to orient aid toward development rather than charity. As Simon put it, these examples "show the futility of making voluntary contributions to world relief, while ignoring public policy decisions."[137] With the growing involvement of the government in food aid programs, the church could be far more effective by influencing the government than by its own charity.

Fund raising—like that of Church World Service—and advocacy— like that of Bread for the World—relied on the support of the people in the churches. To get that support, mainline Protestantism turned to the great liberal panacea: education. Like most liberals, mainline American Protestants were convinced that people would do the right thing, that they could change the world, if only they were properly educated. In the late 1970s and early 1980s the mainline denominations produced curricular materials for children and adults, designed to raise their consciousness about hunger and poverty through a variety of activities that provoked feelings and actions. All of this material came with implicit or explicit theological, political, and economic assumptions.

This educational effort was aimed at a broad variety of audiences. Several curriculum pieces focused on children as young as kindergartners. One asked children to imagine themselves as hungry, and showed a demonstration of drought-induced famine; the curriculum then concluded with a sophisticated political analysis involving international trade and dependency theory.[138] Others were specifically directed to adults, such as a curriculum piece from Bread for the World called *Land and Hunger*, requiring "a moderate level of commitment to the course" and a good deal of advance reading.[139]

Much of this material, however, was aimed at church youth. They were common targets for hunger education, for a variety of reasons. Youth are more likely to be attracted to an issue they think they can do something about. Children also are most often the victims of hunger. Finally, adolescents are always hungry. One educator, relying on developmental psychology, argued that youth were a good audience for hunger education. They "are developing an enlarged ability to think abstractly," for instance. Adolescence "is a time when youth are susceptible, vulnerable and extremely open to external influence." It gives hunger activists "an opportunity to encourage and support youth in developing interest, concern and activity that will mold them to work to address world concerns."[140] For some Christian educators, hunger education gave them an opening to create a new generation of activists.

The substance of these curricula focused on economics and politics, while scripture and theology played a supporting role. To be a good curriculum for Protestants, however, the economics needed a biblical context. For the smallest children games were designed to have them memorize Bible verses about hunger. One program advised teachers to put words from a Bible verse on the floor so children could memorize the words by walking on them or to have children create a mobile of suspended printed scripture verses.[141] Older children read Matthew 25:31-46—the parable of the Great Judgment—in a circle and then listened as their teacher explained "that Christians care about hungry people and try to help them because God cares about us."[142] A Bread for the World study for adults focused on individual texts, asking participants to "read prayerfully" and reflect on several passages from the gospels.[143]

These materials concentrated on what might be called the "hunger canon"—a collection of biblical texts that deal with hunger and justice. This canon included texts from Leviticus about equity and the Jubilee, verses from the prophets, and the gospel accounts of the Feeding of the Five Thousand and the Good Samaritan. A curriculum for youth focused less on individual texts and more on the entire message of the Bible. It told the youth that "stories from the Hebrew and Christian scriptures present ways of looking at the world which jostle and call into question our normal ways of looking at the world. Responses to the problems of hunger in our world are often better evoked by nurturing alternative visions of the world than by imposing sets of duties or obligations."[144] While none of these curricula referred directly to liberation theology, the use of scripture was similar—both concentrated on the call to justice and on God's care for the poor.

Aside from these biblical references, however, these hunger curricula had little theological content. There were no references to the tradition of the church or to contemporary theological thought. While the work of the liberation theologians may have informed the writing of the curricula, there were no explicit references to that—or any other—school of theology. For the most part, faith served Christians as a motivation to care about hunger rather than as a lens for analyzing and understanding it. One curriculum for junior high children notes that any hunger curriculum "should help them care about hungry people with deeper understanding of what hunger means; of what causes it and what it does to people's lives; of how our lives connect with theirs; and of how we can help." A church school curriculum, on the other hand, also must include understanding "the roots of caring and the reasons for acting in justice and compassion that lie in the insights and teachings of our faith."[145] For these mainline Protestants, faith encouraged Christians to care about hunger, a theological task that paled alongside Sider's understanding of hunger as a manifestation of systemic sin and his call to repentance.

If the hunger curricula were theologically weak and biblically predictable, they drew heavily on political and economic analysis for understanding the causes of hunger—usually from a liberal if not socialist perspective. The Bread for the World curriculum for adults referred to articles from the *New Internationalist* and reports from the World Bank and the Worldwatch Institute. Almost all the pieces—for both children and adults—referred extensively to the work of Frances Moore Lappé and her Institute for Food and Development Policy. Inspired by Lappé, one curriculum tells very young children that "moneylenders, landlords, bureaucrats, military officers, city-based speculators and foreign corporations" are the prime beneficiaries of the current system. "We must face up to the real questions: Who controls the land? Who cultivates it? A few, or all who need to?"[146] A program for youth refers the teacher to *Global Reach,* "a look at the power of multinational corporations," and *Towards a Global Economy That Works* from the United Nations. It argues that "to work effectively at the problem of world hunger one must understand the basic economic principles that govern the distribution of food" and proceeds to analyze the impact of supply and demand on world imports and exports and the proposal for a New International Economic Order.[147] The analysis is sophisticated for a young audience, and none of it has much good to say about American-style free market capitalism.

Influenced by these international development experts, most of the curricula centered on explanations for the origins of hunger. Almost all agreed that the problem was not underproduction or overpopulation, despite the "eco-doomsters."[148] Rather, they taught their students that "inadequate food distribution (as opposed to food production) is the major cause of world hunger."[149] An adult curriculum tied the problem more directly to issues of land ownership and tenure in developing countries.[150] Almost all of the curricula placed a great deal of the blame on the wasteful "life-style" of North Americans.[151] (The next chapter examines this lifestyle material in greater depth.) Given these causes, junior high children were told, addressing the problem of hunger "require[s] an increase of resources available to the poor. Most ways require changes in governmental policies both in developing countries and in developed countries like the United States."[152] Drawing on their economic analysis, these materials traced the problem of hunger to patterns of both individual consumption and international trade.

To convey these lessons about the Bible and world trade, these curricula used a wide variety of methods. The children's material in particular employed games, songs, crafts, and stories to teach about the causes and results of world hunger. One writer observed in an introduction that games about starvation might seem a bit morbid. "Hunger is no game," she acknowledged. The goal of her book, however, was to personalize hunger, make it more than just statistics. While things we read rarely sink in, educators report that "we remember approximately *ninety* percent of anything we do. This became real for me when I realized that the hunger facts I remembered best were those I had learned in hunger workshops through short, to-the-point games." Through such games, she concluded, "hungry people cease being, vaguely, 'They' and become 'We.'"[153] One resource argued that games were particularly important in working with children, who "like DOING, MAKING, MOVING, SHOWING, TELLING: They like ACTION and they like it NOW!"[154] Another curriculum cited the work of Latin American educator Paulo Freire, whose *Pedagogy of the Oppressed* (1970) played an important role in the formation of liberation theology. Freire, the curriculum writers noted, "outlines an understanding of education which he describes as problem-posing. It is a dialogical education, not imposed on the student from without, but born of the student's perception of the world from within."[155] A retreat program for youth asked the young people to get themselves in a group knot and then untangle themselves; the leader was then to ask, "What was necessary for this to work?" "Accept all answers, but especially look for: willingness to play the game, willingness to stay together, cooperation, planning, and work. Point out that these are the same things needed to solve the problem of world hunger."[156] Another used "Stir the Soup," in which each child impersonated an ingredient for soup and was called into the circle in a variety of combinations, as a "get-acquainted food game."[157] "The Global Web" asked participants to mark on a map where their food and clothing come from, to "identify and understand ways in which we are connected with the entire human family, especially those in the Third World."[158] All of these games focused on experience-based education.

The younger children did crafts as well as games. *Hunger Activities for Children* suggested that teachers have their children build huts out of construction paper, complete with thatched roofs like those in Africa. "At the craft table the teacher can emphasize the living conditions of people in India or Africa who must stay in such buildings. Contrast those with our houses and their furnishings." Another idea was to fill a Big Mac carton with reminders of the work of a relief agency.[159] Several of the craft suggestions were meant to teach scripture lessons, such as the "parable put-ups," "posters, banners, collages, or cartoons" suggested by Jesus' parables about food and justice.[160] Others focused on the facts about world hunger, such as a project in which the children glued "each of the causes of world hunger . . . on a world map. All group members should contribute to the creation of the art work done on small pieces of paper."[161] These crafts helped to teach using visual and tactile senses as well as reading and hearing.

Stories were another way to get across the message about hunger. *Ending World Hunger* used several stories to help children understand what it is like to starve. The diary of an impoverished Brazilian mother tells of her sorrow over her inability to bake a birthday cake for her child. A Peace Corps volunteer reported on being the guest in a drought-stricken community in Ecuador, where he was served the only egg in a starving household.[162] *Hunger Activities for Children* used drama, as the students were asked to "hear or read descriptions of people in a poverty setting. Then discuss possibilities for enacting a play about these people; practice enacting roles in the situation; and 'play the story.'"[163] A curriculum for junior high and younger children began with tape recordings of several Third World children telling about their lives and their hunger. The teacher was then to ask the students if they had ever been hungry. "Ask children to bring next week some pictures of well-fed children, hungry children with empty bowls, and children eating different kinds of food." It also encouraged role-playing, suggesting "Act out what a poor family does during the day."[164]

Participants in these curricula were encouraged to sing about the hungry as well. Some songs were traditional church music, hymns out of the social gospel tradition—"Where Cross the Crowded Ways of Life"—or from the camp songbook—"He's Got the Whole World in His Hands."[165] Others offered new songs written specifically for children about the issue of hunger. *Hunger Activities for Children* included a song called "To Care." "To look at our life styles we see how unequal / All of our comforts when we compare. / To see is to care and to care is to dare / To order our living to spare and to share."[166] Another song in the confessional mode, for "The Hungry Child," chorused, "Jesus fed the multitude and He showed us what to do. / Yet still we look from face to face as if nobody knew."[167] These songs were designed to make children feel responsible for helping the hungry.

The most important element of the hunger curricula, emblematic of all this material, was the simulation game. Usually designed for larger groups and often aimed at teenagers, these games aimed to teach the systemic causes of hunger by re-creating those systems on a classroom scale. A book that included several simulations noted that the games were designed to "teach concepts, strategic thinking, conflict resolution, bargaining, need to compromise, etc." Most of the games began with dividing the group unequally, giving more food or other resources to the smallest group (representing the developed world) and the least to the largest group (representing the Third World) and then analyzing reactions. "Discuss the experience," one curriculum directed. "What happened? Why? What does this mean? Could we have divided the food another way? How did the participants feel? If this is the way the world is, what implications does this have for our world? Can we do anything about it?"[168] After the unequal distribution, one curriculum advised the teacher, "some child will usually say, 'That's not fair. . . .' If it does not occur spontaneously, suggest the idea. Once the injustice of the situation is felt, you have reached the *teachable moment* where the feeling and invested active interest of the learner is at its height. Then the point of the exercise can be made."[169] Another guide suggested acting out domestic hunger, with some teenagers playing poor people, one a welfare worker, one a minister, and several as police. One could be an organizer of the poor.[170] The "World Food Crisis Simulation," designed for up to 100 participants, aimed "to show the predicament of the underdeveloped areas of the world which can't afford to buy food from the few exporting countries."[171] The one adult curriculum was a series of simulation games, showing students the consequences of various land-tenure systems.[172] Powerful if unsubtle, the simulation games were the most important example of Freire's "dialogical education" at work.

Similar to the simulation games were "food experiences that teach," meals—often designed for an entire congregation—that could "also stimulate thinking on the issue of hunger for families and church groups." Most involved dividing the group into First, Second, and Third Worlds, and feeding them the meal those groups get in real life. A "Coffee Break Game" provided different setups for a morning coffee break, ranging from a table with lots to drink, many snacks, and a tablecloth, to an area in the corner with lukewarm water, little coffee, and not enough chairs. A small group was invited to the nicer table, while the rest of the people received little. "Famine—Feast" for a church night supper involved the same principle, with the Third Worlders getting only a cup of tea while the First Worlders get a full menu. "Hunger Surprise!" gave everyone just a cup of rice and tea, while the First World table in the center of the room went untouched. All of these experiences required "debriefing" at the end: "Against whom did you feel what you felt? Might persons in the Third World feel similarly about being born where they are?"[173] An activist working on domestic hunger recommended "a food stamp meal"—spending per diner only what a poor family receives in food stamps. After dinner, he counseled, "give people a cost breakdown of the meal and talk about the problems you had to deal with."[174] The goal of all of these meals was "to show solidarity with the poor."[175] They were designed to provoke visceral reactions; the goal was to change the participants' understanding of hunger politics.

Some "food experiences" aimed at raising money as well as consciousness. A "Fastathon," in which people solicited pledges per hour of fasting, allowed participants to "experience to some degree what hunger actually feels like, and begin to identify with hungry people" as well as raise a good deal of money. During the fast they educated themselves about the causes of world hunger and came up with possible responses. Those fasts often ended with communion. As noted in chapter 1, however, grape juice and white bread were not very filling.[176] In a variant on "Hunger Surprise!," guests at a "hunger restaurant" ordered a full meal from a printed menu but received only tea and rice. When the bill came they paid for what they had originally ordered; the income went to Church World Service. By using dramatic readings, groups could turn "your Hunger Restaurant into a Hunger Dinner Theatre. Have fun!"[177] Such programs weren't limited to congregational settings; families could raise money for hunger relief together, by tithing their grocery bill or by having a "Third World Evening," making a simple dinner and donating the cost of a more expensive dinner to a relief organization.[178] These nonfood meals turned the church social into political theatre—and raised money, to boot.

All of these materials aimed at teaching information, but more importantly, they were intended to stimulate feelings. Almost all of the curricula encouraged the participants to "get in touch with feelings of hunger." One told the teacher to read a brief passage about hunger and have the children "tell about times when they felt that way. Ask what colors they felt like then."[179] Another encouraged the teacher to ask the students, "what do you think it is like to be a hungry child? What do you think hungry children think about? What do you think they worry about?"[180] One curriculum based on research into the motivations of hunger activists stressed the importance of empathy. "How a person feels about hunger is important. Empathy with the hungry is an element of motivation for persons active in hunger elimination."[181] A CROP program noted that statistics were "helpful in learning about hunger" but that exploring feelings would help "participants get more fully into the issue by understanding hunger on an emotional, rather than factual level." It asked participants to "imagine that you have to decide between paying rent on your farm or feeding your family." "How does such a decision make you feel?" it asked.[182] Perhaps in reaction to lifeboat ethicists, who argued that there was a great distance between Americans and the Third World poor, these curricula stressed the connections among all people. The suggested introductory speech for a youth hunger retreat announced that "this weekend we'll see that all the world is interrelated, connected. We are connected to hungry people, and they are connected to us. Being connected can seem a frustrating mess, but it can also be a circle of concern and love."[183] These feelings of connection were meant to stimulate feelings of responsibility. One reference acknowledged that it did not "have many answers to the world hunger situation. What it does have is ways for well-fed people and groups to begin identifying with hungry people until we all care enough to start making our own answers."[184]

These materials went beyond feelings to suggest actions in response to world hunger. The curricula struggled with a delicate balance. To impress their readers with the importance of the issue, the writers offered harrowing statistics outlining the threat of global hunger. This approach, however, risked making the problem overwhelming, certainly beyond the control of the average junior high Sunday school student. To keep students from despair, the curricula insisted that the situation was not hopeless and that there were things people could do. "Most authorities . . . agree that the worst aspects of hunger and malnutrition can be eliminated within one generation if the human community acts cooperatively and decisively," one stated. "We CAN make a difference!"[185] And so, after describing in incredible detail the systemic causes of world hunger, these hunger curricula offered some actions students could take to help solve the problem.

Several of the curricula, for instance, focused on changing the lifestyles of the students, including pledging a simpler life and changing one's diet.[186] The goal of one class session, for instance, was "to gain more understanding of, respect for, and even pleasurable appreciation of typical Third World food in good protein combinations."[187] Another encouraged students to analyze their family food purchases and "keep track of your household's consumption of 'luxury' food."[188] Chapter 5 looks more closely at these "lifestyle" issues.

Several courses encouraged children to support political action. One connected food stamps and Meals on Wheels with the Old Testament concept of the Jubilee. "Explain what a federal food plan is and point out which programs belong in this category. Ask the children to sit down in circles on the floor with Bibles. Ask if they know that there were programs like this in Bible times."[189] One of the *Hunger Activities for Children* was to write a letter to a legislator. "Christians should understand pending legislation. Then, by writing letters to congress people and the president, they can generate support for valid programs."[190] These curricula encouraged the political education of children, aiming to create a new generation of hunger activists.

Most important, however, the curricula encouraged financial support of hunger relief organizations. *Ending World Hunger* included presentations on Church World Service and the Heifer Project, among others. "Knowledge about hunger alleviation organizations motivates people to become involved in them. Most people become involved in hunger alleviation when invited to do so by another person."[191] Another curriculum combined lifestyle and fund raising, suggesting that "by eating less beef and substituting more efficiently produced protein foods, we can save money and send part of that money to a humanitarian agency such as the United Nations Children's Fund."[192] In the end, these hunger curricula ended up being stewardship materials—designed to increase donations to the church by convincing students about the importance of world hunger.

Through a wide variety of experiences, these educational materials aimed to both stimulate feelings and encourage action to deal with global hunger. In a time of limits for the church, for the country, and for the world, American mainline Protestant churches tried to get the support, both financial and political, of the people in the pews for relief and policy programs dealing with hunger. Some of these approaches were theological; some, institutional; and some, emotional; each, however, aimed at inculcating a moral duty to help the hungry in a world where the abundant American breadbasket was no longer the solution to global poverty.

In their fasting the young people in the California church basement—introduced at the beginning of this chapter—lived out whitebread Protestantism's hunger politics. They spent their thirty-hour fast learning about the causes of hunger; this education sought to convince them of the need for political and social change. The fast went far beyond education, however, to a personal and spiritual experience of hunger. Ultimately, the fast was about raising money, contributing to the Protestant institutional response to world hunger. The fund raising allowed them personally to contribute to hunger's solution, as they experienced its pains. With its concentrations on education, personal experience, and fund raising, this fast contained all the elements of Protestant hunger politics.

During the second half of the twentieth century, whitebread Protestants developed a politics of hunger. Shaped by both a biblical vocation to care and a responsibility born of great wealth, they sought to feed the world's hungry. They started out sharing the abundance of America with former allies and enemies in Europe. In time their sharing extended around the world. As the international situation changed, however, so did their response. In the 1970s ethicists and denominational officials developed a political analysis of world hunger, an analysis that led them to critique the global economy. In their efforts at fund raising, advocacy, and education, they put this analysis at the heart of whitebread Protestant hunger politics.

It's not clear whether the average whitebread Protestant shared this political perspective. To be sure, liberal Protestants have been almost unanimous in their concern for world hunger. For instance, a survey suggested that 94 percent of all Presbyterian Church (USA) congregations had given money to One Great Hour of Sharing. They were less likely to agree, however, on the causes of hunger or on proper policy responses.[193] Whatever denominational policies and curricula said, whitebread Protestants remained solidly middle and upper class. While these congregations might have all given money for emergency relief, they might not have all supported calls for a New International Economic Order. And it's unclear how they felt about Sunday school turning their children into hunger activists.

Protestant hunger politics was most effective, however, not in its economic or systemic analysis but in its opportunity for personal involvement. All the analysis and all the statistics made the problem of world hunger appear insurmountable, too big for even a whitebread Protestant to solve. The fasts, walkathons, and hunger dinner theaters, however, gave these Protestants a sense that they could do something to make a difference. Even if the contributions were small in comparison to the problem, they assuaged people's sense of responsibility and responded to the call of God. The last chapter reveals the ultimate stage in this personal involvement—the lifestyle movement, part of a long history of American diet reforms.

CHAPTER FIVE

MORAL FOOD:
EATING AS A CHRISTIAN SHOULD

AT A RECENT FACULTY DINNER, the servers brought out the dessert—a cream and cake concoction, sprinkled with chocolate. A colleague—a minister and professor of religion—laughed and declared, "That looks sinful, but Luther urged us to sin boldly." He and the rest of the people at the table tucked into the evil confection, while the college president, seated nearby, received praise for resisting the dessert's temptation. Around that table, food was a moral issue.

Whitebread Protestants—and all Americans—live in the world's richest country, feasting off the productivity of the North American continent. In our abundant society, what happened at the faculty dinner is common: Food carries a moral value in America. In this culture, a particular foodstuff is not only good or bad for your body but also can be good or bad for your soul. Whether based on popular culture or on scientific studies, personal food choice becomes an ethical calculation. Food marketers are conscious of this moralism, shown in the line of snack foods called "Sweet Temptation" and the dessert on many restaurant menus called "Chocolate Decadence" or "Chocolate Sin." They know that some foods are "guilty pleasures." More seriously, this food moralism drives millions of Americans to diet and some to starve themselves. It also can involve social ethics as well as personal behavior, as governments deal with hunger and agriculture policies.

The preceding chapters have shown that food has moral meaning for white mainline Protestants. Grape juice and the individual cup prevailed over wine and the common cup because they fit the participants' understanding of what it meant to be a Christian. Churches created social events, often centered on food, because they wanted to create a setting for a Christian social life. Mainline Protestants founded institutions to feed the hungry—at home and abroad—because of a clear biblical mandate and a vague feeling of privilege when they were faced with extreme need. In all these settings, food practices in whitebread Protestant churches have been shaped by moral convictions, by the need to behave the way Christians should.

While previous chapters looked at the way institutions—churches and governments—behaved, this chapter examines individual behavior. It finds that some whitebread Protestants have taken this moral focus to heart, challenging the way they eat. In the face of American abundance or world hunger, activists and church leaders have challenged the diets of American Christians to mixed success. In this realm of food moralism, social responsibility—politics—meets individual food choice—personal decisions.

To examine the complexity of food moralism, this chapter looks at two moments in American food history. First, it examines a set of nineteenth-century diet reform movements, featuring such luminaries as Sylvester Graham and John Harvey Kellogg as well as the reformers of the Women's Christian Temperance Union. For these Victorians, diet shaped the state of the soul. Then the chapter looks at the "lifestyle" movement of the 1970s and early 1980s, when whitebread Protestant churches urged their members to eat morally, in a way that was sensitive to the impact of their food choices on the planet and its hungry people. While widely separated in time and in theology, both of these movements pushed Americans to control their appetites in the midst of abundance.

DIET REFORM: FOR THE SAKE OF THE SOUL

The earliest European settlers of the North American continent were amazed by its richness. The waters were full of fish and the forests full of game. Familiar and strange fruits and vegetables hung from the trees and bushes. To refugees from an overcrowded Europe, survivors of a two-month diet of dried beef and hardtack, the new land seemed like Eden. The Dutch of New Amsterdam reported six-foot-long lobsters. John Smith stated that the settlers at Jamestown found an "abundance of fish, lying so thicke with their heads above the water, as for wants of nets . . . we attempted to catch them with a frying-pan." A later Virginian described the territory as having "so happy a Climate and so fertile a soil, that no Body's poor enough to beg, or Want Food, though they have an abundance of People that are lazy enough to deserve it."[1] North America offered a rich larder.

In the eyes of later observers, especially European visitors, Americans took almost obscene advantage of this plenty. In the nineteenth century English writer Charles Dickens journeyed on a canal boat in Pennsylvania, where he found the entire company sitting down "to tea, coffee, bread, butter, salmon, shad, liver, steak, potatoes, pickles, ham, chops, black-puddings and sausages." The same meal was offered for breakfast, dinner, and supper. The natives' table manners were as amazing as the abundance of the table. "The gentlemen thrust the broad-bladed knives and the two-pronged forks farther down their throats than I ever saw the same weapons go before except in the hands of a skilful juggler." Every breakfast on his tour of America featured "a deformed beefsteak . . . swimming in hot butter." Sometimes the quantities of food had to compensate for the lack of variety. American novelist Henry Adams remembered that "the ordinary rural American was brought up on salt pork and Indian corn, or rye; and the effect of this diet showed itself in dyspepsia."[2] The American way of eating, especially on the frontier, drew on the abundance of the continent and often made its consumers ill.

In the early decades of the nineteenth century, however, some evangelical Christians began to question the morality of the American diet. Evangelical Protestantism, the ancestor of the modern mainline, became a dominant faith in the first half of the century, as revivals spread through cities and villages through the preaching of such evangelists as Charles Grandison Finney. Its adherents not only found forgiveness of their sins; they also heard the call to perfect society as they perfected themselves. They threw themselves into new social reform movements, including abolition and temperance.[3]

For many of these evangelical reformers, the American diet was as scandalous as slavery and drunkenness. With its abundance of meat and grease, it aroused diners' animal passions and destroyed their digestion. Most of the diet reformers drew their inspiration from a clergyman crusader, Sylvester Graham, advocate of a variety of social causes. Born when his minister father was seventy-two, he was a sickly child—explaining, perhaps, his long interest in health and diet. Graham was ordained a Presbyterian minister in 1829 in New Jersey but soon he became an itinerant speaker on a variety of health issues.[4] He lectured on alcohol, chastity, and diet reform up and down the East Coast.[5] In his addresses he blamed his own ill health—and that of many Americans—on ignorance of God's design and the onslaughts of modern civilization. Only by living in a natural state, in accordance with God's laws, Graham believed, could people find health and vigor. He recommended loose clothing, cold baths, fresh air, and abstinence from alcohol and tobacco. Like some utopians of the age, he advised men to guard their health by conserving their "vital force," forbidding masturbation and limiting their sexual activity within marriage.[6]

Graham was best known, however, for his dietary concerns. The stomach, he argued, was the greatest victim of civilization. In 1833 he wrote that "almost every circumstance and influence in civic life, tend to the development of preternatural irritability and diseased sensibility in these nerves." American society, growing in size and complexity, led to "undue excitements and exercises of the mind, and of the passion; all excessive indulgences of the appetites; improper qualities and quantities of food." Worst of all, he argued, was "the habitual use of artificial stimulants, such as the heating and irritating condiments of the table, and more particularly the various narcotic and alcoholic substances." All these irritants "act upon the stomach to disturb its functions . . . to develop and establish in it a diseased excitability and irritability, resulting often in chronic or acute inflammation." Under this onslaught the stomach did not suffer alone, "being, as it were, a kind of retina or sensorium to the nerves of organic life, the whole system of those nerves, and consequently all the organs supplied by them, sympathize powerfully in all its conditions and affections, partake of all its irritations, and suffer a consequent debility." The result, Graham warned, was "diseased irritability and inflammation, painful sensibility, and, finally, disorganization and death."[7] An excessive indulgence of the appetites—consuming the continent's abundance—could lead only to disaster.

To survive the assaults of civilization, Graham argued, Americans had to change their eating habits. Graham's study of man in his "pure" state, including Native Americans and Pacific Islanders, convinced him that humans were naturally herbivorous. Therefore, meat—especially the pork loved by frontier Americans—was out. So were gravies, fried foods, and pies of all descriptions. The best diet, Graham believed, should focus on bread—made from whole wheat, never refined flour— along with vegetables, fruits, and nuts. Water was the only proper liquid to wash all this down.[8] Graham's longest-lasting legacy was flour with the rolled but unbolted product of the entire wheat kernel, known as Graham flour—the main contents of Graham crackers. This regimen, reminiscent of medieval monasteries, rejected the traditional American diet of salt pork and hard cider.

In this reform era, Graham's ideas had substantial impact. In 1837 a group of Boston reformers, inspired by Graham, founded the American Physiological Society. They noted that "several ministers of the gospel" were "beginning to inculcate with much zeal, the importance of yielding a strict obedience to the natural laws, as a part of the grand system of Jehovah, and as no less obligatory upon us than his revealed laws."[9] Within several years the faithful across the country founded "Graham boarding houses," where residents could eat the evangelist's recommended diet.[10] Finney, president of Oberlin College, put his students on the diet, to a mixed reception.[11]

Graham's influence spread through another nineteenth-century religious movement, rooted in millennial excitement and disappointment. In the late 1830s William Miller, a Baptist minister, predicted that Christ would return in 1843, bringing about the end of the world and the Kingdom of God. The message spread like wildfire, and many evangelical Christians prepared themselves for the beginning of the Savior's reign on Earth. When the fateful day came and went without the end of history, Miller revised his calculations and predicted a new date the following year. After the second failure, most of Miller's followers fell away. Ellen White, a Millerite and visionary from Maine, organized the faithful remnant under the banner of the Seventh-Day Adventists.

Several of White's visions concerned health, particularly diet. After a revelation in 1863 she testified "against tobacco, spirituous liquors, snuff, tea, coffee, flesh-meats, butter, spices, rich cakes, mince pies, a large amount of salt, and all exciting substances used as articles of food." Like Graham, she argued that meat excited the "animal passions." "When the animal propensities are increased," she said, "the intellectual and moral powers are diseased. The use of the flesh of animals tends to cause a grossness of body, and denumbs the fine sensibilities of the mind." Similarly, stimulants like alcohol, tobacco, coffee, and tea excited "the brain to undue activity, only to leave it weaker and less capable of exertion. The after-effect is prostration, not only mental and physical, but moral."[12] While the Adventists based their health code on White's visions, they clearly had much in common with Graham's prescriptions.

White's more general concern for health brought the Graham diet to its apotheosis—the corn flake. The Adventist prophet's health visions went beyond diet; at her instruction the church founded a network of hospitals, most prominent among them the Western Health Reform Institute in Battle Creek, Michigan. In 1876 John Harvey Kellogg, a member of the church, became the director of the institute, later known as the Battle Creek Sanitarium—the San, for short. Kellogg described himself as "a sort of umpire as to what was true or correct and what was error in matters relating to hygienic reform, a responsibility which has often made me tremble, and which I have felt very keenly."[13] Diet reform was an essential part of Kellogg's agenda for patients at the San, with a particular focus on breakfast. He blamed many of Americans' worst problems on their heavy and grease-laden breakfasts of meat and pies, and searched for a substitute. In 1895 the doctor and his brother, W.K., invented the corn flake, a grain-based food meant to replace meat on the breakfast table. It soon made the Kelloggs and Battle Creek famous.[14] Kellogg attributed much of the Adventist interest in food to Graham.[15] The ideas of an evangelical diet reformer, filtered through a new religious community, changed the American breakfast.

While Graham's ideas ultimately had a wide impact, at the time they influenced only a limited circle. At the middle of the nineteenth century the Graham diet was popular among a small but determined cadre of devotees. Similarly, Ellen White's vision of a proper diet influenced only the small group of Adventists. But they were not the only Christian diet reformers. Reforming women, more within the mainstream, also wanted to change the way Americans ate. While they did not create movements like Graham or White, they did try to make the American diet more Christian—which for them meant more refined and polite, more genteel.

In some cases these genteel reformers provided recipes as well as prescriptions. In 1858, for instance, Mary Mann, the wife of education reformer Horace, wrote *Christianity in the Kitchen: A Physiological Cookbook*. Despite her epigraph from the Bible, "There's death in the pot" (2 Kings 4:40), Mann aimed "to show how healthful, nutritious, and even luscious food can be prepared, without the admixture of injurious ingredients." In her introduction she acknowledged that "the pleasures of the appetite are legitimate pleasures. God did not implant the sense of Taste in man to ruin the beautiful structure of his body, or to impair the noble faculties of his soul." But she also warned that "like all the other appetites, the appetite for food may be abused." Through such abuse, "the loss of power, premature decay, and untimely death, are inevitable." In sum, Mann argued that "there is no more prolific,—indeed, there is no *such* prolific cause of bad morals as abuses of diet."[16]

The key, believed Mann, was controlling the animal appetites. Reflecting the diet reformers' common obsession with over consumption, Mann warned that "the profusions of *nature* tempt the appetite of man. The productions of all the earth are at his command. But, for the control of his appetites, man is endowed with reason and conscience."[17] Unlike animals, humans could control their appetite for excess, for rich and spicy food. To do so, she believed, was only Christian—rooted in the experience of the Last Supper.

> Is it is not a reasonable explanation of the request which Christ made to his disciples, to remember him "as often" as they assembled at the social board, that he wishes to associate together the life that subsists by eating bread, and the life that feeds upon "every word that proceedeth out of the mouth of God," —thus ensuring temperance? Is it not certain, that if that voice were in the ear of every Christian as he sits down to the social meal, if every "grace before meat" should recognize that we are to eat, not to gratify ignoble appetites, but to build up purely and devoutly these temples of the Holy Spirit, which our bodies were designed to be, we should be less likely to pervert God's beautiful provision of enjoyment in eating?[18]

If Christians ate as if Christ were at the table with them for every meal, they would control their self-indulgence. For Mann and the genteel reformers, eating should be a spiritual act, not just a physical one.

Mann centered her work on two themes common to the diet campaigners. First, she was concerned with digestion. She believed that "compounds, like wedding cake, suet plum-puddings, and rich turtle soup, are masses of indigestible material, which should never find their way to any christian table." She defended her ethical stance. "If asked why I pronounce these and similar dishes *unchristian*, I answer, that health is one of the indispensable conditions of the highest morality and beneficence."[19] Indigestion was a moral issue, on the level of drunkenness. "Why is not dyspepsia disgraceful, like *delirium tremens?*"[20] To preserve the digestion, Mann advised her readers to cook simply and to limit the use of spices. Excessive use makes "a stimulus to appetite by a conglomeration, which is a most unnatural one, and gradually injures

John Harvey Kellogg, Adventist physician and co-inventor of the corn flake,
inspired countless diet reformers—both secular and religious—at the end
of the nineteenth century.
(Photograph courtesy the Kellogg Company)

the very power of digestion." She also recommended boiling vegetables
for half an hour to an hour at least—for digestion's sake.[21] Keeping the
digestion strong was healthy, therefore moral, therefore Christian.

Anticipating the "natural" cookbooks of a later time, Mann also
recommended the purest possible ingredients. Warning her readers of
contamination by processed foods, she advised that "the first object of a
housekeeper should be, to procure unadulterated articles." In a truly
scientific kitchen, Mann believed, every cook would have a microscope
to help detect tainted food. Because the flour used by professional bakers
was adulterated with soda, alum, and metals, Mann insisted that "bread
should be home-made. In this country, it is the general custom to make

bread in families, but as our domestics are not scientific, it is absolutely necessary that it should not be left to them."[22] These recommendations, common to all the genteel reformers, reflected the anxieties of a traditional cook in an increasingly industrial and urban society.

Similar prescriptions appeared in an 1886 essay in *Good Housekeeping*. Margaret Sidney won $250 for her essay on "How to Eat, Drink, and Sleep as a Christian Should." She based her work on the theological conclusion that "Christ, while living the human life, always acted intelligently." Thus, she concluded, "His professed followers cannot be excused from using their reasoning powers in all the affairs of life." For Sidney, being Christian meant behaving reasonably—or, as she put it, "religion might be termed 'sanctified common sense.'"[23] As chapter 1 showed, temperance advocates assumed that Christ was a teetotaler, and sanitation crusaders assumed that he was clean. For these genteel reformers, Christ ate in a reasonable and healthful way.

Sidney's warnings and recommendations echoed Mann's and Graham's. Reflecting on the petitions of the Lord's Prayer, "give us this day our daily bread" and "deliver us from evil," Sidney exalted in "the healthful, nutritious food, the cool and juicy raw fruit, that would Christianize our table—what good daily bread it is!" But, she went on, "how we love the evil—Satan's own emissary in the guise of the toothsome fried dishes."[24] While God was in fresh produce, Satan himself was in the frying pan.

As with Mann, Sidney's priority was protecting the digestion. "There is no reason to doubt the statement often made that Americans, in general, are doing their best to ruin the digestive organs with which their bodies are supplied." She was critical of businessmen who overloaded their lunches with meat instead of light soups and well-made bread, and overworked mothers who nibbled cold leftovers instead of a more relaxed luncheon. She recommended improving the family digestion by decorating the table with flowers and nice linens; "they shed a Christian influence over every thought and act."[25] In short, for Sidney, "eating as Christians should" meant eating like genteel middle-class Americans.

While Mann and Sidney told whitebread Protestant mothers how to Christianize their kitchens, organizations also advocated diet reform—most notably, members of the Women's Christian Temperance Union (WCTU). Issues of diet and nutrition were on the organization's agenda from its early years, and it established a Department of Sanitary and Economic Cookery in 1894. This concern arose out of the union's central goal of limiting alcohol consumption. A bad diet, it believed, encouraged people (mainly men) to drink. The director of the department told the WCTU's 1894 convention that "if the food elements required by the body are not supplied or are improperly proportioned or cooked, disease, weakness, or a longing for stimulants, often all combined, are the result."[26] In a healthy body, however, "nutrition is the enemy of intemperance. It satisfies the child and man, and the healthy, unperverted system neither craves for nor likes condiments or stimulants."[27] Her successor told members that, by satisfying "our fathers, brothers, husbands, sons and all beloved ones" with "well-cooked, well-served, wholly nourishing meals at home[,] that salted lunches shall find no one to eat and the bottled demons shall fling up their corks in despair, there being none to drink."[28] A healthful diet could save American men from the saloon.

Members of the WCTU identified several culprits in the American diet that led to alcoholism and despair. The most important, reminiscent of Graham and the earlier reformers, was overeating. In 1883 the wife of corn flake king John Harvey Kellogg, herself a dedicated member of the WCTU, argued that "intemperance in eating is a round on the ladder, and but a few steps above, that which leads down to the drunkard's ignominious grave; an over-indulgence of a natural appetite soon leads to the creation and indulgence of wholly unnatural desires." Gratifying the desire for food led inexorably to gratifying other debased appetites. Like Graham, Mrs. Kellogg warned against wallowing in the continent's bounty. "God has provided a bountiful supply and plentiful variety of substances for man's nourishment, but he did not design that man should partake of all this variety at a single meal. The use of too great a variety of tempting viands is without doubt responsible for most of the surfeiting and excesses in eating."[29] The abundance of America—both in quantity and variety—remained a snare for these diet reformers.

Part of the blame for overindulgence, some WCTU members felt, lay in the use of condiments and spices. Their purpose, after all, was to whet the appetite. "The very fact that condiments do create appetite," Mrs. Kellogg warned, "is a sufficient argument against their use." Condiments and spices, by changing the taste of food, were clearly against God's plans; adding anything to food implied "that it did not fit the purpose for which the creator evidently designed it." Returning to the focus of the WCTU's work, Mrs. Kellogg concluded that "the use of condiments is unquestionably a strong auxiliary to the use of intoxicating drinks."[30] Instead of "mustard, ginger, pepper, pepper-sauce, Worcestershire sauce, cloves, spices and other similar substances," WCTU members recommended pure fare, prepared simply—the way God designed it.

Like Graham and the earlier reformers, several of the WCTU diet activists also questioned the eating of meat. In 1883 Mrs. Kellogg criticized the "great excess in the use of animal food, which is deleterious to health, exciting the nervous system, and thus producing a tendency to the use of artificial stimulants."[31] Ten years later a WCTU member responsible for the Scientific Nutrition in Cookery department questioned "the frequent use of beef which tends to inflammatory conditions and excitement of nerve for people of sedentary habits."[32] For these reformers, as for Graham, meat was bad because it stimulated animal passions and unhealthy appetites. Another WCTU member, however, recommended vegetarianism, simply for the sake of the animals.[33] Advocating vegetarianism on religious grounds was a radical move for nineteenth-century America.

Bread—more properly, bread commercially produced from white flour—was also a target for the WCTU diet reformers. One advocate of whole-wheat bread argued that "the imperfect nutrition of the white bread" helped lead to "a fearfully craving appetite" for alcohol. She considered "the introduction of the entire wheat flour one of the most important improvements of the times."[34] Another offered "lessons on bread-making from the entire wheat—the elements of which form a perfect food and feed not only muscle and bone, but repair also the waste and strain upon brain and nerve."[35] One WCTU member was the founder of the Bread Reform League, "a purely uncommercial association, organized to spread a knowledge of wholesome, nourishing foods."[36] This concern for pure unadulterated bread led the WCTU to advocate the passage of a "Pure Food" bill at its 1901 convention.[37]

While WCTU members concerned themselves with such details as spices and bread, at its heart their concern was a moral one; the question of what to eat—and how much—was a question of right and wrong. One of the WCTU's leading diet reformers, a medical doctor, wrote in the organization's newspaper in 1903 that "our eating, the waste and worse than waste from the overplus, and the diseases engendered tend to the undoing of nations." Since she was "humbly devoted to the spread of the gospel of our Lord Jesus Christ," she pleaded "for a reform in favor of a natural diet. It is a moral as well as a national question and has a bearing upon the life to come as well as that which now is; it is to be rightly classed among the greater problems which confront the church of God."[38] For these diet reformers, the question was one of both Christian morality and national survival.

These Victorian diet reformers—from Graham to the WCTU—wanted Americans to eat as they believed Christians should. They were all critical of overeating, seeing it as an inability to control the animal appetites. They all advocated simple eating, suspicious of spices and condiments. They never said exactly what made their diets Christian, but their worldview is unmistakable. For them, eating like a Christian meant eating like a middle- or upper-class Anglo-American. They opposed the food of the barroom and its attendant immorality. They opposed the strong spices and exotic flavors of immigrant cooking. All around them, immigrants and lower-class natives indulged their sensory appetites, risking damnation—or, at the very least, indigestion. To save their stomachs and their souls, the Christian diet reformers advocated practical asceticism.

LIFESTYLE: FOR THE SAKE OF THE HUNGRY

The religious food reformers of the nineteenth century struggled with abundance. The abuses they preached against—overconsumption and rich food—were rooted in the richness of the American continent. In many cases, Americans ate as much as they did simply because they could. The religious food reform campaigns of the late twentieth century also struggled with abundance—specifically, with the guilt caused by American abundance in a world of scarcity. As we saw in the last chapter, in the 1970s Americans—particularly white mainline Protestants—were overwhelmed with the problem of world hunger. In the face of starvation around the world, they felt powerless. Hunger activists worked to convince these middle-class Americans that hunger was caused by their own diet. While world hunger seemed insurmountable, these church leaders told their members that they could cure it by changing the way they ate.

As chapter 4 showed, American Protestants had long been concerned about feeding the world's poor and hungry. They built large institutions to share the wealth of the American breadbasket with the rest of the world. But every year there seemed to be more hunger. Experts warned that the 1970s would see unprecedented starvation. In the late 1960s a British statesman predicted local famines by the end of the decade; "at worst the local famines will spread into a sea of hunger." One agronomist and Nobel Peace Prize winner told Congress in 1974 that "fifty million people, perhaps more, could perish from famine."[39] These apocalyptic predictions mocked American relief efforts.

Whitebread Protestants and others debated the cause of this hunger. Some blamed the hungry—specifically, overpopulation in the Third World. One American Baptist layman wrote to his denominational magazine that "we are trying to treat the symptom and not the disease! The real problem is *overpopulation* and it is time we recognized it!"[40] Meanwhile there was less food to feed more people. Lester Brown, a widely quoted food authority, pointed out that in a few years world grain reserves had dropped quickly, to just twenty-six days by 1974, while prices of grain rose. "Between late 1972 and the end of 1973 the world prices of wheat and rice tripled. Soybean prices doubled in a 24-month period."[41] Inflation and the shock caused by the oil embargo had disrupted the global economy, driving up grain prices as supplies fell.

In Brown's eyes, the real problem, however, was not overpopulation in the Third World but overconsumption in the First World. He argued that "rising affluence has now emerged as a major new claimant on the world's food-producing resources." He pointed out that people in less-developed nations consume only about 400 pounds of grain in a year, most of that eaten directly. "By contrast, the average North American consumed nearly one ton of grain per year"—most of that indirectly in the form of milk, meat, and eggs.[42] In previous famines Americans had seen themselves as saviors, sharing from their agricultural abundance. Brown argued, however, that they were the cause of famine rather than the solution.

An influential book took up that banner and in the process shifted the hunger debate from agronomy to lifestyle. Frances Moore Lappé's *Diet for a Small Planet* first appeared in 1971; republished several times over the next few decades, the book was part political tract, part ecological screed, and part cookbook. Like Brown, Lappé laid the blame for world hunger at the feet of wealthy Americans—specifically American meat eaters. To save the hungry, Americans would need to do more than simply raise money and ship some cows overseas—they would have to change the way they ate. Lappé's book did not talk about hunger from a Christian perspective, but her work caught the attention of mainline Protestant hunger activists, helping to create the lifestyle movement.

Lappé was a graduate student at the University of California at Berkeley in the late 1960s when she became concerned about the problem of world hunger. She quit her studies and turned her energies to the problems of agriculture and nutrition. In the basement of the university's agriculture library, she made what she considered to be an amazing discovery—"the amount of humanly edible protein fed to American livestock and not returned for human consumption approached the whole world's protein deficit!"[43] "The increased appetite of the richer countries for more grain-consuming livestock products" had driven up the price of grain in the early 1970s "beyond the reach of those with real food needs."[44] While the hunger relief agencies of the postwar era saw Americans as benevolently sharing the nation's breadbasket, Lappé portrayed them as the greedy consumers of more than their share of the world's protein production.

The book's argument turned on two basic facts. First, the innocent steer is "the *least* efficient among his fellow ruminants as a converter of plant protein to animal protein." Cattle consume sixteen pounds of grain and soy to produce one pound of meat. In comparison, other animals, such as pigs, chickens, and turkeys, are far more efficient.[45] Second, half of American grain harvests are fed to livestock in feedlot operations. "Here the steer is taught the business of getting rid of over a ton of grain." This forced feeding of grain was a recent invention, suggested Lappé, devised in the 1950s as an easy way to get rid of surplus American grain the rest of the world could not afford to buy.[46] All this led to some "startling statistics." "Although we lead the world in exports of grain and soy, this incredible volume 'lost' through livestock was twice the level of our current exports. It is enough to provide every single human being on earth with more than a cup of cooked grain each day of the year!"[47] As a result, Lappé concluded, the poor "pay" for our steaks. Although American agriculture was abundant enough to ensure every American enough plant protein regardless of income, she believed, we had created an economy where the rich overconsumed protein in the form of meat while the poor, who could not afford meat, were inadequately fed.

Meat production would be far more efficient—and healthier for the consumer—if cattle spent less time in the feedlot consuming grain, Lappé argued, because feedlot beef has more fat. Livestock are good at grazing land unsuitable for cultivation and turning grass into protein. In fact, they can get by on garbage instead of grain and grass. Proposals to discourage feedlot fattening, however, met with "resistance by the vested interests as well as consumer suspicion born of ignorance."[48] It is possible to raise meat without wasting grain, but, Lappé noted ominously, corporate America had prevented it.

Lappé's book went beyond American methods of raising cattle, to questioning what she called "The Great American Steak Religion." Modern Americans, she argued, were meat obsessed. They believed that they must have meat at every meal and prized steak as a status symbol. Lappé stated that these "myths" led Americans to waste protein, causing "the very institutionalization of waste" in the face of world starvation. "Can we go on consuming a meat diet that uses up the food that could have fed five people when we have just seen a child starve before our eyes on television?"[49] The "Steak Religion" made Americans responsible for world hunger. The last myth fell, she reported some years later, when she learned that "much of what I had grown up believing about a healthy diet was false." It was not true that humans need lots of protein to be healthy, she concluded, and it was not true that meat was an essential part of every meal.[50]

In Lappé's eyes, meat was bad news from every angle. Supplying the American meat-centered diet was environmentally destructive, wasting water and causing soil erosion. Grain that could have fed hungry children around the world was feeding cows to make meat for American tables. That meat caused cancer and heart attacks because of its high fat and cholesterol content. Meat was not only bad for the hungry, it was bad for Americans.

Lappé developed this dietary and environmental argument into a comprehensive social critique. The carnivorous diet reflected systemic injustice. "The World Food Problem," she argued, "is in large part only a reflection of the World Wealth Problem and . . . therefore, a recasting of all our monetary, trade, and military ties to the poor world is necessary to redress the growing maldistribution of world wealth."[51] In a later edition Lappé added that the American "Steak Religion" was shaped by the demands of agribusiness. Americans ate unhealthful, fat- and additive-laden processed foods because it satisfied the corporate need for profit.[52] The solution lay in political and economic changes, making the food system responsible for feeding people, not for generating profit. "Until the production of our basic survival goods is consciously tied to the fulfillment of human need there can be no solution to the tragedy of needless hunger."[53] Starting with the social and environmental dangers of meat, Lappé ended up challenging the economic and political structure of American society. And then she offered a rich collection of meatless recipes.

Although Lappé was not writing for a church audience, church hunger activists took her message to heart. They were looking for an explanation of hunger in an abundant world, and they were looking for something they could do. Lappé provided both. Children around the world were starving because Americans were eating meat, she told them, and Americans could prevent that starvation by becoming vegetarians. Although Lappé's book consisted mainly of arcane protein tables and recipes for Rice-Cream-and-Sesame Cereal and Crusty Soybean Crowd-Pleaser, it was ultimately a morality tract. Their wasteful lives, she scolded her readers, were causing hunger around the world. But there was a path to salvation: They could end hunger by changing their lifestyle.

"Lifestyle" became a common word among whitebread Protestants in the 1970s. More recently it has described fashion and entertainment—as in the "lifestyle" sections of many newspapers—or has been a code word in the family values debate—as in the "homosexual lifestyle." But for mainline American Protestants in the 1970s, "lifestyle" meant living so that you consumed resources responsibly. It meant eating less meat, decreasing one's energy use, and spending less on luxuries. Like the Christian diet reform movements of the nineteenth century, it called on people to change the way they ate for moral reasons. It called them to a new asceticism, restricting their behavior for a moral cause. Unlike the earlier movements, however, the moral cause was not spiritual purity but saving the hungry. Lifestyle was the Christian diet reform movement for an age of scarcity.

The language of lifestyle first appeared in the evangelical world. In 1973 a group of activist evangelicals led by ethicist Ron Sider signed the Chicago Declaration of Evangelical Social Concern. Among its statements was a consideration of lifestyle and justice. "Before God and a billion hungry neighbors, we must rethink our values regarding our present standard of living and promote more just acquisition and distribution of the world's resources."[54] A year later, at the peak of the world hunger crisis, a Congress on World Evangelization met in Lausanne, Switzerland. In its final covenant the congress stated that it was "shocked by the poverty of the millions and disturbed by the injustices which cause it. Those of us who live in affluent circumstances accept our duty to develop a simple lifestyle in order to contribute more generously to both relief and evangelism."[55] These statements set the tone for Christian responses to hunger, for both evangelical and mainline Protestants: Americans needed to change the way they lived, for the sake of justice and for the sake of the hungry.

Sider placed the lifestyle question at the climax of his influential 1977 book *Rich Christians in an Age of Hunger,* stating that "simple personal lifestyles are crucial to symbolize, validate and facilitate our concern for the hungry."[56] He drew his inspiration in part from John Wesley, who argued that Christians should give away all but "the plain necessities of life." Such a life is difficult, Sider wrote, in modern America, however. "We have become ensnared by unprecedented material luxury. Advertising constantly convinced us that we really need one unnecessary luxury after another." The theological problem, Sider concluded, was idolatry. "The standard of living is the god of twentieth-century America, and the ad man is its prophet."[57] Consumption-minded American culture, Sider believed, clashed with Christian faithfulness.

The book included suggestions "for living an uncompromisingly Christian lifestyle." Sider's own family practiced a graduated tithe, identifying the income required for a simple standard of living and then tithing increasing percentages of any income over that amount. "The ultimate goal should be to reduce total expenditures to the point where you enjoy a standard of living which all persons in the world could share."[58] He noted that other Christians made more radical changes in their lives, selling their homes or founding communes. "Communal living releases vast amounts of money and people-time for alternative resources."[59] Other suggestions included gardening rather than shopping, walking rather than driving, resisting consumerism, refusing to keep up with clothing fashions, and—citing Lappé—"substituting vegetable protein for animal protein."[60] Effectively, Sider asked American Christians to adopt a Third World lifestyle.

He made it clear that "simpler living is a biblical imperative for contemporary Christians in affluent lands." It is an ethical demand. But, as was also suggested in the Lausanne Covenant, simpler living also had a practical consequence—it freed up more money for church mission and hunger work. Sider wrote that "the gulf between what affluent Northern Christians give and what they *could* give is a terrifying tragedy."[61] Increased giving could help to solve hunger around the world. This practical issue remained an essential part of the lifestyle movement. Lifestyle was a fund-raising—or, in church language, a stewardship—issue.

Although it first appeared among activist evangelicals, mainline Protestants also took up the lifestyle issue in their magazines, curricula, and policy pronouncements. For Thanksgiving 1974 an American Baptist minister in Seattle preached a sermon on the story of Lazarus at the rich man's gate (Luke 16:19–31). He told his congregation that "we are the rich man—we are six percent of the world's population consuming 35 percent of the world's resources. . . . It's a moral issue—over-consumption in a world of scarcity!" He suggested that "we can adjust our life style. We can eat a bit less and live more simply. Since we have a loaf of bread, why want more?" Among his suggestions was cutting down on eating beef, citing the same kinds of statistics Lappé used. He recommended reducing drinking alcohol. "The grain used annually to produce alcoholic beverages in this country would keep a half million in South Asia alive for a year." Challenging Americans' sentimental side, he suggested reducing "the number of pets we support. Our household pets consume about 3.5 million tons of food annually." He even suggested having a simple meal on Thanksgiving instead of the usual feast. And, as many of these texts do, the preacher concluded by suggesting donating "the money we save in these ways to our American Baptist World Relief Fund, designated to feed the starving."[62] His sermon made food behavior a moral issue in a hungry world.

The following month Roger Shinn, an ethicist, reported that a World Council of Churches conference had called for a "new asceticism."

The conference concluded that "an appropriate 'asceticism' for our time will not be a punishing of the body for the sake of the soul" but rather, Shinn stated, "a recognition of the futility of the scramble for unlimited wealth and a recovery of some of the simple joys that have delighted people through the centuries." Among the results of such asceticism, said Shinn, would be "major changes in diet." He repeated the same statistics about grain fed to animals and asked, "When grain and soybeans could save people from starvation, can we afford to feed them to cattle?" He asked the same question of cultivating tea, coffee, and grain for alcohol. At the very least, he urged his readers to "undertake some symbolic acts of restraint." He acknowledged that such acts "will not transform the world. But they will raise our own consciousness and contribute to raising the social consciousness of the world's needs." And, in the typical refrain, he noted that "if we contribute the cash savings from such acts to the direct relief of hunger or to political efforts to meet human need, we can make a real difference."[63] This new asceticism continued Christianity's spiritual tradition, but now it was with a different goal—it would change the world rather than simply purify the soul.

Chapter 4 described how mainline Protestants taught their children about world hunger with Sunday school curricula, trying to teach empathy with the hungry as well as the economic and geopolitical causes of hunger. Some of these curricula taught the children about lifestyle as well. An example is *Have You Ever Been Hungry?* an ecumenical curriculum prepared for elementary and junior high youth in 1978.

Like much of the mainline hunger material, the curriculum quotes Lappé, focusing particular attention on the question of meat eating and grain consumption. The introduction noted that "most of the world's people live on grain-based diets which can be healthy if the diet is properly balanced." It included the usual statistics, stating "the average North American consumes five times as much grain as the average resident of a Third World country, most of it indirectly through meat, dairy products, and eggs."[64] Various activities drove home the point. One game had the children play "Find the Protein." Each child was to play a food product—"soybean, rice, cheese"—which then had to find a complementary protein. In the discussion that followed, the teacher's guide advised, "explain that these are the Third World foods. If these provide protein, why are so many people malnourished? (Part poverty; part ignorance.)"[65] The game helped introduce children to dietetics for a hungry world.

With this nutrition lesson setting the stage, the curriculum focused the lifestyle questions on the ethical implications of eating meat. The purpose of one session was to "gain new insights into our own personal lifestyles and into ways we might become better stewards for God and God's hungry people." It asks, "Why do hungry people in the rest of the world look on the North American and European meat customs as greedy and unjust? Is it greedy to eat meat?" Expanding the question beyond human consumption, it also wondered, "Can we be better stewards both in the number of pets we have and in the way we feed them?" It concludes, "The most direct way that changing our dietary customs can help the hungry is to donate the money we save from eating less or less expensive meat to agencies and programs like Ten Days for World Development, Church World Service, UNICEF, the Heifer Project, or CARE."[66] Meat was the heart of the lifestyle—and stewardship—issue.

The curriculum's liturgical experiences reinforced and expanded the lifestyle question. One session concluded with a fairly gut-wrenching prayer.

> O God, I thoroughly enjoy being rich enough to eat regularly and wear shoes and have indoor plumbing. Why don't you leave me in peace to enjoy you and these gifts? Must hungry eyes and thoughts of bulging, worm-filled bellies face me over the dinner table? Are you the One haunting me with the agony of the mother who has only cornbread or ricewater—or perhaps nothing—to give her child, mealtime after mealtime? What do you want me to do about it?[67]

One can only imagine the dinner table conversations when the children got home from that church school lesson. At the end of the last session the children were asked to read the "Shakertown Pledge," a common lifestyle affirmation from the mid-1970s. "Recognizing that life itself is a gift, and a call to responsibility, joy, and celebration," the child pledged a variety of things, including committing her- or himself to become "a world citizen" and "to lead a life of creative simplicity and to share my personal wealth with the world's poor."[68] These are remarkably grown-up commitments for middle-class American children.

In *Have You Ever Been Hungry?* hunger education was the major focus, with lifestyle a part of the larger topic. A Presbyterian curriculum for children, on the other hand, made lifestyle the central theme. *Life-Style Change for Children,* published in 1981, was the companion piece to an adult curriculum, *A Covenant Group for Life-style Assessment.* Its goal was to give parents interested in lifestyle concerns "ways to interpret their new convictions to their families," while "some churches may hope to begin with young persons and use their interest as a springboard from which to involve parents and other adults."[69] The author sought to enlist "kid power" in the lifestyle campaign, using children to commit their parents to lifestyle change. The author acknowledged that this strategy had potential complications. "Certainly the leader will want to take pains to avoid encouraging children to sit in judgment upon their parents."[70] And yet the curriculum finds some subtle ways to encourage reeducation. In one session, for instance, the notes suggest that "if some child seems reluctant to undertake energy conservation because of indifference at home, invite a parent of that child to be a classroom helper this week."[71] This is Sunday school subversion.

The curriculum looked beyond the specific issues of hunger and food to question the social-economic order. For the author lifestyle change involved "conserving and redistributing the world's resources and restructuring its institutions to meet everyone's basic needs" and replacing "wasteful production and consumption of material goods with creativity and pride in the ability to make things." This approach was given a theological justification. "A life-style of sufficiency is a present-day extension of the life-style adopted by the early followers of Jesus the Christ, whose deeds and words showed them how to live in a world filled with injustice and great inequality between rich and poor."[72] For the writer of this curriculum, Sunday school was to be about more than Bible stories and finger painting. *Life-Style Change for Children* introduced middle-class American Presbyterian children to the redistribution of income and a more just global economic system. It's an American Protestant adaptation of Marxism.

The first session revealed the agenda of the piece. The children acted out two scenarios for the future, describing American society in the 1990s. The first presumed that society would continue on its present path of consumption and economic injustice. As a result the country is under the shadow of food and fuel shortages, incredible inequalities, and rampant crime. The children chant at the beginning and end:

> Our world is in an awful mess;
> The reason why we try to guess.
> Our days are bleak, our nights are long
> Oh, when, or what did we do wrong?

The second scenario shows the results of lifestyle change. Children harvest corn they've grown themselves and dry it with solar crop dryers, the church has been turned into a community center and food co-op, and a good vacation is one close to home. Life is good, they're convinced, because "people have less money to spend, and fewer things to spend it on." They sing:

> Our world has problems, but we care;
> We plan and work; we give and share;
> To live for all humanity
> Takes brave new persons—you and me.[73]

A better world could come, the play implied, through a more Christian lifestyle, brought about through the creation of "brave new persons." As the scenarios suggested, lifestyle has a broad definition. The curriculum encouraged children to question the materialism of American society and to "experience the joy of shared fun in simple games and pastimes" instead of television and expensive toys. It suggested staying close to home rather than traveling around the world.[74] In this worldview, a Christian lifestyle required a social revolution.

Food was an important part of the lifestyle revolution in *Life-Style Change for Children.* After listing "luxury" foods, such as imported beef, bananas, and winter produce, families were urged to "think of ways we together can consume less of these foods, and transfer the money saved to the church's hunger program." They could also "introduce the family to a new main dish recipe based on rice or beans, the staple foods of over half of the world family."[75] A session called "Getting What We Need— And Giving the Rest Away" took "a forthright look at what we have and what we actually need" and sought to encourage "freer, more unselfish giving." The children made a recipe for "good-tasting, inexpensive, and nourishing food" and made banks for a hunger offering.[76] The "eat less meat and give money to the church" connection was a common theme in mainline Protestant approaches to lifestyle.

But for the author of *Life-Style Change,* solving hunger was more difficult than that. A take-home sheet told children and parents that "to solve the world's problems we will have to do a lot more than giving away extra food and money to help people who are already undernourished. We may have to give up some things we like but do not really need, so that what is left of our scarce resources can go to more people all over the world. Some money and a lot of work will have to go toward changing the wrong things that are happening in our world family."[77] According to this material, one less hamburger a week would not solve the problem; the world needs systemic change. The final lesson argued that "the power of human solidarity transcends the barriers created by current economic practices and political structures." The subversive language returned in the curriculum's conclusion, which stated that "hard work, cooperation, and immediate action will be the earmarks of New Persons who emerge, not out of the blue, but out of our own homes, schools, and churches, to assume responsibility for our common future."[78]

The language of lifestyle reached beyond the Sunday school classroom, into the sacred precincts of the church kitchen. As chapter 2 showed, during the twentieth century American mainline Protestants had developed a variety of food-centered social events in their churches, designed to strengthen the community and provide an alternative to secular entertainment. These meals, like the rest of the American diet, were often lavish, expressing the abundance of the continent. Recall, for instance, the 1913 men's banquet at St. Pauls Church, which featured a four-course menu, complete with trout and beef tenderloin and concluding with cigars.[79]

But as hunger activists called whitebread Protestants to change their eating at home, they realized that their eating at church would need to change as well. In 1983 a Presbyterian laywoman published a cookbook for churches concerned about hunger and lifestyle issues. As noted in chapter 2, *Simply Delicious* encouraged "local churches to be responsible about serving food." This responsibility included two lifestyle agendas. First, in a hungry world the church dare not waste food. Second, the church should help people make better choices about their diets. Food-centered social events could be more than fun—they could be "an excellent opportunity to *model* good stewardship of our bodies and of the earth's food resources."[80] The book offered meals for the socially responsible church, whose members were encouraged to restrain their appetites.

Most of the book's suggestions echoed those of other lifestyle writers—not to mention the food reformers of the nineteenth century. Citing Lappé's authority, it stated that churches should serve healthier food, with more fruit, vegetables, and whole grains and less meat and fat. "Alternative proteins" are not only good for us but are more just because our meat habits consume an unfair amount of grain. "At least four persons, eating grain direct, could survive a whole day on what we use to produce four 'quarter-pounder' hamburgers."[81] So the cookbook's menus included more fresh dishes, main dishes with complementary nonmeat proteins, simpler desserts, and homemade breads with whole-wheat flour, while avoiding convenience foods and refined sugar. Suggested main dishes included Broccoli Noodle Parmesan, Tofu Stroganoff, and Layered Spinach Supreme.

The author had particular advice for church socials. Threatening generations of tradition, she suggested giving children celery, fruit, banana bread, and fruit juice in place of cookies and Kool-Aid. In place of coffee and sweet rolls for their parents she offered raw vegetables, cheese and crackers, and herbal teas. For church social events, "simple does not mean dull or glum or deadly serious." Instead she recommended a "Stone Soup Night" for "church night supper" or a baked potato bar for Sunday after church. Instead of celebrations centered on abundance, "the most celebrative thing about a church meal is the people who are there. . . . The food, which can be simple as well as delicious, brings us together to enjoy our differences while affirming our unity."[82] These proposals required a rethinking of many church food traditions.

The editor acknowledged that these changes would lead to conflict. One contributor told of an affluent church that struggled with lifestyle issues and its food events. After a retreat had focused on lifestyle, some of the converts tried to change the traditional church night suppers, suggesting one meatless meal a month. Resistance came from the church's hostess and cook, who were anxious that trying new recipes would require additional work. After one meatless meal the cook refused to cook any more, and the church backed off from its plans. The traditions were too well rooted.[83] Nevertheless, the author recommended perseverance. A simple meal "affirms our solidarity with all our fellow human beings, many of whom are hungry. The horizons of our church dining room or fellowship hall become global."[84] The result would be a more just church social life.

During the 1970s, lifestyle became policy as well as practice. Whitebread Protestants also discussed their concerns about hunger and lifestyle at their national denominational meetings, frequently passing resolutions drafted by their denominational hunger offices. The passing of resolutions is a familiar practice in liberal Protestant churches; resolutions are a common way to express concern about social and political issues. The resolutions theoretically reflect the convictions of the entire church on concerns ranging from hunger, to pornography, to foreign policy. In some cases they commit the denomination to a particular course of action, but usually they are designed simply to educate the church about the issue. Sometimes the resolutions have an impact on the church as a whole; more often they salve the consciences of those voting at the meeting.

Like the curricula, the resolutions passed by mainline denominational meetings in the mid-1970s responded to the perceptions of dwindling resources and left little doubt who was at fault. A resolution considered (and ultimately defeated) by the 1975 General Synod of the Reformed Church in America began by noting that "the proliferation of shortages, present and projected, of food as well as fossil fuels and other non-renewal resources requires a re-examination of Christian life style as we have known it for the past quarter century in the American church." The self-indulgent diets of whitebread Protestants contributed to the hunger of people around the world, the General Synod concluded. "Our over-consumption of non-nutritive products, such as coffee, tea, chocolate, tobacco, etc., affects the ability of the desperately poor of the world to get enough food to survive."[85] The General Assembly of the United Presbyterian Church in the USA (the "northern" Presbyterian church) confessed in 1976 that "many of us have been overconsuming food resources while paying little attention to the bitter facts and root causes of starvation and malnutrition among the poor overseas and in the United States."[86] Americans were no longer the cultivators of the world's breadbasket but the consumer of all the world's bread.

The self-criticism in these resolutions became almost self-flagellation. The Reformed Church of America's 1975 resolution pointed out that church members were unimaginably better off than the poor of the Third World, which limited the effects of American evangelization. "The witness of those of us who own adult toys such as pleasure boats, trail bikes, snowmobiles, stereo sets, golfing or ski equipment which total in cost more than we have ever given in our lifetime to such direct relief agencies as Church World Service must inevitably be quite incredible to people who watch their babies bloat with malnutrition." The same is true, the resolution continued, for our churches. "How do we justify our carpeted sanctuaries," the resolution asked, "in a world where tens of millions are stunted and retarded due to childhood malnutrition?" Continuing the lament, the resolution stated that even well-intentioned efforts aren't enough. "Our responses to date, an occasional extra collection for world relief, a meatless meal once a week, etc., are pitiably inadequate in the face of the magnitude of the need." The resolution asked rhetorically and dramatically, "What must God make of our ritual intercessions for the hungry and poor while in the pockets of our fashionable new suits our wallets are stuffed with tens and twenties we refuse to share?"[87] This intense self-criticism is almost reminiscent of revolutionary movements.

As in the curricula, these resolutions blame the self-indulgent lifestyle on the larger culture—specifically, a consumer capitalism designed to manufacture needs through advertising. The Presbyterian resolution urged "legislative bodies to provide incentives for simplified food processing and packaging and disincentives for advertising that stimulates wasteful consumption."[88] The Reformed Church in America, echoing the call for "New Persons" in *Life-Style Change for Children*, argued that "as individuals we must come through a whole process of re-education." Such an education would be difficult, the resolution admitted, in a society where advertising bombards us, "designed to convince us that we want and even need things which are not essential, and that, contrary to the teachings of our Lord, true life does consist in abundance."[89] Although we might be guilty of overconsumption, these resolutions confessed, Madison Avenue made us do it.

The resolutions offered more than just confession; they also urged action, with commitments to changed lifestyles and increased sharing with the hungry. The United Presbyterians pledged "to evaluate our personal, family, and institutional styles of life and to reduce our consumption of the planet's limited resources, and to cut down on our waste of food and other scare resources."[90] A 1974 resolution of the Reformed Church in America's General Synod urged "individual members of the RCA to recognize the Biblical, moral, and humanitarian responsibility to re-evaluate their own life styles and values in order to shape the conscience of the church and society."[91] The unsuccessful 1975 resolution went further, stating that "each family should observe several meatless days each week" and "vegetarian life styles should be seen as important viable options for our time." It also noted that "individuals could curtail their intake of certain alcoholic beverages which use a sizeable amount of this country's grain supply. By doing this it would free up grain to be used for more food calories." As part of the larger lifestyle concern, the resolution also urged families to be "more creative about the way they spend their times of recreation and vacation . . . as they attempt to stay true to their sensitivity of the world resource situation."[92] The following year the synod adopted a less far-reaching resolution, which nevertheless urged families to "make consistent, extensive, and varied use of food stuffs that are lower on the food chain, such as lentils, soy, and vegetables, etc." and to raise hunger awareness "by observing one or more meatless days each week as well as short periods of fasting or reduced intake."[93] As their proposals to decrease meat consumption in order to free up grain supplies shows, these resolutions echo Lappé's analysis.

The suggestions went beyond individual diet, to concerns about the church's social life. The Reformed Church in America's 1975 resolution suggested that "church dinners usually consisting of beef, ham and chicken should be the objects of different menu options."[94] While a committee of the 1976 General Assembly of the northern Presbyterians recommended tabling a resolution entitled "On Reducing Food Consumption at Denominational Functions and Allocating the Money Saved to the Hunger Program," it did so because it would require budgetary changes, not just a resolution. The assembly acknowledged, however, that "some judicatories and groups that meet in churches, with the participants paying for their own meals, are now asking the churches to serve modest meals and requesting the participants to make a voluntary offering."[95] Since the resolutions' confessions included criticism of congregational eating habits, the solution required changes of those habits.

The goal of all this lifestyle change was not just to make eating more moral. As with the lifestyle curricula, it aimed at increasing donations to the church's fund-raising for hunger concerns. The 1975 RCA resolution, after urging families to eat meatless several times a week, pointed out that "since in the immediate future our salaries aren't going to be cut because we chose not to eat meat, the money spent for meat should be donated to relief organizations."[96] The 1976 resolution of the northern Presbyterians told church members "that saving, i.e., withholding from consumption," only helps "when it is channeled into programs of development and production coupled with systems of effective redistribution which deal with the root causes of hunger at home and abroad."[97] Nevertheless a committee of the same General Assembly stated that "reduced food consumption and more modest expenditures for life needs are important objectives for church groups in themselves, as a means of experiencing and affirming the truth that we do not live by bread alone." It concluded that "the value of simplified life-style should be stressed for its own sake as well as for its potential in releasing more resources for sharing."[98] In general, however, most of the resolutions focused on increased giving.

These lifestyle resolutions did provoke reactions—not from the agribusiness executives and government policymakers who were their primary targets, but from the farmers within the churches. An American Baptist laywoman, also a cattle rancher, lamented to the denominational journal that "we have jumped on the wrong bandwagon. Meatless days won't help the hungry. . . . Cows are not wasteful food producers."[99] William Rambo, a delegate to the 1976 Presbyterian General Assembly, was a pastor to a rural church in western Nebraska. He remembers that "my congregation was very concerned about the position the church had taken." The ranchers objected to the strong anti-meat strain—rooted in Lappé—in these resolutions. His members "were not without sympathy for the hungry of the world. They just felt they had been unfairly singled out and targeted as villains in the scheme of things." Hearing his congregation's concern, Rambo "initiated an action at that time to change the Hunger Program, to take the reference to meat out of it." He objected to the simplistic arguments of some hunger crusaders that "beef is bad."[100] Rambo was not alone; at the previous General Assembly, a committee recommended tabling a resolution "On Adopting Meatless Wednesdays and Fridays and One Day of Fasting During Lent, and Giving the Money Saved to the One Great Hour of Sharing." The committee recognized "the symbolic value in limiting the use of food, yet we feel the overture singles out (discriminates against) one particular industry."[101] The denominational leadership had to balance the concerns of lifestyle crusaders and cattle ranchers in the church.

As quickly as it appeared, the lifestyle movement disappeared. After 1982 there was little discussion of lifestyle in denominational resolutions or in Sunday school curricula. In the mid-1980s the mainline churches were still concerned about world hunger—that was the era of the Ethiopian famine and the rock fund-raising song "We Are the World"— but lifestyle played a small role in the churches' response. The 1970s were a time of limitations, with a series of energy crises, inflation, the failure in Vietnam, and the seizure of American hostages in Iran. It all fed what President Carter called the national "malaise." In the 1980s, however, President Reagan declared that it was once again "morning in America"; the lead character in *Wall Street,* a hit movie of 1987, caught the spirit of the age when he declared that "greed is good." In such a time of confidence and a return to apparent abundance, mainline Protestant churches again focused on generosity rather than lifestyle change as their response to world hunger.[102]

During its heyday, however, "lifestyle" was an important topic in the ethical reflections of whitebread Protestants, bringing together a variety of themes current in the culture. In its focus on decreased consumption and living lightly on Earth, it reflected the concerns of the environmental movement that hit its stride in the 1970s. With its desire to identify with the poor around the world, the lifestyle movement represented an early influence of Latin American liberation theology on the American church. And its focus on community and simple living was the last gasp of the 1960s counterculture as it tried to influence the lives of mainstream Americans.

Unfortunately, it is hard to gauge the impact of the lifestyle movement on the lives of middle-class mainline Protestants. It aimed to change the way they shopped, cooked, ate, and spent their leisure time. Material such as *Life-Style Change for Children* looked to shape children in Sunday school into "New Persons" who would be community-focused, generous, and critical of consumer capitalism. It would be fascinating to know what difference the curricula made in the lives of those children. It would be even more interesting to know how their parents felt as the church taught their children to question their lifestyles and the economic system.

The first four chapters of this book showed how whitebread Protestants combined eating and moralism in their church life. Moral stances changed the way they celebrated communion and encouraged them to organize church socials. Ethical convictions motivated them to feed the hungry both at home and around the world. This food moralism shaped the institutional life of middle-class American Protestants in the nineteenth and twentieth centuries.

This last chapter shows how two groups of diet reformers—genteel Victorians and twentieth-century hunger activists—asked Protestants to bring those food convictions home, to take their commitments to heart ... and to stomach. By eating pure and simple foods, said the Victorians, Americans could survive the assault of modern society. By giving up beef and simplifying their lives, lifestyle campaigners believed, whitebread Protestants could feed the hungry and create a just world. In both cases, these activists urged their followers to eat as Christians should.

These diet reform movements reflected the worldview that created them. According to the Victorian reformers, nineteenth-century America was dangerous to the healthy digestion and the settled soul. It was full of stress, intoxication, and unnecessary excitement. Overindulgence of the senses risked indigestion and possibly one's life. The lifestyle reformers confronted a much bigger problem: world hunger. Liberal Protestants wanted to make a difference, but the systemic causes of starvation—injustice in global economic and social structures—were beyond the control of the average American. The answer for both

Although most Protestant denominations backed away from the lifestyle
campaign in the early 1980s, some Christians still advocated vegetarianism as a
solution to world hunger. *Seeds,* a magazine for Christian hunger activists,
used this image in 1989 to advocate a vegetarian diet.
(Image by Louise Britton, from Seeds of Hope Publishers, used with permission.)

movements was a change in diet. They responded to their worlds by
giving personal food choices moral weight, by asking whitebread Protestants to match their diets to their beliefs.

How does one eat like a Christian? There are no official rules. While
most religious traditions forbid certain foods—pork in Islam, pork and
shellfish in Judaism, any kind of meat in Hinduism—Christianity has
no food taboos. The religion's founder deliberately rejected Jewish
kosher laws and told his followers, "It's not what goes into the mouth
that defiles a person, but what comes out of the mouth that defiles."[103]

The apostle Paul qualified that, however. "All things are lawful for me," he acknowledged, but he quickly added, "not all things are beneficial."[104] While he knew that Christianity had no food taboos, he believed that eating certain foods would lead weak believers into temptation. These whitebread Protestant diet reformers followed Paul's lead, creating unofficial food taboos. None of these reform movements, of course, had much long-term impact on the American diet. Americans still eat large amounts of beef and wash it down with alcohol. Our diets are full of both exotic spices and chemical additives. But the food moralism remains. Our desserts are still sweet temptation.

CONCLUSION

IT WAS A TYPICAL SUNDAY in a whitebread Protestant church. At the beginning of the service the congregation's children wandered through the pews, collecting canned goods for the local food pantry; when they were done they piled the food under the communion table. During the prayer time a member encouraged donations for flood relief in Africa, especially for the hungry there. Later in the service the congregation celebrated communion—with both wine and grape juice. After the service they all gathered in the social hall for coffee and conversation.

All of these food events weren't planned just because I was there and because I was writing a book about food and religion. It was a typical Sunday at a typical whitebread Protestant church. In that church, as in mainline Protestant churches across the country, people eat and talk about eating; their eating practices express the church's deep faith convictions and reveal the whitebread Protestant world.

At the end of the nineteenth century and again at the end of the twentieth, American Protestants debated the proper celebration of communion. These debates showed a distinctive mark of mainline Protestantism—its openness to options and variations from traditional practices. By choosing grape juice over wine, they showed their loyalty to the temperance cause rather than to the tradition of the church. By using individual cups rather the common cup, they opted for sanitation and purity rather than community.

In church basements across the country, whitebread Protestants gather for coffee hours, congregational potlucks, and youth group pizza feeds. Through these social events the church offers an alternative to the distractions of secular entertainment. The meals reinforce social roles within the congregation and reflect the nature of its community.

Thousands of those congregations use the same basements to feed hungry strangers as well as members. Christian faith motivates church members to found soup kitchens and food pantries, although it plays a small role in their ordinary operations. For these congregations, food symbolizes larger ideas, such as charity, community, and choice.

In the decades after World War II, whitebread Protestants developed an understanding of global hunger and hunger politics. Stimulated by world need and American abundance, churches raised both money and consciousness around the issue of hunger. This hunger politics changed as the world changed.

Protestant diet reformers in the nineteenth century and in the 1970s tried to change the way Americans ate. The Victorians felt that indulging the appetites was bad for the soul, while lifestyle activists believed that overconsumption was immoral in the face of world hunger. Both groups encouraged Protestants to eat as Christians should.

All of these food experiences reflect the world of whitebread Protestants. It is a world that focuses on cleanliness rather than theological tradition. It is a world of well-ordered social lives. It is a world of Christian obligation and institutionalized charity. It is a world of incredible wealth—and guilt over that wealth. And it is a world of self-control and symbolic action in response to systemic injustice.

Food plays important symbolic roles in the church. It reveals the theological and political convictions of American Protestants and it opens a window onto belief and practice. Church food events are full of meaning, ripe for anthropological research.

The participants in these meals, of course, don't think of it this way. They're just eating. Around the church's tables, church members find fellowship and familiar tastes—grape juice and Wonder Bread, Jell-O and three-bean salad, Coke and pizza. Hungry strangers find a warm meal. Starving children receive rice and a cup of milk. Assuming a stance of objective analysis and using technical language, a scholar may look at these food events and say "This is all about boundary maintenance in a free-market religious system." To the participants, however, such analysis sounds lifeless or pointless. For them, food is food—it is the sensuous experience of taste and the emotional experience of community.

As I said in the acknowledgments, one of the unanticipated benefits of working on this book has been hearing stories about food and religion—about church suppers, casserole recipes, and Sunday school snacks. Such stories connect the scholar and the community the scholar is studying. Michael McNally, another historian of American religious practice, observes that "such connections speak to a web of life in which practices . . . are inextricably related in lived experience. These connections remind those of us in the business of theorizing that our inquiries place boundaries around phenomena that are otherwise seamlessly woven into all of life."[1] Studying food is one more way to hear the stories of the community of faith.

I'll conclude with one more story about food, this time from the Bible—specifically, the Gospel of Luke. Three days after his death, Jesus' disciples were amazed to find his tomb empty. That evening, two of them encountered a stranger as they walked to a nearby village. They described to him the sorrowful events of the preceding week and the confusing disappearance of Jesus' body. The stranger invited them to join him for a meal; when he blessed the bread and offered it to them, they recognized the stranger as Jesus. The gospel account concludes, "he had been made known to them in the breaking of the bread."[2]

We can learn a lot from a meal. Many Christians encounter God at the Communion table. We know Christian community in a potluck. Strangers find hospitality in a soup kitchen. The world's hungry receive compassion from half a world away. Around all these tables, whitebread Protestants—and many others—discover that they are God's people. We can learn a lot from a meal.

NOTES

CHAPTER ONE

1. Thomas Aquinas, *Summa Theologia,* Third Part, Question 74, Article 5 (New York: Benziger Brothers, 1947), 2443.
2. John Calvin, *Institutes of the Christian Religion,* 4.17.43 (Philadelphia: Westminster Press, 1960), 1421.
3. Leigh Eric Schmidt, *Holy Fairs: Scottish Communions and American Revivals in the Early Modern Period* (Princeton, NJ: Princeton University Press, 1989), 90.
4. Cited in Theodore G. Tappert, *The Lord's Supper: Past and Present Practices* (Philadelphia: Muhlenberg Press, 1961), 26.
5. Cited in ibid., 25.
6. Schmidt, *Holy Fairs,* 196.
7. W. J. Rorabaugh, *The Alcoholic Republic* (New York: Oxford University Press, 1979), 8.
8. Schmidt, *Holy Fairs,* 196-197.
9. Charles A. Johnson, *The Frontier Camp Meeting: Religion's Harvest Time* (Dallas: Southern Methodist University Press, 1955), 214.
10. The former argument comes from Glenn C. Altschuler and Jan M. Saltzgaber, *Revivalism, Social Conscience, and Community in the Burned-Over District: The Trial of Rhoda Bement* (Ithaca, NY: Cornell University Press, 1983); the latter from Paul Johnson, "Bottoms Up: Drinking, Temperance, and the Social Historians," *Reviews in American History* 13:1 (March 1985), 49.
11. Rorabaugh, *Alcoholic Republic,* 192.
12. Ibid., 207.
13. Genesis 27:25.
14. Psalm 104:15.
15. Isaiah 55:1.
16. 1 Timothy 5:23.
17. Luke 7:34.
18. John 2:10.
19. Psalm 75:8.
20. Isaiah 5:11.

21. Ephesians 5:18.
22. 1 Timothy 3:8.
23. Frederic Richard Lees and Dawson Burns, *The Temperance Bible Commentary* (London: S.W. Partridge and Co., 1880).
24. Leon C. Field, "Wines of the Bible," *Methodist Quarterly Review* 64:2 (April 1882), 319.
25. Mrs. G. S. Hunt, "What Shall We Drink at the Lord's Table?" *Union Signal,* 31 January 1884, 4.
26. Mrs. H. E. Hollingshead, "Unfermented Wine at the Sacrament," *Union Signal,* 22 September 1910, 10.
27. Moses Stuart, "Dr. Stuart's Essay," *Methodist Quarterly Review* 17:1 (1835), 432. (Emphasis in original.)
28. Ernest Gordon, *Christ, the Apostles, and Wine: An Exegetical Study* (Philadelphia: Sunday School Times, 1944), 23.
29. Leon C. Field, "Jesus Was a Total Abstainer," Part 2, *Methodist Quarterly Review* 64:4 (October 1882), 665.
30. Leon C. Field, "Jesus Was a Total Abstainer," Part 1, *Methodist Quarterly Review* 64:3 (July 1882), 479.
31. Field, "Jesus Was a Total Abstainer," Part 2, 661, 663.
32. T. H. Tabor, "The Passover Wine," *Union Signal,* 4 September 1884, 2-3.
33. Jonathan D. Sarna, "Passover Raisin Wine, the American Temperance Movement, and Mordecai Noah: The Origins, Meaning, and Wider Significance of a Nineteenth-Century American Jewish Practice," *Hebrew Union College Annual* 59 (1988), 273. Sarna states that Noah was "quite wrong." The Talmud, he says, stipulates that "the juice of fruits produces no leavening." There is no doubt, he concludes, that Jews have always used fermented wine in the Passover. Sarna argues that Noah, eager to be accepted as a Jew by evangelical Protestants, was used by temperance crusaders.
34. Field, "Wines of the Bible," 289.
35. Ibid., 287.
36. Stuart, "Dr. Stuart's Essay," 429.
37. Review of Norman Kerr, *Wines: Scriptural and Ecclesiastical* (New York: National Temperance Society and Publication House, 1883), in *Methodist Quarterly Review* 65 (January 1883), 179.
38. Field, "Wines of the Bible," 298.
39. Paper published in *National Temperance Advocate,* March 1882, 37; cited in Field, "Jesus Was a Total Abstainer," Part 2, 667.
40. *Union Signal,* 3 October 1895, 5.
41. Minutes, Ninth Annual Meeting, Women's Christian Temperance Union, October 1882, xxxix.
42. Dr. Richardson, "Agricultural Chemistry," cited in Field, "Jesus Was a Total Abstainer," Part 1, 471.
43. Gordon, *Christ, the Apostles, and Wine,* 22.
44. Lees and Burns, *Temperance Bible Commentary,* xlv. (Emphasis in original.)

45. Stuart, "Dr. Stuart's Essay," 412.

46. Charles Hodge, *Systematic Theology,* Vol. 3 (Grand Rapids, MI: William B. Eerdmans Publishing Company, 1952), 616.

47. Archibald Alexander Hodge, *Outlines of Theology* (New York: A. C. Armstrong and Son, 1897), 633.

48. J. Clarke Hagey, "The Elements of the Lord's Supper," *Methodist Quarterly Review* 63:3 (October 1881), 694.

49. F. D. Hemenway, "Bible Wines," *Methodist Quarterly Review* 60:2 (July 1878), 481.

50. John Maclean, "Bacchus and Anti-Bacchus," *Biblical Repertory and Princeton Review* 31 (1841), 269.

51. Lees and Burns, *Temperance Bible Commentary,* ix.

52. R. A. Esmond, "Unfermented Wine," *Union Signal,* 6 September 1888, 5.

53. Hemenway, "Bible Wines," 484.

54. Dunlop Moore, "Sacramental Wine," *Presbyterian Review* 3 (1882), 106.

55. William B. Sprague, *Dr. Sprague's Reply* (Albany, NY: Packard and Van Benthuysen, 1835), 27. (Emphasis in original.)

56. Maclean, "Bacchus and Anti-Bacchus," 268.

57. Frances E. Willard, *How to Win: A Book for Girls* (New York: Funk and Wagnalls, 1888), 54. My thanks to Carolyn De Swarte Gifford for the citation.

58. Anna M. Hammer, "The Brother That Hath Need," *Union Signal,* 8 January 1885, 6.

59. "Unfermented Wine at the Sacrament," *Union Signal,* 18 March 1886, 7.

60. Mrs. Mary C. Nobles, "Department of Unfermented Wine at the Lord's Table," *Union Signal,* 24 March 1887, 12.

61. Isabella H. Irish, "Unfermented Wine," *Union Signal,* 27 August 1885, 7.

62. R. A. Esmond, "Unfermented Wine Department," *Union Signal,* 22 January 1891, 12.

63. Stuart, "Dr. Stuart's Essay," 424, 428. (Emphasis in original.)

64. Ibid., 439. (Emphasis in original.)

65. Minutes, Second Annual Convention, Women's Christian Temperance Union, November 1875, 61.

66. "Course of Study for Local Unions," *Union Signal,* 5 April 1906, 4.

67. Hunt, "What Shall We Drink at the Lord's Table?"

68. *Union Signal,* 3 January 1884, 12.

69. *Union Signal,* 17 November 1892, 13.

70. R. A. Esmond, "Unfermented Sacramental Wine," *Union Signal,* 27 February 1890, 12.

71. Report of the Department of Unfermented Wine, *Union Signal,* 17 November 1892, 13.

72. Altschuler and Saltzgaber, *Revivalism, Social Conscience, and Community,* 96.

73. Ibid., 101.

74. Ibid., 140.

75. Minutes, Third Annual Convention, Women's Christian Temperance Union, October 1876, 112.

76. Hunt, "Department Sacramental Wine."

77. Esmond, "Unfermented Wine Department." The white ribbon was the emblem of the WCTU, analogous to the red ribbons of modern AIDS activists.

78. Report of the Committee on Unfermented Wines, Minutes, Sixth Annual Meeting, Women's Christian Temperance Union, October 1879, 95.

79. Hunt, "What Shall We Drink at the Lord's Table?"

80. Hunt, "Department Sacramental Wine."

81. *Union Signal,* 24 May 1888, 9.

82. Jeannette G. Hauser, "The Social and Economic Uses of Unfermented Wine," *Union Signal,* 6 June 1895, 2-3.

83. William Chazanof, *Welch's Grape Juice: From Corporation to Co-operative* (Syracuse, NY: Syracuse University Press, 1977), 2.

84. Ibid., 8.

85. Ibid., 18.

86. Ibid., 31.

87. Ibid., 76-77.

88. Ibid., 146.

89. Robert P. Teachout, *Wine, the Biblical Imperative: Total Abstinence* (Columbia, SC: Richbarry Press, 1983), 61; cited in *Bibliotheca Sacra* 141 (1984), 367.

90. Everett Tilson, *Should Christians Drink?* (New York: Abingdon Press, 1957), 36.

91. Robert G. Rayburn, *O Come, Let Us Worship: Corporate Worship in the Evangelical Church* (Grand Rapids, MI: Baker Book House, 1980), 266-267.

92. Robert C. Fuller, *Religion and Wine: A Cultural History of Wine Drinking in the United States* (Knoxville, TN: University of Tennessee Press, 1996), 96.

93. William H. Willimon, *Sunday Dinner: The Lord's Supper and the Christian Life* (Nashville, TN: The Upper Room), 40.

94. John Howard Spahr, "I Smell the Cup," *Christian Century* 92 (12 March 1975), 257.

95. Howard L. Stimmel, letter to the editor, *Christian Century* 92 (14 May 1975), 509.

96. Lester S. King, "Germ Theory and Its Influence," *Journal of the American Medical Association* 249:6 (11 February 1983), 794-798.

97. Suellen Hoy, *Chasing Dirt: The American Pursuit of Cleanliness* (New York: Oxford University Press, 1995), 112.

98. Josiah Strong, *Our Country: Its Possible Future and Its Present Crisis* (New York: American Home Missionary Society, 1885), 43.

99. Willard, *How to Win.*

100. Hoy, *Chasing Dirt,* 99.

101. Mary Douglas, *Natural Symbols: Explorations in Cosmology* (New York: Pantheon Books, 1982), 65.

102. *Religious Telescope*, 25 March 1895, 195.

103. M. O. Terry, "The Poisoned Chalice," *Physicians and Surgeons' Investigator* 8:6 (15 June 1887), 163-165.

104. "The Poisoned Chalice," *Annals of Hygiene* 3:1 (1885), 31. Given the anti-Catholic sentiment of the time, this suggestion is surprising.

105. "Each Communicant a Cup," *The (Rochester) Sun*, 3 June 1894, cited in Betty O'Brien, "The Lord's Supper: Traditional Cup of Unity or Innovative Cups of Individuality," *Methodist History* 32:2 (January 1994), 82. O'Brien's article provides some important and helpful resources, but my argument moves in different directions.

106. O'Brien, "The Lord's Supper," 80.

107. Ibid., 83.

108. Howard S. Anders, "Prophylaxis in Churches Needed by the Adoption of Individual Communion Chalices or Cups," *Proceedings of the Philadelphia Medical Society* 15 (1894), 345-352.

109. Howard Anders, "The Progress of the Individual Cup Movement, Especially Among the Churches," *Journal of the American Medical Association* 29 (1897), 789-794. (Emphasis in original.)

110. J. M. Buckley, "The Common Cup, or Individual Cups, Part II," *Christian Advocate*, 31 January 1895, 2.

111. J. M. Buckley, "The Common Cup, Or Individual Cups?" *Christian Advocate*, 24 January 1895, 1.

112. Buckley, "The Common Cup, or Individual Cups, Part II."

113. J. M. Buckley, "The Common Cup, or Individual Cups? Part V," *Christian Advocate*, 21 February 1895, 2.

114. J. M. Buckley, "The Common Cup or Individual Cups," *Christian Advocate*, 1 September 1898, 8.

115. Buckley, "The Common Cup, Part V."

116. J. M. Buckley, "Is the Communion a Source of Disease?" *Christian Advocate*, 28 February 1895, 2.

117. J. M. Buckley, "Was the Infidel Right?" *Christian Advocate*, 30 June 1898, 5.

118. J. M. Buckley, "The Common Cup or Individual Cups," *Christian Advocate*, 1 September 1898, 6. (Emphasis in original.)

119. J. M. Buckley, "The Common Cup or Individual Cups? Part III," *Christian Advocate*, 7 February 1895, 1. (Emphasis in original.)

120. Buckley, "The Common Cup or Individual Cups," *Christian Advocate*, 1 September 1898, 6.

121. Joseph Pullman, "The Individual Cup and the Common Cup," *Christian Advocate*, 6 October 1898, 13.

122. J. M. Buckley, "The Common Cup, or Individual Cups? Part IV," *Christian Advocate*, 14 February 1895, 1.

123. Ibid.

124. Pullman, "The Individual Cup and the Common Cup."

125. E. W. Ryan, "Individual Communion Cups," *Christian Advocate*, 21 March 1895, 4. (Emphasis in original.)

126. W. C. Holliday, "The Common Cup, or Individual Cups?" *Christian Advocate*, 21 March 1895, 4. (Emphasis in original.)

127. J. D. Krout, "The Individual Communion Cup," *Lutheran Quarterly*, reprinted in *United Brethren Review* 17:2 (March-April 1906), 102. (Emphasis in original.)

128. C. B. Schuchard, "The Individual Communion Cup Question," *Lutheran Church Review* 29:3 (July 1910), 571.

129. Krout, "The Individual Communion Cup."

130. Arthur T. Michler, "The Individual Communion Cup," *Lutheran Church Review* 34:3 (July 1915), 398.

131. Schuchard, "The Individual Communion Cup Question," 569.

132. Ibid., 572.

133. Ibid., 573.

134. Michler, "The Individual Communion Cup," 396.

135. George Drach, "Have Individual Communion Cups Any Historical Justification," *Lutheran Church Review* 26:3 (July 1907), 568.

136. Michler, "The Individual Communion Cup," 400.

137. Lewis Seymour Mudge, "How to Conduct the Communion," in Cleland Boyd McAfee, ed., *The Communion Service: A Manual of Helpful Suggestions to Aid Ministers in Their Communion Practice* (Philadelphia: Board of Christian Education of the Presbyterian Church in the United States of America, 1937), 10.

138. "Practical Helps and Suggestions," in McAfee, *The Communion Service*, 25.

139. Luther D. Reed, *The Lutheran Liturgy* (Philadelphia: Muhlenberg Press, 1947), 374.

140. J. M. Buckley, "The Common Cup, or Individual Cups? Part VII," *Christian Advocate*, 7 March 1895, 2.

141. Albert W. Palmer, *The Art of Conducting Public Worship* (New York: The Macmillan Company, 1931), 142.

142. Mudge, "How to Conduct the Communion," 11.

143. Mrs. H. E. Hollingshead, "Was the Supper Served Right," *Union Signal*, 15 February 1912, 10.

144. John G. Kirby, *Word and Action: New Forms of the Liturgy* (New York: Seabury Press, 1969), ix, provides a brief introduction to the liturgical reform movement.

145. An exhaustive history of these developments among the Presbyterians is in Stanley R. Hall, "The American Presbyterian Directory for Worship: History of a Liturgical Strategy," Ph.D. dissertation, University of Notre Dame, 1990.

146. Clyde Reid and Jerry Kerns, *Let It Happen: Creative Worship for the Emerging Church* (New York: Harper & Row, 1973), 69.

147. Willimon, *Sunday Dinner*, 108.

148. J. J. von Allmen, *Worship: Its Theology and Practice* (New York: Oxford University Press, 1965), 301.

149. Xavier Leon-Dufour, S.J., *Sharing the Eucharistic Bread: The Witness of the New Testament* (New York: Paulist Books, 1987), 164. (Emphasis in original.)

150. Lawrence E. Martin, "This Cup Is the New Testament," *American Lutheran* 48:11 (November 1965), 7, 25.

151. Horton Davies, *Bread of Life and Cup of Joy: Newer Ecumenical Perspectives on the Eucharist* (Grand Rapids, MI: Wm. B. Eerdmans Publishing Company, 1993), 130-131.

152. Willimon, *Sunday Dinner,* 1-4, 70.

153. William H. Willimon, "Communion as a Culinary Art," *Christian Century* 94 (21 September 1977), 829.

154. Scott Francis Brenner, *The Art of Worship: A Guide in Corporate Worship Techniques* (New York: The Macmillan Company, 1961), 46.

155. Reid and Kerns, *Let It Happen,* 69.

156. Grady Hardin, *The Leadership of Worship* (Nashville, TN: Abingdon Press, 1980), 77.

157. Edward J. Kilmartin, S.J., *The Eucharist in the Primitive Church* (Englewood Cliffs, NJ: Prentice-Hall, 1965), 43.

158. Reid and Kerns, *Let It Happen,* 71.

159. Marianne H. Micks, *The Future Present: The Phenomenon of Christian Worship* (New York: Seabury Press, 1970), 144.

160. Philip H. Pfatteicher and Carlos R. Messerli, *Manual on the Liturgy: Lutheran Book of Worship* (Minneapolis: Augsburg Publishing House, 1979), 244.

161. Letters to the editor, *The Lutheran,* 21 June 1978, 33.

162. George Michaelsen, "I Think," *The Lutheran Standard,* 4 November 1983, 16.

163. Letters to the editor, *The Lutheran Standard,* 6 January 1984, 17.

164. "Communion Cup Study," Luther Northwestern Theological Seminary, May 1984. Courtesy of the Archives of Luther Theological Seminary.

165. "Communion Cup Discontinued," *Christian Century* 102 (6 November 1985), 994.

166. Frank C. Senn, "AIDS and the Common Cup," *Dialog* 25:1 (Winter 1986), 4-5.

167. Patrick R. Keifert, "Common Cup, Noch Einmal," *Dialog* 25:3 (Summer 1986), 165.

168. Kenneth J. Doka, letter to the editor, *Lutheran Forum* 21:2 (Pentecost 1987), 7.

169. Frank C. Senn, "Reply to Keifert," *Dialog* 25:4 (Fall 1986), 299.

170. Frank C. Senn, "The Cup of Salvation: Take and Drink," *Lutheran Forum* 20:3 (Reformation 1986), 23.

171. Gordon W. Lathrop, "Chronicle: AIDS and the Cup," *Worship* 62 (1988), 164.

172. "AIDS and Communion," *Christian Century* 102 (9 October 1985), 888.

173. "Keep Common Cup," *Christian Century* 103 (1-8 January 1986), 9.

174. Donald M. McLean, "The Church in Our Time: Common Communion Cups as Possible Infection Hazard," *Crux* 23:1 (March 1987), 27.

175. Jeffrey R. Harris, "The Common Communion Cup," *Journal of the American Medical Association* 247:17 (7 May 1982), 2434.

176. Thomas Grigg-Smith, *Intinction and the Administration of the Chalice* (Portsmouth, England: Grosvenor Press, 1950), 14.

177. David Randall Boone, "To Dip or Not to Dip?: Intinction Among Reformed Churches," *Reformed Liturgy and Music* 22:4 (Fall 1988), 204.

178. Grigg-Smith, *Intinction*, 4.

179. "Infection and the Common Cup," *The Lancet* 248 (4 February 1950), 236.

180. Walter Lowrie, *Action in the Liturgy: Essential and Unessential* (New York: Philosophical Library, 1952), 271.

181. Boone, "To Dip or Not to Dip?" 205.

182. *Book of Worship* (New York: United Church of Christ Office for Church Life and Leadership, 1986), 33.

183. Boone, "To Dip or Not to Dip?" 206.

184. John Shelby Spong, "Understanding the Gay Reality," *Christian Century* 103 (22 January 1986), 62.

185. Ruth A. Meyers, "The Common Cup and Common Loaf," in David R. Holeton, ed., *Revising the Eucharist: Groundwork for the Anglican Communion* (Bramcote, England: Grove Books Ltd., 1994), 46.

186. "Prepackaged Communion Takes Off," *Christianity Today* 40:5 (29 April 1996), 58.

187. Willimon, *Sunday Dinner*, 104.

CHAPTER TWO

1. Paul K. Conkin, *Cane Ridge: America's Pentecost* (Madison, WI: University of Wisconsin Press, 1990), 84-86.

2. Charles A. Johnson, *The Frontier Camp Meeting: Religion's Harvest Time* (Dallas: Southern Methodist University Press), 217.

3. Editorial, "Preparing Food For Camp-Meetings," *Western Christian Advocate*, 26 July 1839, cited in Johnson, *Frontier Camp Meeting*, 215.

4. For more on these events, see Gwen Kennedy Neville, *Kinship and Pilgrimage: Rituals of Reunion in American Protestant Culture* (New York: Oxford University Press, 1987).

5. E. Brooks Holifield, "Toward a History of American Congregations," in James P. Wind and James W. Lewis, eds., *American Congregations: Volume 2, New Perspectives in the Study of Congregations* (Chicago: University of Chicago Press, 1994), 39.

6. For more on this, see R. Laurence Moore, *Selling God: American Religion in the Marketplace of Culture* (New York: Oxford University Press, 1994), 117.

7. Albert Ben Wegener, *Church and Community Recreation* (New York: The Macmillan Company, 1924), 104.

8. William Ingraham Haven, introduction to Annie E. Smiley, *Fifty Social Evenings for Epworth Leagues and the Home Circle* (New York: Eaton and Mains, 1894), 7.

9. E. O. Harbin, *The Fun Encyclopedia* (Nashville, TN: Abingdon-Cokesbury Press, 1940), 7, 87.

10. Haven, introduction to Smiley, *Fifty Social Evenings*, 7.

11. Clyde Merrill Maguire, *The Cokesbury Dinner and Banquet Book* (Nashville, TN: Abingdon-Cokesbury Press, 1953), 7.

12. Smiley, *Fifty Social Evenings*, 7.

13. Arthur M. Depew, *The Cokesbury Party Book* (Nashville, TN: Cokesbury Press, 1932).

14. E. O. Harbin, *Gay Parties for All Occasions* (Nashville, TN: Abingdon-Cokesbury Press, 1950), 7.

15. Clyde Merrill Maguire, *Abingdon Party and Banquet Book* (Nashville, TN: Abingdon Press, 1956), 158.

16. Maguire, *Cokesbury Dinner and Banquet Book*.

17. Harbin, *Fun Encyclopedia*, 87.

18. Depew, *The Cokesbury Party Book*, 46-52.

19. Arthur M. Depew, *The Cokesbury Stunt Book* (Nashville, TN: Cokesbury Press, 1934), 7.

20. Maguire, *Abingdon Party and Banquet Book*, 89.

21. Lora Lee Parrott, *Christian Etiquette* (Grand Rapids, MI: Zondervan Publishing House, 1953), 70-74.

22. Depew, *Cokesbury Party Book*, 159.

23. Parrott, *Christian Etiquette*, 74.

24. Maguire, *Abingdon Party and Banquet Book*, 141.

25. Depew, *Cokesbury Party Book*, 141, 144.

26. Jack B. and Edith Fellows, *A Calendar of Parties* (Nashville, TN: Broadman Press, 1951), 35.

27. Harbin, *Fun Encyclopedia*, 920.

28. The primary source for St. Pauls' history is Thomas R. Henry, *Making a Joyful Sound in the City: The History of St. Pauls United Church of Christ* (Chicago: St. Pauls United Church of Christ, 1996).

29. Program, "The Annual Dinner of the Men's Club," 21 January 1913, Records of St. Pauls Church (hereafter SPC).

30. Laura Shapiro, *Perfection Salad: Women and Cooking at the Turn of the Century* (New York: Farrar, Straus, and Giroux, 1986), 102.

31. For a feminist-ethical reflection on the connection between meat-eating and masculinity, see Carol J. Adams, *The Sexual Politics of Meat: A Feminist-Vegetarian Critical Theory* (New York: Continuum, 1990).

32. Program, "The Annual Dinner of the Men's Club," SPC.
33. *St. Pauls Bote* 29:2 (February 1918), 71, SPC.
34. "Men's Club," *St. Pauls Bote* 51:6-7 (June-July 1939), 154, SPC.
35. "The Men's Club," *St. Pauls Bote* 60:1-2 (January-February 1948), 27, SPC.
36. "Men's Club," *St. Pauls Quarterly,* June 1958, 11, SPC.
37. Invitation for 27 March 1958, SPC.
38. "The Dorcas Society," *St. Pauls Bote* 41:6 (June 1930), 253, SPC.
39. "Dorcas Society," *St. Pauls Bote* 50:8-9 (September-October 1938), 254, SPC.
40. Jane Kirk, *How to Plan Church Meals* (Westwood, NJ: Fleming H. Revell Company, 1962), 57.
41. Shapiro, *Perfection Salad,* 100.
42. "Dedication Tea," *St. Pauls Bote,* Spring 1952, 20, SPC.
43. "Women's Guild Smorgasbord," *St. Pauls Quarterly,* June 1961, 5, SPC.
44. Program, 17 May 1934, SPC.
45. Programs, 13 May 1959 and 11 May 1960, "Daughters of Ruth," *St. Pauls Quarterly,* Summer 1962, 8, SPC.
46. Program, 24 May 1963, and "Mother and Daughter—Father and Son Banquets," *St. Pauls Quarterly,* Summer 1966, 6, SPC.
47. Patricia Tracy, *Jonathan Edwards, Pastor: Religion and Society in Eighteenth-Century Northampton* (New York: Hill and Wang, 1979), 111.
48. E. O. Harbin, *Phunology: A Collection of Tried and Proved Plans for Play, Fellowship, and Profit* (Nashville, TN: Cokesbury Press, 1923), vii.
49. Henry, *Making a Joyful Sound in the City,* 16.
50. *St. Pauls Bote* 35:1 (January-February 1924), 22, SPC.
51. "We Were Hosts to the Young Peoples Federation," *St. Pauls Bote* 51:10-12 (October-December 1939), 251, SPC.
52. "Our Thanksgiving Supper," *St. Pauls Bote* 51:10-12 (October-December 1939), 251, SPC.
53. "Junior Congregation Corner," *St. Pauls Bote* 53:1-3 (January-March 1941), 37, SPC.
54. Form letter, 30 April 1956, SPC.
55. "Young Adults," *St. Pauls Quarterly,* Spring 1959, 8, SPC.
56. "Senior Youth Fellowship," *St. Pauls Quarterly,* March 1961, 17, SPC.
57. "Senior High Youth Fellowship," *St. Pauls Quarterly,* December 1964, 10, SPC.
58. *St. Pauls Newsletter,* June 1964, SPC.
59. "Here and There," *St. Pauls Quarterly,* March 1962, 15, SPC.
60. Flyer, 29 September 1963, SPC.
61. "Family Night," *St. Pauls Quarterly,* March 1966, 9, SPC.
62. "'International Celebration' Proves Fun for All!," *St. Pauls Quarterly,* Summer 1967, 6, SPC.
63. "Young Adults," *St. Pauls Bote,* Christmas 1952, 7, SPC.

64. John L. Mixon and Rosalie W. Mixon, "A Study of St. Paul's Church and Community with Recommendations for the New Building," 15 December 1947, SPC.

65. Benjamin Franklin Olson, "The Architect Reports," *St. Pauls Bote*, Dedication Issue, 1952, 3, SPC.

66. Report from Pastor Henry to the Church Council, 24 February 1975, SPC.

67. *Now You Know*, November 1977, SPC.

68. Memorandum to members of the Session, 23 April 1984, SPC.

69. "From the Program Director," *St. Pauls Quarterly*, Autumn 1960, 8, SPC.

70. *Now You Know*, May 1978 and Pastor's Report to Council, 18 November 1971, SPC.

71. Reports to the Annual Meeting of the Congregation, 25 January 1976, SPC.

72. Minutes, Board of Elders, 25 February 1980, SPC.

73. *Now You Know*, May 1980, SPC.

74. *Now You Know*, February 1986, SPC.

75. "Mothers Club," *St. Pauls Quarterly*, Autumn 1967, 6, SPC.

76. Minutes of the Congregational Life Committee, 9 May 1985, SPC.

77. Reports to the Annual Meeting of the Congregation, 23 November 1986, SPC.

78. Gibson Winter, *The Suburban Captivity of the Churches: An Analysis of Protestant Responsibility in the Expanding Metropolis* (Garden City, NY: Doubleday and Company, 1961), 102, 94, 79.

79. Martin E. Marty, *The New Shape of American Religion* (New York: Harper & Brothers, 1958), 135.

80. "Annual Meeting of the Congregation," *St. Pauls Bote* 52:1-2 (January-February 1940), 4, SPC.

81. *Now You Know*, November/December 1978, SPC.

82. *Now You Know*, December 1979, SPC.

83. "St. Pauls and REACH," *St. Pauls Quarterly*, Summer 1968, 4, SPC.

84. "Emergency Needs Center," *St. Pauls Quarterly*, Summer 1967, 2, SPC.

85. *Now You Know*, June 1976, SPC.

86. *Now You Know*, September 1979, SPC.

87. *Now You Know*, March 1983, SPC.

88. *Now You Know*, December 1983, SPC.

89. Henry, *Making a Joyful Sound in the City*, 46.

90. *Now You Know*, March 1985, SPC.

91. *Now You Know*, June 1986, SPC.

92. *Now You Know*, Easter 1988, SPC.

93. *Now You Know*, September 1988, SPC.

94. *Now You Know*, May 1991, SPC.

95. *Now You Know*, February 1988, SPC.

96. Minutes of the Board of Elders, 22 February 1988, SPC.

97. *Now You Know*, November 1985, SPC.

98. *Now You Know*, February 1989, SPC.

99. *Now You Know,* October 1992, SPC.
100. *Now You Know,* March 1983, SPC.
101. Grace Winn, ed., *Simply Delicious: Quantity Cooking for Churches* (Ellenwood, GA: Alternatives, 1983), 2.
102. *Now You Know,* June 1990, SPC.
103. *St. Pauls Bote* 34:7 (15 April 1923), 154, SPC.
104. *St. Pauls Bote* 39:5 (May 1928), 211, SPC.
105. Report of the Frauen-Verein, *St. Pauls Bote* 48:1 (January 1937), 3, SPC.
106. "Fiftieth Anniversary of the Frauen Verein," *St. Pauls Bote* 52:9-12 (December 1940), 191, SPC.
107. "Mothers Club," *St. Pauls Quarterly,* December 1964, 16, SPC.
108. Kirk, *How to Plan Church Meals,* 28-29, 17.
109. Virginia Lobdell Jennings, *By These Stones: A Narrative History of the First Presbyterian Church of Baton Rouge, Louisiana* (Baton Rouge, LA: First Presbyterian Church, 1977), 168.
110. Interview with Carolyn Clayton, Atlanta, Georgia, 5 February 1997.
111. Interview with Frank Scimeca, South Barrington, Illinois, 16 July 1996.
112. Frederick Buechner, *Wishful Thinking: A Theological ABC* (New York: Harper & Row, 1973), 12.

CHAPTER THREE

1. Kurt Helmcke, "What's in a Survey?" *Church and Society,* March-April 1994, 5.
2. At the Atlanta Union Mission I interviewed Robert Hunter, a program director, on 17 May 1999. At Druid Hills Presbyterian Church I interviewed staff members Jerry and Caroline Coling and volunteer Bob on 23 May 1999. At the Atlanta Community Food Bank I interviewed Bill Bolling, the executive director, Sherrill Terry, the administrative coordinator, Kathy Palumbo, the community services director, and Kathleen Kelly, the volunteer coordinator, on 20-24 May 1999. At the Midtown Assistance Center I interviewed Dorothy Chandler, director, and Maria Carmody, a volunteer, on 27 May 1999. At Café 458 I interviewed executive director Thomas Reuter and volunteers Dawn, George, and Saralyn on 19 May 1999.
3. For an excellent recent history of the Salvation Army's mission, see Diane Winston, *Red-Hot and Righteous: The Urban Religion of the Salvation Army* (Cambridge, MA: Harvard University Press, 1999).
4. "Fourteen Years With God," c. 1956, Atlanta Union Mission files (hereafter AUM).
5. "The Atlanta Union Mission: Seeking the Least, the Last, the Lost," c. 1976, AUM.
6. Steven Beeber, "Give Thanks," *Creative Loafing,* 26 November 1988, 2.

7. Rebecca Perl, "Mission Changes Its Focus," *Atlanta Constitution,* 9 October 1990.

8. Beeber, "Give Thanks."

9. Minutes of the Session, Druid Hills Presbyterian Church, 16 September 1974, Druid Hills Presbyterian Church History Room (hereafter DHPC).

10. Report of the Division of Outreach, Minutes of the Session, 15 September 1975, DHPC.

11. Letter to the editor from Lila Bonner Miller, c. February 1980, DHPC.

12. Yearbook, 1986, DHPC

13. Deuteronomy 14:29.

14. Luke 16:19-31.

15. Acts 6:1.

16. Jo-Ann Eccher, "Adding Justice to Our Charity," *Seeds,* October 1988, 4.

17. Janet Poppendieck, *Sweet Charity?: Emergency Food and the End of Entitlement* (New York: Viking, 1998), makes this argument at some length.

18. Bill Bolling, "A New Time—A New Mission," *Foodsharing,* November/December 1993, 3, Atlanta Community Food Bank (hereafter ACFB).

19. *Foodsharing,* November 1997-January 1998, 4, ACFB.

20. *Foodsharing,* February-April 1998, 11, ACFB.

21. Bill Bolling, "Creative Collaboration in the Land of Disney," *Foodsharing,* August-October 1995, 3, ACFB.

22. "Fourteen Years with God," c. 1956, AUM.

23. "Our Twenty Years with God," c. 1961, AUM.

24. *Molders of Men* (November 1968), 4, 8, AUM.

25. "The Atlanta Union Mission: Seeking the Least, the Last, the Lost," clipping c. 1976, AUM.

26. Beeber, "Give Thanks."

27. Emma Edmunds, "A Room of One's Own," *Atlanta Weekly,* 16 May 1982, 24.

28. Perl, "Mission Changes Its Focus."

29. *The Light,* July 1996, AUM.

30. Adam Gelb, "Union Mission Faces Uphill Battle as It Retools to Treat Drug Addiction," *Atlanta Constitution,* c. 1990, clipping at AUM.

31. Bill Bolling, "In Giving We Receive and Learn," *Foodsharing,* August-October 1997, 3, ACFB.

32. Ibid.

33. Proposal to Fulton County for Human Services Grant, 10 February 1999, Café 458 records.

34. *Foodsharing,* August-October 1995, 5, ACFB.

35. *The Light,* Fall 1997, 3, AUM.

36. *Foodsharing,* August-October 1995, ACFB.

37. "Bringing in the Food," *Foodsharing,* July/August 1987, 2, ACFB.

38. Sherrill Terry, "Riding with Atlanta's Table," *Foodsharing,* May-July 1995, 4, ACFB.

39. *Foodsharing,* August-October 1998, 7, ACFB.

40. *Foodsharing,* July/August 1988, 4, ACFB.

41. The baby version of the parable is told—and analyzed at some length—in Poppendieck, *Sweet Charity?* 288-296. Another version, involving a dangerous mountain road, is in Beverly Phillips, "An Offering of Letters," *Church and Society,* March/April 1994, 72-73.

CHAPTER FOUR

1. "Long Beach Fasters Feast on Food for Thought," *CROP Service News,* March 1975, 6, Records of Church World Service, Elkhart, Indiana (hereafter CWS).

2. Samuel McCrea Cavert, *Church Cooperation and Unity in America: A Historical Review, 1900-1970* (New York: Association Press, 1970), 186, 190.

3. Harold E. Fey, *Cooperation in Compassion: The Story of Church World Service* (New York: Friendship Press, 1966), 13, 24, 27.

4. Stanley I. Stuber, "When Emergency Spells Opportunity," *Missions,* November 1945, 488.

5. "3 Church Groups Form New Agency," *New York Times,* 20 May 1946, 20.

6. Fey, *Cooperation in Compassion,* 29.

7. On refugees, see Haim Genizi, "Problems of Protestant Cooperation: the Church World Service, the World Council of Churches and Post-War Relief in Germany," in Hubert G. Locke and Marcia Sachs, eds., *Holocaust and Church Struggle: Religion, Power, and the Politics of Resistance* (Lanham, MD: University Press of America, 1996). On church aid, see Fey, *Cooperation in Compassion,* 38.

8. "Youth Shares with Youth," *Missions,* October 1946, 503.

9. Stanley I. Stuber, "A Unified Program of World Relief," *Missions,* September 1946, 425.

10. Cavert, *Church Cooperation,* 194.

11. Quoted in Ronald E. Stenning, *Church World Service: Fifty Years of Help and Hope* (New York: Friendship Press, 1996), 4.

12. "CROP Gives the Answers," brochure, n.d. (c. 1948), CWS.

13. *CROP Newsletter,* 1 July 1956, 1, CWS.

14. Stenning, *Church World Service,* 5-6.

15. "Not Gratitude But Pangs of Conscience on Thanksgiving Day," *Missions,* November 1945, 475.

16. "Titanic Feasting in America and Gigantic Hunger in Europe," *Missions,* January 1946, 33.

17. "The Grim and Devastating Ride of the Third Horseman of the Apocalypse," *Missions,* April 1946, 223.

18. William B. Lipphard, "Misery and Hunger in Postwar Germany," *Missions,* November 1946, 529.

19. Harold Schock, "How Would You Like to Live Here?" *Missions,* January 1950, 17.

20. Romans 20:17; "The Overwhelming Tide of Misery in Central Europe," *Missions,* March 1946, 141.

21. "CROP Gives the Answers," brochure, n.d., (c. 1948), CWS.

22. "Church World Service 1953" (annual report), cover, CWS.

23. "Farmers Share with Needy Through CROP," *Ohio Farm Bureau News,* August 1950, 15.

24. "Food for Thought: How Europeans Eat," *Columbus (Ohio) Citizen,* 15 December 1949, 1.

25. *CROP News Iowa,* December 1956, CWS.

26. CROP flyer, c. 1954, CWS.

27. *CROP News,* September 1961, CWS.

28. Ruth Davenport, "Love in Deed," *Missions,* May 1962, 33.

29. "Corn Syrup Enroute to Eight Countries," *CROP Information Services,* November 1962, CWS.

30. *CROP News Montana,* 22 February 1956, CWS.

31. Schock, "How Would You Like to Live Here?" 18-19.

32. "Your Gifts Provided These Exports," *CROP News,* June 1965, 4, CWS.

33. "A More Excellent Way," *The Messenger,* 31 July 1951. (editorial)

34. R. E. D., "Two Cent's Worth," *Hooker (Oklahoma) Advance,* 4 September 1952.

35. "Christ, Food, Clothing to Block India's Reds," *Denver Post,* 10 December 1952, 3.

36. "What CROP Is," *CROP Newsletter,* June 1956, 3, CWS.

37. *CROP News Montana,* 6 December 1956, CWS.

38. *CROP Newsletter,* 1 October 1956, 2, CWS.

39. *CROP News Texas,* June 1956, 2, CWS.

40. *CROP News Montana,* 6 December 1956, CWS.

41. Stenning, *Church World Service,* 11.

42. Fey, *Cooperation in Compassion,* 69.

43. Stenning, *Church World Service,* 13.

44. Ibid., 11.

45. Ibid., 10.

46. "Church World Service 1953," 33, CWS.

47. Advertisement, *Missions,* February 1950, 130.

48. "Make It One Great Hour!" *Christian Century* 67 (22 February 1950), 232.

49. For these developments, see Sydney E. Ahlstrom, *A Religious History of the American People* (Garden City, NY: Image Books, 1975), 2:444f.

50. Stenning, *Church World Service,* 15, and Robert R. Sullivan, "The Politics of Altruism: The American Church-State Conflict in the Food for Peace

Program," *Journal of Church and State* 11 (1969), 47f., discuss the origins of PL 480.

51. *The CWS Reporter,* June 1954, CWS.
52. G. E. Blackford, "Churches to Send U.S. Surplus Abroad," *Missions,* October 1954, 54.
53. *CROP News,* November 1961, CWS.
54. "C.W.S. Magically Multiplies Bread," *Christian Century* 78 (1 November 1961), 1293.
55. Stenning, *Church World Service,* 16.
56. "Christian Charity Knows No Iron Curtain!" *Christian Century* 65 (21 April 1948), 343.
57. *Wait a Minute,* CROP filmstrip, n.d. (c. late 1950s), CWS.
58. Davenport, "Love in Deed," 33. (Emphasis in original.)
59. Cavert, *Church Cooperation,* 198.
60. Fey, *Cooperation in Compassion,* 92, 84.
61. "How to Make CROP Publicity More Effective" (booklet, June 1954), CWS.
62. *Service News,* March 1968, 2, CWS.
63. "Industry Helps, Too," *CROP News,* September 1966, 4, CWS.
64. Stenning, *Church World Service,* 52.
65. "Team Notes," *Service News,* October 1967, 2, CWS.
66. *CROP News,* May 1960, 4, CWS.
67. *CROP News Texas,* November 1957, CWS.
68. "Pennies into Pounds," *CROP News,* December 1964, 3, CWS.
69. Elizabeth Allstrom, *Children's Kit 1959* (Elkhart, IN: Church World Service, 1959), CWS.
70. *Children's Kit 1960* (Elkhart, IN: Church World Service, 1959), CWS.
71. Elizabeth Allstrom, *Children's Kit 1961* (Elkhart, IN: Church World Service, 1961), CWS.
72. *Wait a Minute,* CROP filmstrip, n.d. (c. late 1950s), CWS.
73. *Everyone Likes to Eat,* CROP filmstrip, n.d. (c. late 1950s), CWS.
74. *A Birthday Cake for Rima,* CROP filmstrip, n.d. (c. late 1950s), CWS.
75. *Our World—And Theirs,* CROP filmstrip, n.d. (c. late 1950s), CWS.
76. *On The Move,* CROP filmstrip, n.d. (c. late 1950s), CWS.
77. Stenning, *Church World Service,* 69.
78. Fey, *Cooperation in Compassion,* 105.
79. For Cold War concerns, see "Hunger and Sacrifice," *Christian Century* 80 (10 July 1963), 875. Aid statistics from Fey, *Cooperation in Compassion,* 140.
80. Jo Carr, *Come Meet Our New Neighbors in Ghana and Nigeria* (Elkhart, IN: Church World Service, 1964), CWS.
81. Jo Carr, *Hello Friends* (Elkhart, IN: Church World Service, 1966), CWS.
82. Frances S. Smith, "The Churches and Relief," *Christianity and Crisis* 22 (25 June 1962), 106.
83. John B. Housley, "Protestant Failure in Chile," *Christianity and Crisis* 26 (31 October 1966), 244.

84. "CWS-CROP Aid to Biafra Stepped Up," *Service News,* October 1968, 1, CWS.
85. Stenning, *Church World Service,* 50.
86. *Missions,* April 1966, 37.
87. Stenning, *Church World Service,* 48.
88. "The Time of Famine," *Service News,* April/May 1968, 3, CWS.
89. Advertisement for "Campaign to Check the Population Explosion," *Mission,* March 1969, 51.
90. Lester R. Brown, "The Agricultural Revolution in Asia," *Mission,* November 1968, 40.
91. John W. Abbott, "Church World Service," *Christian Century* 77 (2 March 1960), 268-269.
92. Cavert, *Church Cooperation,* 201.
93. "Promoting Family Planning," *Christian Century* 82 (11 August 1965), 980.
94. See, for instance, the picture of a starving Biafran child in *Service News,* October 1968, back cover, CWS. A later CWS official condemned this "starving-baby syndrome." Larry Hollon, "Selling Human Misery," *Christian Century,* 26 October 1983, 968.
95. Stenning, *Church World Service,* 42.
96. *Hunger or Hope,* CROP filmstrip, 1974, CWS.
97. *The Road to Zapotal,* CROP filmstrip, 1981, CWS.
98. *The Root of the Matter,* CROP filmstrip, n.d. (c. early 1970s), CWS.
99. Anthony H. Cordesman, *The Changing Geopolitics of Energy,* Part VII (Washington, DC: Center for Strategic and International Studies, 1998), 28.
100. Ronald J. Sider, *Rich Christians in an Age of Hunger: A Biblical Study* (Downers Grove, IL: Intervarsity Press, 1977), 17.
101. Helena Stalson, "The U.N. and the (Economic) Education of Henry Kissinger," *Worldview* 19:1 (January-February, 1976), 7.
102. *Facts on File* 34:1774 (9 November 1974), 922-923.
103. Michael Harrington, *The Other America: Poverty in the United States* (New York: Macmillan, 1962), 1.
104. Alan C. Mermann, "When Did We See Thee Hungry?" *Christian Century* 86 (9 April 1969), 473-474.
105. Alan C. Mermann, "Feed My Sheep," *Christian Century* 86 (2 July 1969), 901.
106. Nancy Amidei, "And a Hungry New Year," *Christianity and Crisis,* 28 December 1981, 357.
107. "Hunger in the U.S.?" *Seeds,* January 1984, 3.
108. Garrett Hardin, "Carrying Capacity as an Ethical Concept," *Soundings* 59 (1976), 130, 132.
109. George R. Lucas Jr., "Famine and Global Policy: An Interview with Joseph Fletcher," *Christian Century* 92 (3-10 September 1975), 756. (Emphasis in original.)
110. James Sellers, "Famine and Interdependence: Toward a New Identity for America and the West," *Soundings* 59 (1976), 110.

111. Daniel Callahan, "Doing Well by Doing Good: Garrett Hardin's 'Lifeboat Ethic,'" *Hastings Center Report* 4:6 (December 1974), 3.
112. Sellers, "Famine and Interdependence," 112.
113. Walter W. Benjamin, "A Challenge to the Eco-Doomsters," *Christian Century* 96 (21 March 1979), 312.
114. Sellers, "Famine and Interdependence," 113.
115. Benjamin, "A Challenge to the Eco-Doomsters," 313.
116. Glenn R. Bucher, "Scarcity and Starvation: Solidarity and Survival," *Religion in Life* 62 (Spring 1977), 96, 101.
117. H. Wayne Pipkin, "The Neo-Evangelical Alternative: (Re)discovering A Social Gospel," *Midstream* 22 (1983), describes the rise of these radical evangelicals and the founding of the Evangelicals for Social Action.
118. Sider, *Rich Christians*, 133.
119. Ibid., 26-27.
120. Ibid., 133, 47.
121. Ibid., 82.
122. Ibid., 87, 95, 93.
123. Stenning, *Church World Service*, 54.
124. Ibid., 120.
125. Leslie Withers, "How to Plan a Hunger Walk," *Seeds*, February 1986, 25.
126. Stenning, *Church World Service*, 78.
127. Ibid., 63.
128. James M. Wall, "Strategy Conflict at Church World Service," *Christian Century* 91 (17 July 1974), 715.
129. James M. Wall, "'Integration' Sparks NCC Showdown," *Christian Century* 104 (4 November 1987), 955-956.
130. Doug Hostetter and Michael McIntyre, "The Politics of Charity," *Christian Century* 91 (18 September 1974), 845-850.
131. Michael Marchino and Robert K. Musil, "Food for Peace or Food for Power?" *Christian Century* 94 (17-24 August 1977), 714f.
132. Rael Jean Isaac, "Do You Know Where Your Church Offerings Go?" *Reader's Digest*, January 1983, 120-125.
133. "A Year of Major Tests for Evangelical Relief Agencies," *Christianity Today,* 17 January 1986, 33
134. Robert Wuthnow, *The Restructuring of American Religion* (Princeton, NJ: Princeton University Press, 1988), 318.
135. Arthur Simon, *Bread for the World* (New York: Paulist Press, 1984), 158.
136. Patrick R. Bruns et al., *Ending World Hunger: The First Steps* (Nashville, TN: United Methodist Discipleship Resources, 1983), 51.
137. Simon, *Bread for the World*, 161-163.
138. Kaaren St. Armour Gray, *Children Hungering for Justice* (Baltimore, MD: Office on Global Education, Church World Service, 1991), 4.
139. *Land and Hunger: A Biblical Worldview* (Washington, DC: Bread for the World, 1987).

140. Patrick R. Bruns, "Youth and World Hunger," *Religious Education* 78 (Spring 1983), 235.

141. Phil Lersch, Jean Lersch, and Bonnie Munson, *Hunger Activities for Children* (St. Petersburg, FL: Brethren House, 1978), 12-14.

142. Patricia L. Kurtzner and Linda Stoerkel, *Have You Ever Been Hungry?* (New York: United Church Press, 1978), 18.

143. *Land and Hunger,* 3.

144. Bruns et al., *Ending World Hunger,* 43

145. Kurtzner and Stoerkel, *Have You Ever Been Hungry?* 9.

146. Gray, *Children Hungering for Justice,* 8-9.

147. Bruns et al., *Ending World Hunger,* 33, 39, 37.

148. Gray, *Children Hungering for Justice,* 8.

149. Bruns et al., *Ending World Hunger,* 3.

150. Land and Hunger.

151. Most overwhelmingly, Doris Lee Shettel, *Life-Style Change for Children (and Intergenerational Groups)* (New York: United Presbyterian Program Agency, 1981).

152. Kurtzner and Stoerkel, *Have You Ever Been Hungry?* 12.

153. Patricia Houck Sprinkle, *Hunger: Understanding the Crisis Through Games, Dramas, and Songs* (Atlanta: John Knox Press, 1980), 10. (Emphasis in original.)

154. Lersch et al., *Hunger Activities for Children,* 1. (Emphasis in original.)

155. Bruns et al., *Ending World Hunger,* 23.

156. *All Tied Up: A Youth Program on Hunger* (Ellenwood, GA: Alternatives, 1985).

157. Kurtzner and Stoerkel, *Have You Ever Been Hungry?* 17.

158. Ronda Hughes, *Meeting Hunger Hands On: Hunger Awareness Activities for Groups* (Elkhart, IN: Church World Service, n.d. (c. 1990)), 9.

159. Lersch et al., *Hunger Activities for Children,* 24, 25.

160. Sprinkle, *Hunger,* 30.

161. Gray, *Children Hungering for Justice,* 5.

162. Bruns et al., *Ending World Hunger,* 22.

163. Lersch et al., *Hunger Activities for Children,* 60.

164. Kurtzner and Stoerkel, *Have You Ever Been Hungry?* 18, 30.

165. Ibid., 18.

166. Lersch et al., *Hunger Activities for Children,* 71.

167. Kurtzner and Stoerkel, *Have You Ever Been Hungry?* 52.

168. Bruns et al., *Ending World Hunger,* 4.

169. Kurtzner and Stoerkel, *Have You Ever Been Hungry?* 54. (Emphasis in orignial.)

170. All Tied Up.

171. Sprinkle, *Hunger,* 100, 102.

172. Land and Hunger.

173. Sprinkle, *Hunger,* 119-134.

174. Kelly Owen, "'What's For Dinner?' How to Conduct a Hunger Meal," *Seeds,* September 1994, 28.

175. Patricia Houck Sprinkle, "How to Have a Hunger Meal," *Seeds,* August 1986, 40.

176. Sprinkle, *Hunger,* 114.

177. Hughes, *Meeting Hunger Hands On,* 15.

178. Sprinkle, *Hunger,* 136.

179. Kurtzner and Stoerkel, *Have You Ever Been Hungry?,* 17.

180. Gray, *Children Hungering,* 5.

181. Bruns et al., *Ending World Hunger,* 21.

182. *Hunger: Learning for Action,* (Elkhart, IN: Church World Services, n.d. (c. 1991), 9.

183. All Tied Up.

184. Sprinkle, *Hunger,*11.

185. Gray, *Children Hungering,* 18.

186. Kurtzner and Stoerkel, *Have You Ever Been Hungry?* 46.

187. Ibid., 33.

188. Shettel, *Life-Style Change,* 18.

189. Kurtzner and Stoerkel, *Have You Ever Been Hungry?* 24.

190. Lersch et al., *Hunger Activities for Children,* 110.

191. Bruns et al., *Ending World Hunger,* 49.

192. Kurtzner and Stoerkel, *Have You Ever Been Hungry?* 56.

193. Kurt Helmcke, "What's in a Survey?" *Church and Society,* March-April 1994, 7.

CHAPTER FIVE

1. Waverly Root and Richard de Rochemont, *Eating in America: A History* (New York: William Morrow and Company, 1976), 51, 52, 54.

2. Ibid., 122, 124.

3. This connection between evangelical faith and social reform is the main theme of Timothy Smith, *Revival and Reform: American Protestantism on the Eve of the Civil War* (New York: Harper & Row, 1957).

4. John B. Blake, "Health Reform," in Edwin S. Gaustad, ed., *The Rise of Adventism: Religion and Society in Mid-Nineteenth-Century America* (New York: Harper & Row, 1974), 36.

5. Gerald Carson, *Cornflake Crusade* (New York: Rinehart and Company, 1957), 46.

6. Louis J. Kern, *An Ordered Love: Sexual Roles and Sexuality in Victorian Utopias* (Chapel Hill, NC: University of North Carolina Press, 1981), 224.

7. Sylvester Graham, *A Lecture on Epidemic Diseases Generally, and Particularly the Spasmodic Cholera* (New York: Mahlon Day, 1833), 10-11, cited in Blake, "Health Reform," 38.

8. Blake, "Health Reform," 39.

9. Ibid., 43.

10. Richard Harrison Shryock, "Sylvester Graham and the Popular Health Movement, 1830-1870," in *Medicine in America: Historical Essays* (Baltimore, MD: The Johns Hopkins Press, 1966), 117.

11. Martin E. Marty, *Pilgrims in Their Own Land: 500 Years of Religion in America* (New York: Little, Brown, 1984), 321.

12. Ronald G. Numbers, *Prophetess of Health: A Study of Ellen G. White* (New York: Harper & Row, 1976), 160-166.

13. Ibid., 169.

14. For a full—if cynical—account of the Battle Creek Sanitarium, Kellogg, and the corn flake, see Carson, *Cornflake Crusade.*

15. Carson, *Cornflake Crusade,* 57.

16. Mrs. Horace [Mary] Mann, *Christianity in the Kitchen: A Physiological Cookbook* (Boston: Ticknor and Fields, 1858), 1. (Emphasis in original.)

17. Ibid., 3. (Emphasis in original.)

18. Ibid., 5.

19. Ibid., 2. (Emphasis in original.)

20. Ibid., 2.

21. Ibid., 11.

22. Ibid., 14.

23. Margaret Sidney, "How to Eat, Drink and Sleep as a Christian Should," *Good Housekeeping,* 9 January 1886, 125.

24. Ibid., 126.

25. Ibid., 128.

26. Sara C. Bull, "Sanitary and Economic Cookery," *Minutes of the Twenty-First Annual Convention* (1894), 500-501.

27. Sara C. Bull, "Scientific Nutrition in Cookery," *Union Signal,* 2 February 1893, 4.

28. Abbie Kusel Richardson, "Sanitary and Economic Cookery," *Minutes of the Twenty-Third Convention* (1896), 193.

29. Mrs. J. H. Kellogg, "What to Eat," *Union Signal,* 2 February 1883, 5.

30. Mrs. J. H. Kellogg, "Condiments," *Union Signal,* 4 April 1885, 5.

31. Kellogg, "What to Eat."

32. Bull, "Scientific Nutrition in Cookery."

33. Sidney M. Beard, "The Dawn of a Better Day," *Union Signal,* 8 January 1896, 5.

34. Lucinda H. Corr, "Whole Wheat Flour Again," *Union Signal,* 11 January 1883, 12.

35. Richardson, "Sanitary and Economic Cookery."

36. "Leader of the W.C.T.U. Food Reform Movement," *Union Signal,* 19 December 1895, 10.

37. Louise C. Purington, "Health and Heredity," *Minutes of the Twenty-Eighth Annual Meeting* (1901), 213.

38. Louise C. Purington, "Food Economics," *Union Signal,* 1 January 1903, 6.

39. Cited in Lee Ranck, "Much More Than Relief," *Engage/Social Action* 3:2 (February 1976), 18.

40. David Berdan, letter to the editor, *American Baptist,* December 1974, 6. (Emphasis in original.) Some Baptists, reflecting traditional anti-Catholicism, blamed much of the overpopulation on the anti-birth control stance of the Roman Catholic hierarchy.

41. Lester R. Brown and Erik P. Eckholm, "The World Food Problem," *Christianity and Crisis* 34:1 (3 February 1975), 2.

42. Ibid.

43. Frances Moore Lappé, *Diet for a Small Planet* (New York: Ballantine Books, 1975), 3.

44. Ibid., 4-5.

45. Ibid., 9. (Emphasis in original.)

46. Ibid., 12.

47. Ibid., 13-14.

48. Ibid., 18.

49. Ibid., 41-43.

50. Ibid., 9.

51. Ibid., 50.

52. Frances Moore Lappé, *Diet for a Small Planet* (New York: Ballantine Books, 1991), 140f.

53. Ibid., 14.

54. Ronald J. Sider, *Rich Christians in an Age of Hunger: A Biblical Study* (Downers Grove, IL: Intervarsity Press, 1977), 171.

55. Ronald J. Sider, ed., *Lifestyle in the Eighties: An Evangelical Commitment to Simple Lifestyle* (Philadelphia: Westminster Press, 1982), 9.

56. Sider, *Rich Christians,* 170.

57. Ibid., 174.

58. Ibid., 178.

59. Ibid., 180.

60. Ibid., 182.

61. Ibid., 187. (Emphasis in original.)

62. August M. Hintz, "Lazarus at the Gate," *The American Baptist,* November 1974, 10-11.

63. Roger L. Shinn, "Asceticism for Our Time," *A.D.* 3:12 (December 1974), 42-46.

64. Patricia L. Kutzner and Linda Stoerkel, *Have You Ever Been Hungry?* (New York: United Church Press, 1978), 11.

65. Ibid., 37.

66. Ibid., 43-44.
67. Ibid., 45.
68. Ibid., 75.
69. Doris Lee Shettel, *Life-Style Change for Children (and Intergenerational Groups)* (New York: United Presbyterian Program Agency, 1981), 1.
70. Ibid., 2.
71. Ibid., 15.
72. Ibid., 2.
73. Ibid., 13-14.
74. Ibid., 45.
75. Ibid., 18.
76. Ibid., 35.
77. Ibid., 22.
78. Ibid., 55.
79. Program, "The Annual Dinner of the Men's Club," 21 January 1913, St. Pauls Church.
80. Grace Wynn, ed., *Simply Delicious: Quantity Cooking for Churches* (Ellenwood, GA: Alternatives, 1983), 2. (Emphasis in original.)
81. Ibid., 5.
82. Ibid., 9, 14.
83. Ibid., 4.
84. Ibid., 14.
85. Report of the Christian Action Commission, "Holy Living in Time of Famine," *Minutes of the 169th General Synod of the Reformed Church in America* (1975), 195-199.
86. Report of the Advisory Council on Church and Society, "United States Food Policy Objectives and Guidelines," *Minutes of the 188th General Assembly of the United Presbyterian Church in the USA* (1976), 501-505.
87. "Holy Living in Time of Famine."
88. "United States Food Policy Objectives and Guidelines."
89. "Holy Living in Time of Famine."
90. "United States Food Policy Objectives and Guidelines."
91. *Minutes of the 168th General Synod of the Reformed Church in America* (1974), 71-72.
92. "Holy Living in Time of Famine."
93. *Minutes of the 170th General Synod of the Reformed Church in America* (1976), 184-185.
94. "Holy Living in Time of Famine."
95. *Minutes of the 188th General Assembly of the United Presbyterian Church,* 128-129.
96. "Holy Living in Time of Famine."
97. "United States Food Policy Objectives and Guidelines."
98. *Minutes of the 188th General Assembly of the United Presbyterian Church,* 128-129.

99. Janette Hopper, letter to the editor, *The American Baptist,* June 1975, 7.
100. Interview with William Rambo, Clinton, NY, 3 November 1999.
101. *Minutes of the 187th General Assembly of the United Presbyterian Church in the USA* (1975), 147.
102. Some of the same language has reappeared in the context of ecological concerns. A recent CWS publication on global warming used some of the same simulation exercises common in hunger material of the 1970s.
103. Matthew 15:11.
104. 1 Corinthians 6:12.

CONCLUSION

1. Michael McNally, "The Uses of Ojibwa Hymn-Singing at White Earth: Toward a History of Practice," in David D. Hall, ed., *Lived Religion in America: Toward a History of Practice* (Princeton, NJ: Princeton University Press, 1997), 150.
2. Luke 24:13-35.

INDEX

lifestyle and, 205-206, 210-211
resistance to, 215-216
social events and, 87, 210-211, 214
world hunger and, 199-202, 204-206, 210-211
Vietnam, and Church World Service, 169
volunteers
church kitchens and, 93
hunger ministries and, 106, 107, 114, 125-126, 129-130, 131-132, 134
weight loss, and food moralism, 186
Welch, Charles, 28-29
Welch, Thomas, 28
Welch's Grape Juice Company, 28-29
White, Ellen, 189, 190
whitebread Protestants. *See* Protestants, whitebread
Willard, Frances, 24, 33
Willimon, William, 49, 56
Willow Creek Community Church, 92-95
wine
controversy over, 11-31
diluted, 24
social acceptance of, 30
wine at Communion
Catholic Church, 11-12
Episcopal Church, 12, 23-24
Lutheran churches, 12
Methodist churches, 23, 28
Presbyterian churches, 13, 23, 24
Reformation churches, 12-13
Winter, Gibson, 84
women
diet reform by, 191-197
food moralism by, 191-197
poverty of, 115, 119
reform movements of, 191-197
working at camp meetings, 63

working in kitchen, 74, 83, 88-90
women's activities 65, 71
See also St. Pauls United Church of Christ, women's activities
Women's Christian Temperance Union (WCTU), 14, 20, 23, 46-47
Communion refused by, 26
Communion wine and, 17
denominational politics and, 25-26
diet reform and, 195-197
education and lobbying by, 24-26
food moralism and, 195-197
manufacture of grape juice by, 27
reform and, 33
working poor, and hunger ministries, 108, 115, 109
World Council of Churches
lifestyle and, 204-205
world hunger and, 140, 141, 204-205
World Food Conference (1973), 162-163
world hunger. *See* hunger, world
World Relief, 170
World War II. *See* hunger, post-war
Wuthnow, Robert, 170
Young Men's Christian Association (YMCA), 65, 66
youth, 66, 71, 76
courtship at activities, 65, 70, 71, 77
food moralism for, 205-209
fund raising by, 78 86, 137, 154
lifestyle for, 205-209
teaching about world hunger, 137, 154, 172-182
See also Christian Endeavor Society; Epworth League; St. Pauls United Church of Christ, youth activities

CPSIA information can be obtained
at www.ICGtesting.com
Printed in the USA
FSOW02n1349240817
37962FS